REFLECTIONS
OF A DIGGER

The author at his home, Oldhay, in Cornwall, England.
Photograph courtesy of the author.

REFLECTIONS

OF A

DIGGER

FIFTY YEARS OF WORLD ARCHAEOLOGY

Froelich Rainey

PUBLISHED BY
THE UNIVERSITY MUSEUM OF
ARCHAEOLOGY AND ANTHROPOLOGY
UNIVERSITY OF PENNSYLVANIA

Design and Production
  Bagnell & Socha

Editing
  Publications Department, The University Museum

Printing
  Cypher Press

Binding
  Hoster Bindery

Front cover: The author (left) discussing the progress of the excavation at
Hasanlu, Iran in 1970 with Bob Dyson, director of the excavation.
Photograph courtesy of the Hasanlu Project of The University Museum.

Library of Congress Cataloging-in-Publication Data

Rainey, Froelich G. (Froelich Gladstone), 1907-
  Reflections of a digger: fifty years of world archaeology/by Froelich Rainey.
p.cm.
  Includes bibliographical references\ISBN 0-924171-15-4
  1. Rainey, Froelich G. (Froelich Gladstone), 1907-
2. Archaeologists-United States - Biography. I. Title.
CC115.R35A3 1992
930.1'092-dc20
[B]   92-12150 CIP

To my daughter, Penny,
and my granddaughters, Patricia and Pamela.

Contents

Foreword

For some thirty years The University Museum flourished under the distinguished directorship of Froelich Rainey who revived it after World War II and made it pre-eminent in this country as an institution devoted to excavation and innovative technology applied to archaeology around the world.

The University Museum, with the generous help of Otto Haas, is delighted to be able to produce this volume of memoirs recounting Fro Rainey's career and his own personal view of the trajectory of archaeological research during his lifetime. As a practicing archaeologist and the former Director of The University Museum he brings a unique autobiographical perspective to this period of time. Because of this, although the Museum as a routine matter does not usually publish biographical works as such, we decided it would be appropriate to do so in this instance to honor a major figure in our institutional history and a man who was a major influence in the practice of field archaeology around the world.

—*Robert H. Dyson*
The Charles K. William II Director
The University Museum of
Archaeology and Anthropology

Preface

In essence Fro Rainey wrote his own introduction to Reflections of a Digger nearly four decades ago. At that time—the mid 1950s—Fro came into my life, as he came into the lives of so many others, via his highly successful television series "What in the World." I remember clearly the first time I saw the show; for it was wonderful departure from the usual programming, and to me, at the age of ten or eleven, utterly absorbing.

Looking back on "What in the World," I find it amazing that a small group of experts could have been even remotely interesting as they sat stiffly under severe studio lights, discussing the provenance of obscure artifacts—yet for a vast number of people they were fascinating, and for many young people, including myself, Fro's production helped to launch us on careers in anthropology and archaeology.

More importantly however, Fro opened the eyes of his audience to the fundamental importance of conducting research into all aspects of mankind's history and development, while at the same time he managed to put a human face on these arcane pursuits. As one of the central figures of twentieth century archaeology, Fro did great service for our discipline and simultaneously was instrumental in broadening its base of support throughout the globe.

Today, recalling my vivid memories of "What in the World," I realize that it broadcast the same compelling qualities that Fro himself continued to radiate in the 1970s when it was my good fortune to have been his student. His intellectual curiosity simply overwhelmed us all and swept us up in the thrills and challenge of research into distant cultures, both ancient and modern. But writ large was his profound respect for all the peoples of the earth and his manifest humanity and utter decency.

My life and the lives of many others have been enriched by our association with Fro. I know I speak for many people throughout the world when I state that I will always be grateful to him and proud to have been associated with such a marvelous human being.

—*John Bockstoce*

The author working as a cowboy on Dan Down's
ranch in Dawson County, Montana in 1925.
Photograph courtesy of the author.

INTRODUCTION

The Rainey family in 1909: from left: C.F. Rainey holds the author's brother,
Rex; the author leans against his mother, Alma.
Photograph courtesy of author.

Time and Space

In 1912, when I was five years old, the cowboys on my father's ranch on the high plains took me to see the first aircraft to appear in eastern Montana. It was brought in by rail and assembled on the prairie just east of Glendive, on the bank of the Yellowstone River. Like the Wright brothers, the pilot sat in a frame out in front of a biplane, with the engine and propeller behind him. The plane belched a lot of blue smoke and rushed across the prairie on bicycle wheels at a great rate. But it could not get into the air. The cowboys, who always became well liquored-up when they rode into town, lost patience, picked up the plane with the pilot, and threw it into the river.

A few years ago, as I watched the live television broadcast of the first man to step onto the surface of the moon, I thought of that first aircraft trundling across the prairie and of the cowboys who thought of time and space as measured by a day's ride on horseback. I tried to think of the distance between the Earth and the moon in relation to the thirty-mile ride in three hours from the ranch to Glendive. It did not work. There is no more relation between the aircraft of 1912 and the rocket of 1969 than there is between a day's ride on horseback and space travel. In one generation something has happened to our whole conception of the scale of things, and with that, to our theories about man's relation to the world about him.

In 1940, I flew for the first time across the frozen Arctic from Fairbanks to Kotzebue in Alaska. North of the timberline we entered a world with no boundaries: unbroken snowfields rippling like the sea, a gray, overcast sky, and no horizon. A crippled altimeter left us fearful of flying straight into the ground. There was no sense of movement through space and little sense of time except for the hammering of the engine. Losing Earth's boundaries and drifting in a white to gray nothingness must give any Earth-grown creature a chilling fear. But in the back of my mind lay the certain knowledge that down there below in all that emptiness human beings have lived for many thousands of years. Fur-clad and wandering in small groups, they are among the most intelligent and humorous people I have ever known. No one really knows how long they have been there. I have seen a flint spearhead imbedded in the skull of a woolly mammoth, but was the man who made it related to those who live there still? After seven years of work with the Eskimos and many long conversations about the nature of the world we live in, they remain for me a timeless people in unbounded space.

North of the Tibesti Mountains in southern Libya there lies a vast area of drifting sand known as the Rebiana Sand Sea. Lifeless and moving slowly with the prevailing winds, it shifts in great swells and combers, a cosmic ocean controlled by a geologic clock.

In 1969, I crossed that sand sea between the Tibesti and the oasis of Rebiana in a farewell visit to a land that for me had its own peculiar magic. Our small group of men in Land Rovers was guided by an enlarged color photo taken from satellite Gemini XI. On one image we could see the Tibesti, the paleozoic outcrops surrounding the sand sea, and in the far distance near the curved horizon, the Nile and the Red Sea. This was a glimpse of our world from outer space, and for me a mind-jolting expansion of a personal concept of space and time. Cosmic space was all about us, and cosmic time, in sparkling gems, lay on the surface of the sand. For 300 kilometers we were seldom out of sight of a small patch of those glittering stone tools and weapons polished by the blowing sand to mirror brightness, reflecting the sun's rays. Millions upon millions of them lay there on the surface to evoke for me the endless generations of men who made them: everything from the most ancient paleolithic hand axes to an occasional pottery fragment to mortars made by the men who raised cattle and grain in what is now a lifeless desert.

People of our generation who live for the most part in the canyons and peaks of vast urban outcrops must come to sense time and space, personally, through the regimented intellectual concept of a computer printout. The ancient Australian, in his wanderings across the desert and with his concept of time and space as interrelated, interchangeable, and reversible, knows a very different world.

Surely, men of all epochs and regions have pondered the nature of space and time, attempting to organize their experience and their emotions into some coherent scheme of life. Some have left us inscriptions—tantalizing relics of their beliefs—that we attempt to fit into our own particular modern scheme. Others have left only vague traces of their passage and nothing of their thoughts. But in our epoch the passion for measuring and recording the infinitely small and infinitely large with a battery of wholly new technological tools, our traditional concept of the past and of the present world about us now, is drastically shifting. We seem to have lost the comfortable human-size scale for our conception of the universe.

For many of us the explosion of the first atomic bomb over Hiroshima meant not only the return from war service to our normal professions but also a realization that science fiction could become reality. Thus, I was surprised but not incredulous when Aristide de Grosse came to my office in The University Museum in Philadelphia with an idea that radioactive isotopes could be used to fix the actual date of human events long before the beginning of written history. At that time, 1948, atomic-nuclear research remained top secret, and most of us on the outside had only the vaguest idea of the nature of the forces locked within the atoms. Aristide and I cut a large piece of wood from an Egyptian coffin, fairly well dated by the recorded Egyptian king lists as early in Old Kingdom times, and he took it to Willard Libby in Chicago. During the next two or three years, together with a geologist and three other archaeologists, I searched through worldwide collections for organic fragments from the past that could be reasonably well dated by various means. These were used by Libby and Arnold in the development of the atomic clock, now known as carbon 14, that has since revolutionized our conception of human events during the past 50,000 years.

And during the thirty years since then, several other atomic clocks, such as potassium-argon and fission-track techniques, have been conceived to measure the history of the Earth in billions of years. Just as we measure the distance from Earth to a certain galaxy in a specific number of light years, so we calculate the time since the origin of life on Earth in thousands of millions of Earth years. We think we know now when the great reptiles disappeared and when the first tiny mouselike mammals originated. In our daily press, accounts regularly appear of new discoveries in East Africa that continue to push back the origin of man and manlike creatures, now to a period of three and four million years ago.

For my generation, perhaps, this rapid shift in the familiar scale of time and space resembles my personal experience flying in the Arctic winter with no horizon and no boundaries, or crossing the endless shifting surface of the Rebiana Sand Sea.

In northeast Thailand, near the Laotian border, in 1973, I looked down into a deep cut upon a number of skeletons lying as they had been found, with clay pots, tools, and weapons, in a vast cemetery below the village of Ban Chiang. Buddhist priests in their bright yellow robes walked about the adjoining wat uninterested in the strangers who probed among the skeletons. But I, knowing from new atomic-nuclear devices measuring the age of ancient things that some of these skeletons were of people who had lived there five or six thousand years ago, drifted off into another world of revolutionary speculation. From what I had been taught, it was all wrong. Everything was in the wrong place and the wrong time. We diggers have known for a century at least that the discovery of metal manufacture was made in the Fertile Crescent somewhere in the Near or Middle East about 5,000 years ago and then introduced into China sometime about 1500 BC Its manufacture in Southeast Asia was supposed to have begun with the introduction of Buddhism and Hinduism a few centuries before Christ.

But there, at Ban Chiang, many bronze objects lay with the deepest and earliest burials, dating up to 5,000-6,000 years ago. With later burials, dating as early as 1800 BC, were many iron objects—probably earlier than any wrought iron found in the Near East. For one of my generation it was almost sacrilegious to expose such ancient metal work in East Asia. It is an article of archaeological faith that the technological advances that have made civilization possible were generated in the West, in the heartland of Western civilization, certainly not in Southeast Asia, thought of by the Chinese as a primitive, retarded cul-de-sac.

The culmination of my own skepticism about the neat, rational theories on the course of human history pieced together by the diggers over the past century and a half probably came during the next two years in East Asia. It was not only the discovery of a very ancient technology of civilization but also the rediscovery of East Asia and the phenomenal changes that had occurred there in the forty-five years since I had first landed in Shanghai. Now I have little doubt that some of the first steps toward civilization were made there and also that, contrary to our Western scheme of things, the center of future cultural development is again rapidly shifting to the Far East.

After fifty years of digging, I know very little about the history of man on Earth. And I am skeptical of what I know. Too many cherished schemes and theories have proved untenable; realms of data have been misinterpreted. History, legend, and theory are scrambled in a tale we wish to think of as factual. What really happened and how? Different societies and different epochs have their own theories.

Biblical Genesis, lineal time, the logical cause-and-effect sequence of unique events, and a Newtonian vision of the universe still dominate much of my thinking. But that comfortable worldview is slipping into a void with no horizon and no boundaries. The behavior of atomic particles in orbit around Mars is the same as that in my own bloodstream. I am composed of the same elements as the algae in ponds and controlled by the same balance of electromagnetic energy. All things and events appear to merge into unity and interrelation. In quantum theory there is now even the possibility of an infinite variety of coexisting worlds.

This account of one man's journey through most of the twentieth century is colored by a preoccupation with the discovery of traces of men in the past, extending, theoretically, over a period of three or four million years. But it is not a treatise on archaeology, even though I have spent more than fifty years as a digger and for thirty of them have had the general direction of more than 200 excavations in the Americas, Europe, Asia, and Africa, launched by The University Museum in Philadelphia.

Nevertheless, it is not the discipline of archaeology with its theories and schemes of history that now dominates my thinking. It is, rather, the personal experience of a workaday world with many people in many countries, and of the new world we have discovered during those fifty years. For my own amusement I have tried to trace the adventure of a mind constantly influenced by people of different cultures and different schemes who are caught up in the revolutionary changes of the twentieth century.

At times I feel that most of us cannot take this world without boundaries, so we scramble for safe cover to ancient religions, political doctrines, or just for more and more material things. But then, as I read of new discoveries about the nature of genetics, biology, atomic-nuclear phenomena, electromagnetic energy, and the behavior of astral bodies in outer space, the excitement of an open universe with no clear horizons in any direction sweeps over me. I can dimly foresee a future of comprehension of what this all means, and a safe world in which men learn to accept what is just now unrolling. Probably it has all come too fast. No wonder fear dominates so many. No wonder we scurry into familiar burrows of ancient beliefs and doctrines when the sky burns with brilliant flashes and the earth rocks with incomprehensible tremors. No one generation can quickly reshape the convictions accumulated over hundreds of generations or easily accept the loss of its firm frontiers. And yet what has happened in this century may, in part, herald a return to a very ancient belief in a universe where all things are interrelated and interdependent; where the natural and the supernatural blend into a new kind of reality; when time, space and energy are indistinguishable, reversible, and curved; and the hard reality of the nineteenth century dissolves into the animistic universe of the many peoples we term primitive.

Only now, trying to comprehend the discussions of theoretical nuclear physicists, do I get a glimmer of what the Eskimos at Point Hope were trying to tell me about their spirit world during those long Arctic nights so many years ago. Now, I think, there must be somewhere a common thread if I could only grasp it. Probably I never shall. But at least I think I have learned that the prevailing theory of a progression from the very primitive to the very modern is nonsense. We confuse accumulating technology with a growth of mentality and assume that progress applies to all things.

If, as I think, the growth of science and technology is rapidly changing our present conception of the universe but not the quality of man's mentality, stabilized long ago, then indeed we have very far to go in our understanding of man's past and his future.

The author (second from left) in Brastagi, Sumatra, 1930.
Photograph courtesy of the author.

PART I

Discovering the Ancient World

Pirates in the straits of Formosa, 1929. The author hit one of these boats with a potato as it passed under the bow of his ship.
Photograph courtesy of the author.

CHAPTER ONE

The Vagabond

It was the summer before the Great Depression of 1929. I was reading Kant and Leibnitz, nineteenth-century poets, and Restoration drama, and itching to be away from the depressing atmosphere of my third university and the deadly Midwestern pursuit of culture. Born and bred in the western United States, I longed to discover for myself another and older world. My father, a very big and jovial Scotch-Irish dreamer who throughout his life sought the "big rock candy mountain" always just beyond the next mountain range, understood perfectly. But his decision was not negotiable. I must take my degree at the university, and then I could become a vagabond with his blessing and support.

By chance, just to fill in those necessary credits, I elected a course in anthropology taught by Ralph Linton. He said once that man was the only animal with the capacity for being bored. Perhaps that was the reason why, one hot summer weekend, he proposed that we drive out to Quincy, Illinois, to get some exercise digging an Indian mound. We were joined by

Duncan Strong, then working at the Field Museum in Chicago. The three of us found Bill Krogman, a graduate student in charge of other students, excavating one of those many huge and nameless earth mounds that are so numerous in the Mississippi Valley. Like all graduate students, he took his system of digging seriously. Only trowels and brushes could be used for precise excavations in a minute section of that vast earth heap. Ralph and Duncan examined the dig with considerable skepticism, and then moved in with picks and shovels. Thus my introduction to digging began with a conflict of opinion about scale and method. (This was a conflict that was to plague me many years later at Tikal in Guatemala, Sybaris in Italy, Ban Chiang in Thailand, and at many other sites around the world.) We got our exercise and also found something.

It seemed an odd sort of business and I was not impressed. Neither Ralph nor Duncan would drive a car, and on that long drive back to Chicago on Sunday, after a hard day with a pick and shovel, they agreed to keep me awake with stories. Archaeology as seen through the experience of two highly intelligent, imaginative, and unconventional men emerged as something quite different from a graduate student dig in an Indian mound. Sometime during the long night, half hypnotized in the light path and by the steady speed across the plains, I began to sense what Ralph and Duncan were getting at. They talked of Madagascar, where at some unknown time Malaysians had arrived in their open boats to create strange cultures off the coast of Africa, and of the ancient hunters of bison on the high plains of America, then known only by the beautifully chipped spearheads they had left in the buffalo grass some ten to twenty thousand years ago. Space and time were opening out for me in the glow of the headlights. The energy of creative, unconventional thinking was just beginning to shred the cobwebs of conventional education, theory, system, and method into those wisps of floating gossamer that pilots sometimes see bearing a tiny spider out into the substratosphere.

Two months later I shipped out of San Francisco for Shanghai as the only passenger on a rusty old tramp freighter, the *Golden Mountain*. For a plainsman who had never until then been on an ocean, the mid-Pacific was awesome: no familiar hills in the distance, a strange smell of sea things so different from sagebrush and hot grass, racing waves and smooth swells reaching outward in an empty world through space that was incomprehensible and in which there was no familiar orientation. We were at sea twenty-nine days from the Golden Gate to the muddy waters of the Yangtze. Captain Hansen, who needed conversation and a chess opponent, tried to teach me navigation as well as chess, and when he wanted exercise we moved his personal pile of Philippine mahogany lumber from the bow to the stern or from the stern back to the bow again. Once we disarmed the first mate, who was trying to shoot the chief engineer. For days, in the officers' mess, we argued as to whether flying fish actually waved their fins like a bird's wings, or whether the fins simply fluttered in the wind.

In Shanghai I learned by cable from my father that the stock market had crashed and that I could expect no more money from him. The expected expedition to Inner Mongolia did not materialize, the Bund was crowded with seamen on the beach, and a job was very hard to find. The one possible chance was to fly the mail plane from Shanghai to Hangchow. However, I could not produce a valid pilot's license because my training was not completed. Then, by chance, I happened upon Captain Hansen in a bar on Bubbling Well Road and a few days later was back on the *Golden Mountain*, which had been delayed in port for rudder repairs, not as a passenger but as a paid deckhand.

At that time, the beginning of the last decade of European

domination in Asia, I was to discover the Orient known to merchant seamen: waterfront dives in the streets, the usual warning that to kill a Chinaman would cost at least twenty dollars (up from a few years before), the short-lived rickshaw men, and, in Hong Kong, the sedan chairs that carried one up the mountain. For a boy raised on the high plains of Montana, where cattle were many, people few, and life precious, the Orient's surging mass of humanity as I saw it on the waterfront had a nightmare quality. Against a background of empty grassland, small groups of cowboys, and lonely ranchers with precious few and much-respected women, as well as those few years in a scholar's dream world, China's waterfront was a harsh lesson in man's callousness. I shall never forget the faces of the poor, starving, and yet beautifully calm and dignified old men and women in the streets of Shanghai, Hong Kong, and Saigon.

Life on a tramp freighter in 1929 was almost as harsh a life as on the streets of Shanghai. The crew, largely Hawaiian, Philippine, Chinese, and Malay, were the dregs of Asian ports. With my change of status from passenger to crew I was demoted from wardroom to crew's quarters and mess, for a time, and discovered that I must fight for food and living space. Among the crew were decent and intelligent men who, like me, disguised their background and accepted the strange society in which we lived. But in Hong Kong and Saigon I went ashore with the officers, who had become my friends, and out of Saigon they decided I should return to the pilot's cabin and the wardroom even though I continued to chip paint, stand watch, and work at odd jobs about the ship as a member of the crew. In the Orient at that time there was a very sharp line drawn between native and white. White officers felt uneasy about a white man in a native crew. We were all relieved when I returned to the normal caste relationship, so strange to me as a western American, yet understandable in the environment of that time and place.

Looking back, I marvel at the rapid social and political changes in the Far East since the Second World War—changes that were inconceivable then, when the West dominated most of the world with very small numbers of British, Dutch, French, and Americans controlling hundreds of millions of natives with the power of their armies and navies but also with a firm conviction of their natural superiority. Watching the behavior of some colonial administrators, many of whom were obviously very small fry in their homelands, I was irritated by their attitude toward Orientals, many of whom were more intelligent, more well bred, and more competent. And yet, just then beginning to learn how the world operates, I was impressed with how so few foreigners of a conquering race could control, dominate, and organize a viable social and political system to bring peace, prosperity, and revolutionary changes. Probably that is a very ancient phenomenon in the history of the relations between races.

On board the *Golden Mountain,* we drifted through warm tropical seas from what seemed to me then one exotic port after another. There was one day only in Hong Kong to pick up supplies and sailing orders, but still time to be carried up the mountain on Victoria Island in a sedan chair and to cruise about the streets of Kowloon in a rickshaw. As we left that bustling port through a seething mass of ships, junks, and sampans, most of the officers were too drunk to appear on the bridge.

But it was my watch and I was at the wheel, very sober, to follow the instructions of the Chinese pilot until we dropped him well clear of the harbor in the setting sun and the blue mist over mainland China. For some reason that evening on the China Sea stands out as the essence of my life as a seaman—the rusty hulk of the ship rolling in a long swell, a lonely bridge, and the glow of the binnacle growing brighter as evening darkened into night. In the darkness ahead lay an unknown land and an unknown future for a young man who, for the first time, was entirely on his own with only a few dollars in his pocket and no one to fall back upon. If you are to be cast adrift, it is well to be part of a ship's company and to sense the loneliness and the excitement of the open sea.

In the Straits of Formosa we had a brief brush with fishermen-pirates when an engine cylinder blew out to leave us a sitting duck until it was repaired. We were surrounded by junks and preparing to repel boarders when the engine finally fired again, and we moved off among the junks hilariously pelting their crew with chunks of coal and potatoes from the bins on the foredeck.

Out of Saigon we steamed straight into a full hurricane, with a near-empty ship rolling wildly and crashing down into troughs between unbelievable waves. I did not see how she could survive. But Captain Hansen's only real worry seemed to be the engine and the driveshaft that took a hard beating when the propeller rose above the water in our dives down the waves. We were four days in the worst of it and actually passed through the eye. Even though I had read about that phenomenon, the sudden stillness with no wind and the breakthrough into bright sunlight under a patch of blue sky was startling. But it was all too brief. Again gray skies closed in over a world of lashing water, rain, and spindrift from crashing waves; green water rushed over the foredeck right up to the bridge.

All this was old stuff to the men in the wardroom, but even they found it difficult to sleep in bunks that sometimes almost stood on end. There were long evenings of discussion and stories, particularly about their night on the town in Saigon, then one of the liveliest ports in the Orient, under French control. The story most appreciated was that of Otto, the chief engineer, who was discovered by Captain Hansen, upon our return to the ship at 3 a.m., scrubbing a Vietnamese girl in the shower with one of the stiffest brushes used on the deck.

In the Philippines we loaded copra in the out islands and were sometimes several days tied up at wharfs where coolies carried the dried coconut aboard in sacks to be dumped into the holds. With the coconuts came the bugs, small black beetles that made their home in everything. In the morning you knocked them out of your tooth- and shaving brushes, and at lunch you whacked the bread and sandwiches against the table to rid them of the ubiquitous bugs. The heat, when we were tied up in harbor, was devastating. My worst day was painting the smokestack of the ship, hung in a breeches buoy underneath a blistering sun.

There was free time to explore ports, like Cebu, with two-wheeled carts pulled by a diminutive horse, and to drink beer in many dockside cafes. Once we tied up next to an English freighter, also loading copra, and I learned of the running fight between Limey and Yank seamen. Sun helmets were necessary as we walked past the English ship, when the crew took to hurling nuts and bolts at unwary Yanks passing by on the deck. In another port we watched a teenage Filipino unpack and assemble a new speedboat and then amaze his watching friends by rushing toward the dock, turning only at the last, breathtaking moment. We were about to start betting when he crashed. His new toy was in splinters and at the bottom of the harbor. The crew laughed about the stupidity of the natives, but I remembered my own teens all too clearly.

Some of the Southern islands were famous for "Binibys," supposedly hermaphrodites who wore men's trousers and a women's-type shirtwaist. I was told that most of the leaders of insurrection among the Muslims of the Southern islands were of this kind. Observing their behavior in harbor cafes, it seemed to me that they were also neurotics and psychotics. Since then, reading about the political leaders in our brave new world, I have often wondered if there is some odd human instinct to follow the strange and abnormal, just as caribou in the Arctic will flock about any strange and abnormal behavior, an instinct that the Eskimos utilize in leading them to destruction. Some of the *Golden Mountain* officers, after an argument about the nature of these odd individuals, lured one on board ship and then reported to the wardroom that they really were true hermaphrodites.

The last shipment of copra was loaded at Legaspi, in the southern part of Luzon Island. From there the ship was to head back across the Pacific to San Francisco. For me it was the end of the line because I had no intention of returning to the States. However, it is against the law to jump ship in a foreign port, and some arrangement was necessary to drop me off without my getting into trouble. Bill Williams from Culpepper, Virginia, was the agent for Texaco Oil in the Legaspi-Albay region, and an old friend of Captain Hansen. Somehow the two of them in a few hours managed the whole affair. I found myself employed as a teacher of English in the Albay High School and also as an unofficial agent of Texaco Oil. Moreover, I was settled in Bill's cottage on the main road between Legaspi and Albay. As we watched the *Golden Mountain* steam out of the harbor, after a farewell party aboard, I had an uneasy feeling that my last direct tie with home was finally broken.

Bill's domestic staff was a houseboy called Victor and a nameless old man simply known as "Cook." The house stood on piles and had latticework for windows. Our neighbor's pigs rooted about under the house with a flock of chickens that we kept as a staple food supply. Soon we added Socrates, a macaque monkey who was chained on the verandah for a few weeks until he adopted the household and could be released to wander about the house and the tops of the palm trees all about us. His house-breaking was simple. If he misbehaved, we scooped him up and threw him out a window. The fall, even for a monkey, was stiff enough to convince him what was proper. For weeks we tried to find him a mate, but all the little females brought in by the native trappers were unacceptable to the irascible old fellow. We decided that he considered himself a cut above the wild monkeys when he began to imitate our human actions about the house. Once during the usual siesta I saw him go screaming up a shuttered window trailing an open bottle of iodine with which he had been brushing his teeth. Victor insisted upon teasing him until Socrates revolted, and Victor almost lost a thumb.

At the school I taught English and literature, including Shakespeare. Ralph Linton, in my aborted anthropology course, had taught me something about the fundamental differences between distinct cultural heritages, but in Albay, trying to explain Shakespeare to teenage Filipinos, I really learned what he had been getting at. All my struggles with *King Lear, The Merchant of Venice*, and *Twelfth Night* produced only blank faces and boredom. American history, taught by others, with its stirring account of revolution, civil war, freedom, and democracy surely caught on like a house on fire. Fueled with such an account, a surge toward Philippine independence was inevitable. Militant youngsters with the fanaticism of the very young were so excited they even got into knife fights among themselves. The school's superintendent chose me, as the youngest member of the staff, to disarm the worst of the troublemakers—an uneasy task requiring the frisking of all the boys for knives each morning when they arrived at school.

Certainly a relief from Shakespeare were other tasks assigned to the new boy. After class in the late afternoon I taught the girls how to play volleyball and the boys to play golf and also military training. I could then march the boys around the golf course on the school grounds following the golf teams.

I could always order a "present arms" while instructing some boy how to make an approach shot or to putt. In that three-ring circus I began to know the Filipino kids and to like them. Regular classes were always rather stiff and formal, also difficult to discipline. It was weeks before I learned how to maintain order. Then I discovered that swearing at them worked magic. They were so shocked and surprised they would quiet down at once and remain so for most of that session.

The moonlighting job with Texaco Oil was literally that. Bill was often in Manila with representatives of other oil companies settling new prices for the five-gallon tins of kerosene that were the big market in the Philippines at that time. Chinese traders in the villages sold this in small quantities, primarily for lighting. After I had met most of Bill's Chinese traders we put his scheme into operation. When it was decided at the meetings that prices were to go up or down, Bill would at once send a coded telegram to me in Legaspi indicating the new price. Then I would set out in Bill's car in the evening to make an all-night circuit of the traders arranging deals for future deliveries; if the price were going up I unloaded at the old price, and if going down I took orders at the new price. Probably the other agents would have done the same thing if they had had a moonlighting schoolteacher in their offices able to make verbal agreements with the same Chinese dealers in the small hours of the night. At the club, later, I would delight to hear Bill commiserate with the Shell, Standard, and other representatives who had found all the dealers stocked up for weeks. The scheme, of course, rested upon trust between ourselves and the traders. It was then that I began to have great respect for the Chinese and their heritage. That respect was enhanced by my encounter with a small, elderly, and roly-poly trader in a tiny isolated village near Tabacco.

Wells, an English boy known as "the Admiral" because of his penchant for sailing, took a bet one night at the Anglo-

American Club that he could sail his double outrigger canoe out of Legaspi Bay into the open Pacific and around the headland to Tabacco. Foolishly I agreed to go as his crew. All went well until we were well out into the Pacific. Then in a sudden gust of wind I tried to jump from one outrigger across the hull to the opposite outrigger, missed it, and rose from the deep dive to find the boat bottom up and Wells clinging to the hull. To our horror we realized that the machete had not been tied to the boat and was then sinking to the bottom. There was no way to cut loose the sail and no way of righting the boat with a wet sail hanging straight down. We were two or three miles off shore in the open Pacific in an unsettled region where sea traffic of any kind was very rare. I was not much of a swimmer and Wells could not swim at all. Fear is a common experience for all of us, but as a landsman who had never seen an ocean until a few months before, the unfamiliar ocean added a kind of terror I had never known. Death seemed inevitable. It was obvious we could not cling to the hull for long with waves washing over us. Moreover it was near sunset and the quick darkness of tropical latitude. We decided we might as well try the impossible swim, with me supporting Wells. In preparation we stripped off all our clothes.

Then, just as I was about to drop off my shirt, we saw passing along inshore another outrigger canoe in the glow of the setting sun. Supported by Wells I stood on the hull, waving the shirt until we saw the canoe turn out to sea toward us. This reprieve was one of those glorious moments when the whole world shines. But with the native outrigger alongside we could see it was loaded almost to the gunwale with dried bark, and after a discussion between the two paddlers, which we could not understand, they began to turn away. Desperate to communicate, I jumped from our hull to their near outrigger and overturned their boat. We all scrambled onto one outrigger and thus righted their boat, empty of the dried bark. As we bailed out the hull, the two natives paddled off toward the shore, leaving our boat and their bark adrift.

With the last light we waded ashore on a sandy beach backed by a village of nippa huts. A crowd of men, women, and children, who had been watching the approach of their boat with four men instead of two, met the two stark-naked white men with curiosity and amusement. But they were exceedingly friendly and showed it by pressing upon us a kind of native beer, food, and cigarettes. One young man could speak a little Spanish, and we gathered that within two or three days the village would travel to the local market somewhere up a nearby river and there we could find a trader who would put us in touch with other white men in Tabacco or Legaspi. In the meantime we could stay with them and even go to a feast and dance at a neighboring village some distance away in the forest. Clothing was unnecessary because the whole village went to bathe in the sea naked both morning and evening. To make us more comfortable they found us two native shirts that did little for modesty but helped against sunburn. That was my first encounter with people living in what was essentially a neolithic level of technology. I was to see more of the forest tribes in the Philippines and to be impressed with their way of life, but not speaking Tagalog, I found the lack of communication always frustrating.

The travel upriver in dugout canoes laden with bark, coconuts, palm hearts, chickens, pigs, and other forest produce became a gay procession of people in boats, chanting, shouting from one to another, and, to judge from the laughter, chaffing each other as country people do the world over. Wells and I were both rather sorry to leave our village and to arrive at the fringe of civilization—a market with a Chinese trader. However, the trader in his own way made up for it. He not only spoke English but was well informed about the whole region, world affairs, politics, religion, and philosophy. Moreover, he had taught his Filipino cook to produce the best of Chinese dishes. We were entertained in grand style. It was indeed odd to make my first real acquaintance with the ancient Chinese civilization in a nippa hut on an unknown river somewhere in the forest of southern Luzon. He would arrange to have Wells' boat salvaged and brought upriver to a road where it could be trucked back to Legaspi. He also outfitted us in his own clothes, which, with his diminutive height and rotundity, left Wells and me looking like two clowns in a circus. After walking overland to a road, we caught a bus into Tabacco and then Legaspi to arrive back at the club several days overdue, in out comic clothing, to a hilarious welcome. We were thought to be drowned but fortunately our families had not been notified. Thereafter I felt at home with all our Chinese traders.

Two of the young teachers in Albay, like me, were eager to explore the back country of Luzon. We heard of an isolated tribe of small, dark bush people known as the Igarote somewhere in the up-country hills, and, with one of our students as guide, found them celebrating a funeral. An old man had died weeks before, but, as was the custom, he had been sealed in a coffin during the long funeral ceremonies. The resin seal of the coffin was not adequate, and the stench permeated the whole compound where dancing and feasting took place on that last day before burial. Our appetites were not good under the circumstances, but we did manage the roasted wild boar, probably the most delicious of all Philippine food. Some communication was possible with our student as interpreter, but was clear that the Igarotes knew little of his Tagalog dialect and only very simple exchanges could be made. Nevertheless I could grasp something of the life of those strange little men who clung to a neolithic life in the wilderness area of the East Asia and Oceania. They are men of many different tribes, physical characters, and customs, but they have in common small stature and a kind of secret, wild, suddenly disappearing quality of night creatures in the deep tropical forest. Many years later, small wild people in the interior of Sumatra were to evoke for me the same reaction.

The three of us also decided to try the ascent of Mount Mayon, an 8,000-foot-high volcano that rose from the sea in a very steep cone to an active crater. Smoke and steam rising from the crater could be seen from the parade ground at Albay. That was my first and only experience in mountain climbing. Before we reached the crater I had decided never to climb another mountain unless I could ride up on a horse. By the end of the first day we had reached the very steep, barren lava two-thirds of the way up. We tried to sleep, clinging to a ledge of crumbling lava, but actually spent most of the long hours of darkness watching the lights go out in Albay and Legaspi, the moon rise, fireflies flickering in the forest below, and the glow of the crater above.

At dawn we split up, each one trying a different route to the summit. None of us succeeded. As we climbed, the lava became more and more friable, breaking away from precarious handholds to roll down ravines all the way to the sea. It also grew hotter and hotter until we could not stand long in one place. Finally, near the lip, in sulphurous smoke and steam, we feared breaking over into the crater itself, gave it up, and reassembled on the ledge of our night camp. The descent was like a toboggan slide. We decided to risk one of the shutelike ravines where powdered lava sand flowed down to the sea. It was fast, sliding on our feet or back, but a bit hair-raising because loosened blocks of lava periodically came bouncing down behind.

At the end of the spring term, I went to spend a week of two with Bill's brother at the Polo Club in Manila, looking for a new and different kind of job in the Philippines. The only possibility was as the assistant superintendent of a button factory—that did not appeal to me—and with all the world beckoning, I took passage on a German freighter sailing west. Later I learned from Bill that the superintendent of that factory died a few weeks after my departure and that probably I would have taken his place. Ten years later the islands were taken over by the Japanese, Bill and his brother were killed in a Japanese prison ship bombed by the Americans, and all the whites were imprisoned there for the duration.

It happened that several friends from Legaspi-Albay and Manila also had passage on the freighter, the *S.S. Trier*, bound for Hamburg via Palangan, Singapore, Sumatra, Ceylon (now Sri Lanka), and Port Said, and the long voyage with stopovers in the ports became a kind of extended house party. In Singapore we went ashore to stay at the famous Raffles Hotel, in Sumatra to travel inland to Brastagi in the mountains, and at Colombo, in Ceylon, to visit the famous spice gardens. Everywhere I was to observe an Orient dominated by Europeans and a colonial world that was so soon to crumble in the upheaval of the Second World War. Colonialism in this generation has become a bad word, but I suspect that there are many old people in the Orient who look back with nostalgia to that period of peace, stability, and growth, in spite of the irritations of domination by outsiders. Surely the termination of that worldwide system must be a watershed of the twentieth century that compounds the crises now plaguing men's minds.

By the time we reached the Red Sea and the Suez Canal, I realized that for me the house party had come to an end. Again, there were only a few dollars in my pocket. Somehow I must find a way to survive in Port Said.

When we anchored there in the harbor and I was making my farewell in preparation for going ashore, a police boat pulled up to the gangway and I heard the commanding officer ask the watch for a man named Rainey. He then came aboard, arrested me, and before the shocked expressions of all those old friends on board the *S.S. Trier*, I disappeared into the police cutter for a silent ride across the harbor to a police court and prison on the waterfront. There were no explanations until I arrived before a magistrate in the court. Then I learned that someone on the ship had reported an automatic pistol in my luggage. Foolishly, I had for some time in the Orient carried that small .32-caliber automatic in a shoulder holster (probably because as a boy in Montana we had often packed a gun of some sort) until I had realized it was ridiculous and stowed it away among the spare socks. There was extensive questioning, particularly about the two bullets missing from the box of ammunition. Eventually the police confiscated the gun and bullets and sent me off to a large common prison block filled with beggars, thieves, drunkards, and prostitutes.

The buoyancy of youth is wonderful. I had started out to discover the Old World and there I was in an Egyptian jail, almost penniless, yet fascinated by the strange characters sitting or lying on the floor about me. The sharp line between white and native certainly had blurred with the approach to Europe. But there was no one who spoke my language, and I could only observe and wonder what next. Sometime during the small hours of the night I noticed the turnkey beckoning to me through the bars of our bull pen. Quietly, hoping not to alert my sleeping companions, I made my way to the gate to find that the man spoke English and was making me a proposition. If I gave him all the money I had with me, he would guide me out of the prison and turn me loose; so, of course, I agreed. Once in the street I gave him the few dollars I had left and then, with a really noble gesture, he returned a few coins so that I could hire a taxi.

Fortunately, I was properly dressed in tropical suit and tie, like any white colonial officer or traveler of those days. It was simple to drive up in a taxi to one of Port Said's best hotels and sign in even at that time of night. The bills and chits would only appear much later with the reckoning. But as the days passed, I could see that Port Said, in what was then a worldwide depression, was just as bad as Shanghai as far as jobs were concerned. As a last resort, I decided to cable my brother, Rex, for a loan. He was lucky enough to have a job and might be able to squeeze out enough at least to get me out of immediate trouble.

However, I had no money to cable and could not put it on my hotel bill. The American consul only laughed when I asked him to cable. Somewhere I had heard that if you were really in trouble, British consuls were much more helpful. Apparently that is correct. A congenial young man in the British consul's office simply said, "But, of course," and sent a cable, saying I could pay him back when I received the money. It arrived, bills were settled, and I headed off for Palestine, where I hoped a temporary job with an expedition from the University of Chicago would be possible.

At that time the normal route to Palestine was by rail, crossing the Suez Canal at Kantara and then a night journey through the Sinai desert to Jerusalem. But, when I landed on the Palestinian side of the canal, customs officials turned me back to Egypt because I had no visa for Palestine. Egyptian officials on the other side also turned me back because I had no Egyptian visa. The canal, of course, is a very interesting waterway, but after several crossings it ceased to be so. Finally, on the Palestinian side, I spotted a young British Army officer and called across to him to explain my ridiculous plight. He grinned, then came aboard the ferry, and explained the custom of "baksheesh" that so easily settles such small problems. With a few coins, papers were stamped and I boarded the train for the desert crossing.

Jerusalem is for me a medieval city entirely associated with the Crusades. Perhaps it is the medieval wall, which at that time, before all the modern buildings destroyed its grandeur, dominated the whole region. Walking the wall with the sun

setting across the dry countryside is my most vivid memory of
the city at that time. Of course, like all tourists, I walked the
Way of the Cross and visited the tomb in the Church of the
Holy Sepulchre, but all that seemed rather phoney, like
fragments of the cross that were still being hawked in the
streets, and in any case had little to do with the city as it then
was. It was very easy to imagine Saladin or Richard walking
these walls or riding through the narrow medieval streets, but
very difficult to imagine the city of King Herod so deeply
buried beneath the centuries.

The cheapest way to reach Megiddo and the expedition was
by bus—then a long, hot, dusty trip in what was still a biblical
country, like all those illustrations in my Sunday school
books—Arab costumes, donkeys, camels, and mud huts. But
on the crowded bus was an elderly Jewish fellow from a
kibbutz, who spoke to me with an East Side New York accent.
His opening remark was, "Where are you taking all these
Arabs?" Obviously, my tropical suit and tie no more belonged
on that bus than in an Egyptian jail.

Ancient Megiddo was then being excavated by the Oriental
Institute in Chicago, still in its plush days of open-handed
financing by Mr. Rockefeller. Thus my first look at a major
archaeological expedition in the Near East was misleading. I
find it difficult to remember the elaborate living quarters, the
servants, the huge crew of workmen and women, but I do
remember the club room with its billiard tables and the
reading rooms. It was a small extension of the University of
Chicago in the dry hills of northern Palestine. For me, as a
recent graduate of the university, there was a warm welcome
and a offer to stay as long as I should wish. Unfortunately the
dig would shortly be interrupted for the hot months of
summer. There was only time for an indoctrination in current
Near Eastern methods of digging and to learn how to record
objects then being excavated in King Solomon's stable.

However, for me, it was only mildly interesting, like the dig in the Indian mound, and certainly led to no burning desire to become a digger.

Alone and footloose again, I found in Joppa a small Greek freighter, the *Iphigenia*, bound for Marseilles via Port Said and Piraeus. Deck passage to Marseilles was only a few dollars, which I could still manage, and perhaps there I could find some way to make a living. The deck was crowded with peasant people of all kinds, plus goats and sheep. We slept under the stars leaning against our baggage and ate the simplest peasant food in the crowded mess room. There I learned for the first time about sheep's eyes floating in the soup or stew. But it was a jovial company who spent the evenings dancing and singing on the deck. Although there was no possibility of speech communication, peasant families were always eager to share their olives, cheese, bread, and wine with the odd fellow who was to them a "Frank" from Europe.

Back at Port Said I thought it would be amusing to try to reclaim my pistol from the police at the prison. Strangely enough, there was no problem. It was returned with smiles and good wishes when they learned that I was on a Greek ship bound for Europe. Only then I realized that the turnkey had shaken me down, pretending to break me out of prison but actually acting under orders. Presumably they had held me just long enough to make enquiries.

Out of Port Said there were new deck passengers including a Greek boy who could speak English. We were firm friends when we anchored in Piraeus, and he became my host for the day the ship spent there. Early in the morning we first called upon his uncle, who was a wine merchant, for breakfast with a lot of wine from the barrels in the cellar. Then, when the barber shops were open, he insisted upon the works—shave, haircut, and shampoo. He then took me to what I suddenly realized was a brothel. With care, I explained that in America it was the custom not to indulge in such matters so early in the morning, and I hoped he would excuse me from that part of his hospitality. We passed on to the next stage—the Acropolis, the Museum, the University, Haephestos Street, and other tourist attractions—interspersed with several cafes and cups of Greek coffee. Late in the afternoon, when the Iphigenia was about to sail, he escorted me aboard and then proposed to bind our friendship with an exchange of shirts. Strange customs are often difficult. His shirt was none too clean, and I really could not spare one of mine. The bright day in Athens was dimmed by my stuffiness, and I steamed off to the West determined to be more pliable.

The next morning I awoke on deck to find an American boy watching me with a puzzled expression. His trenchcoat, hat, and shoes could only be American, and I suppose my own clothing was equally typical. We exchanged explanations over morning coffee, and I learned that he had spent all his money on an ungrateful Coptic girl in Alexandria. He too was bound for Marseilles and then Nice, where his divorced mother was living. By the time we reached the French port, Bruce had devised a scheme for us both to make a living. We arrived at his mother's apartment dead broke and very grubby. Without any discussion she sent us off to the bathroom and our clothes to the cleaners. Then at dinner Bruce explained his plan. His mother was to finance a gambling syndicate composed of the three of us. Each would take a small amount of money to a different roulette table in Nice or Monte Carlo, each morning, and continue to play small stakes so long as he was winning. If he lost his stake he quit. According to Bruce, by the law of averages, one of the three ought to be lucky each day.

Surprisingly, it worked well. For several weeks we lived pleasantly in Nice, going to work each day as to an office. Sometimes, with a very good day, we splurged with dinner in one of the best restaurants; at other times, after a bad day, we ate a meager supper in the flat. But slowly we each accumulated a small stake and a certain confidence in the future. Then I began to sicken, probably with a recurrence of dengue fever, and not wanting to be a burden on Bruce and his mother, I explained that I was becoming restless and wanted to be off to something different. They were good and understanding friends. I left with sorrow.

On a bus, I reached Juan-les-Pins. Then really ill, I went to bed in a tiny pension for several days, looked after by a kindly concierge until I was on my feet again. I had written to a friend from the Philippines who was in Paris. A return letter urged that I come on to Paris where I could live with a Canadian painter in his flat on the Left Bank and perhaps find some occupation.

Paris in 1930, before the full effect of the Great Depression, was still the haven for students of the arts from all over the world. The booming success of the capitalistic system in the 1920s meant that aspiring writers, painters, sculptors, and just the young escapees from Papa's successful business in Birmingham, Stockholm, Chicago, or Amsterdam could be sent to the art capital for a pleasant life on the Left Bank. Perhaps they were the hippies of their generation, but how different. "Bohemian" was still the word, and it was no cop-out. Optimism and enthusiasm still dominated aspiring youth. Interest in communism, socialism, and technocracy came later with the deepening depression. Moreover, Paris was then filled with very active White Russian émigrés and their tales of the Communist holocaust. Like me, many had felt the bite of the stock market collapse, but to us then it was only a monetary setback.

Our crowd was based in the cafe Le Dôme, at the intersection of the boulevards Raspail and Montparnasse, only a hundred meters from the fifth-floor walk-up studio where I lived. Now it seems to me impossible that we could have spent so many hours every day over a stein of beer and endless conversation about life, past, present, and future. There were many farewell parties for those whose remittances had ended, and it was accepted that each should last for a minimum of thirty-six consecutive hours. But there were bright sunny days walking the streets and parks of Paris, and long discussions in the Louvre. I think it was not just youth but an attitude of the time that leaves an aura of gaiety in my memory of that Paris—a gaiety so sadly lacking among my students in the years to follow. There were, of course, good reasons for the change, but those creative years of youth, I think flow better and more effectively if leavened with a spirit of gaiety.

As the gambling gains drained away, some sort of meal ticket became urgent. I learned of the American School of Prehistoric Research in Paris that was supported by a number of universities in the United States including the University of Chicago. An urgent letter to Ralph Linton brought a quick return with an appointment to the school for the late summer and fall. To me, then, the important thing was the stipend that made it possible to eat regularly.

The school was directed by Prof. George Grant MacCurdy, soon to be dubbed by the students "Lady MacCurdy" because we decided that Mrs. MacCurdy wore the trousers. Perhaps, also because of his distress over Professor Mitra—that jovial rotund fellow took seriously the Indian custom of expressing his pleasure in a good meal with resounding belches, great explosions that punctuated Lady MacCurdy's cozy talks after dinner.

For one brought up as a Protestant, and by nature a pagan, it is odd that I should find several Catholic priests so attractive and impressive. Abbé Breuil, the famous interpreter of Paleolithic cave art, was one of them. But there were also the two Jesuits on the *S.S. Trier*, crossing the Indian Ocean, who borrowed my copy of Voltaire's Candide to back up our running discussions, and Padre Carballo, in the Basque country, who spent his life resurrecting the life of Stone Age man. Then, too, years later, there was Father Murray, who had the courage to float down the Yukon River with me on a raft I had made myself from driftwood. For whatever reason, it was Abbé Breuil who set off the first spark of true interest in the remote past.

The Abbé Breuil spoke to us over the Stone Age collections of the museum in St. Germain-en-Laye, and waxed enthusiastic over the cave art in the south of France. Some of this was still suspect, like the now-famous clay bisons discovered by Count Begouen and his sons at Le Tuc d'Audobert, a cave that more than any other prehistoric site in France sticks in my mind as the beginning of my lifelong fascination with human history. We toured the megalithic monuments of the New Stone Age in Brittany that are still associated in my mind with the Iron Age Celts, probably because the Breton Celts on their rocky windswept coast seemed to belong with the menhirs, dolmens, and cromlechs. They still do. But it was the caves and the Old Stone Age art of the Dordogne that caught my imagination.

One of our student group was a Cabot from Boston, and an only son whose parents could not bear to turn him loose in a dangerous world. They followed us everywhere in a large chauffeur-driven limousine. The son was, naturally, revolted. Somehow three of us managed to break him loose, together with the limousine, at Hendaye, on the Spanish border, to spend the first night of liberation in a gambling casino. There we met a charming young lady we thought to be a demimondaine, or, for an American, a semiprofessional scouting out a likely protector in the casino. Thinking of the protective parents, we delightedly proposed that she join us the next morning for the drive to Santander in Spain. At the frontier we learned that the Spanish Crown Prince was expected on the same road, driving from France into Spain. The young lady, with a twinkle, suggested that one of us pretend to be the Prince, sitting on the rear seat alone, with the others in the jump seats and in front with the chauffeur. She thought that I was the most likely pretender because of age and appearance, and so I traveled through the Basque country cheered by villagers lining the road.

In Santander, we conspirators again joined the rest of the School and the distracted parents from Boston. There we met the Abbé Carballo, who was excavating the cave of El Pendo, and arranged to join him in the excavation the next day. But that evening we had an appointment with our lady friend at a cafe designated by her, for a farewell and a postmortem. The five of us were gathered about a table and a bottle of wine when, to our embarrassment, the Abbé Carballo walked in. He smiled benignly, marched up to our table, bowed to the lady, and kissed her hand. After a brief conversation with her in Spanish he laughed, turned to us, and introduced her as the Countess, daughter of the aristocratic family who owned large estates around Santander. They were old friends. We wondered if we really pulled off our hoax, or if all those villagers along the road were simply cheering the Countess, who had been riding with the chauffeur in the front seat.

The Abbé had been digging in El Pendo for many years. To work with him, even for a few days, in a vast chamber with deep deposits containing many bone as well as flint objects of the Upper Paleolithic period was, for me, truly exciting. Moreover he had that quality of enthusiastic explanation and interpretation of what all these things meant to him that, undoubtedly, strikes sparks in the minds of the young. Fifty years ago, before all the popular books and television documentaries on archaeology, these remarkable discoveries in the south of France and northern Spain were little known or understood by most of the world's people. Even for students like us, the work of men like Breuil and Carballo was an exciting discovery of a real world not revealed in our textbooks of that time, nor a part of our historical perspective. For me it was a long leap into a fantastically ancient past where men were already producing great works of art by anyone's standards. And to find the tools and the engravings for oneself, far underground, was the ultimate in reality and truth—the spur toward a new way of thinking that could remain for a lifetime.

Later, we were to continue digging in our own operation, at a rock shelter near St. Léon-sur-Vézère in the Dordogne. But after El Pendo it was dull going. There seemed to be nothing in that site but Mousterian flint scrapers, many of them, and not very interesting to begin with. It was a happy release to end the day of scraping with a small hand tool, by swimming down the Vézère River to the village and to watch the evening descend on the flocks of geese being fed with a stick to enlarge their livers. But the digging and MacCurdy's lectures after dinner soon palled. For a little excitement two of us managed to slip an extra-heavy charge of dynamite into the hole drilled in a boulder so that it would be cracked up and removed from the dig. The result was astonishing. Professor and Mrs. MacCurdy never knew who did it, but serious suspicion centered on me. Life in Paris became more and more attractive.

From Paris Robert de Postetes had written to say that a Franco-German film company was to make a film on the Left Bank, and he was sure we could get a job with them as extras at 100 francs a day. That was my excuse to leave the school so that I could make enough money to return to the U.S. Robert was a White Russian émigré who made a precarious living by teaching tennis. His French was excellent but mine was still almost nonexistent. However, in Paris I learned that as an extra in cabaret scenes I need only mumble something like "Rutabaga, rutabaga," and to appear in a decent suit of clothing. It was pleasant to spend late fall days in Paris street scenes with old friends of many nationalities from Le Dôme. Within a few weeks I had made enough money to pay for a third-class passage on the Paris from Le Havre to New York. At that time the vast decks and lounges of first class on transatlantic liners were almost empty, while third class was jammed with Americans forced to return home because of the depression. A few of us soon learned that first-class stewards were almost glad to have someone about in the empty quarters, so that they made it easy for us to drift through to make use of them, at least, until late in the evening. During the late forties and fifties I was to make many crossings by ship, but none was ever quite so pleasant or exciting as that first. No one could guess at that time that I was seeing the end of an epoch.

For anyone informed about the postglacial period in America it is obvious that from time to time a great drought will hit that vast breadbasket on the high plains of the United States and Canada. The Rainey Land and Cattle Co. in eastern Montana had suffered one of those dust bowl periods, and collapsed in the 1920s. My brother and I would not inherit those rolling hills and lush valleys of buffalo grass or the herds of cattle and horses from our father and his brother. Those two second-generation Irishmen had then turned from ranching and land deals to the promotion of a new type of internal combustion engine, a revolutionary invention that was sure to make a fortune, at least in the dreams of the "big rock candy mountain," as the novelist Wallace Stegner has so well described it.

Back in America at the height of the depression I too was

caught up in the dream. I began by working in the engineering laboratory learning to dismantle, rebuild, and test engines built for motor cars, trucks, and aircraft. Then it was test runs of 500 miles a day through the Midwest, and finally stock sales, mostly in the west, where the dream was endemic. To make a substantial income on commissions from stock sales in the depression was rare. I did, but unfortunately invested it in the stock I sold with such enthusiasm.

My brother, Rex, was then flying an old open-cockpit biplane powered by the new engine, and sometimes I flew with him, taking over the stick control to relearn the aborted flying lessons begun in that exciting year after Lindberg's Atlantic flight. The adventure of "flying by the seat of your pants," as we did in those days, took precedence over stock sales. I went to Rantoul, Illinois, to take the tests for the Army Flying School. Four of us were examined, and at the end of the day the officer in charge called me in and asked, "How would you like to spend your time in the officers' mess with those other three clods?" It is now hard to remember the small country club character of the U.S. Army in the 1930s.

Just before I joined the training school at Kelly Field in Texas, a letter arrived from New Haven proposing that I enroll in Yale's Graduate School and at the same time take a job in the university's Peabody Museum. It came from an irritating sort of fellow, Cornelius Osgood (he had been a colleague in the American School of Prehistoric Research), with whom I had almost come to blows over a bridge game at our first meeting, and with whom I continued to fight during the next four years.

The Army Training School allowed me to postpone my appointment until the next class, so that with some misgivings I could try out a return to academic life in my fourth university. But Yale turned out to be different. Culture, after all, was taken for granted. One studied in the Graduate School because it was interesting, not to "improve" oneself or to find a better job in life, but to enjoy learning for its own sake. Working with Osgood at the museum had its problems, but I soon found other good friends in the museum, in the university, and in New Haven. Probably Hildegard and Norman Donaldson (he was then with Yale Press), Went Eldridge, and John Lobb, as much as the atmosphere of the university, had much to do with my decision to stay there and to give up the adventure of flying. That decision was clinched at Christmas time when I ran into a young army flyer who told me that the depression had hit the army so hard that there was little flying time for him. The army could not afford the gasoline.

I have never been a dedicated scholar, and dislike the label "intellectual." Moreover, I have never been impressed with "professionals." My ambition at sixteen was to remain a cowboy and become a rancher. At twenty there was at least a mild interest in writing, and at twenty-four an enthusiasm for business and flying. Surely, a curious combination of chances, more than any conviction, led me to an academic profession. I have had no regrets, but I think there has always been a half-conscious revolt against the labels, the pattern of thought, and the conventions of the "professionals" and the "experts," who seem to have so much prestige in the late twentieth century.

Author (left) at Barrio Canas excavations in Puerto Rico. 1934.
Photograph courtesy of the author.

CHAPTER TWO

The West Indies

U sually, graduate students in their second year have learned a specialized vocabulary, associated themselves with an in-group, and begun to think of themselves as "professionals." Many will never again take this so seriously, but at the time it is heady stuff. At Yale one highly articulate professor enthralled us all with unfamiliar, esoteric, and impressive words the winged us off into the cloudy realms of abstract propositions, worlds unknown to ordinary mortals. Only later in a bull session would some tough, irreverent student ask, "What the hell was he talking about anyway?"

The specialized jargon never did impress me very much, and the professors I remember are those like Peter Buck, half Irish and half Polynesian, known in New Zealand as Tirangi Hiroa, who did Maori war dances and demonstrated the Polynesian defloration ceremony with a finger inserted under a piece of tapa cloth, thus spellbinding his students. And Bronislaw Malinowski, with his advice to me, "Never write anything without a controversial statement in the first paragraph." Or

Richard Thurnwald, who loved roast pork and sweet potatoes and became profound in his lectures on the economic significance of roast pig and sweet potatoes in Melanesia. (Ten years later I was to find him starving, like everyone else in Berlin at the end of the Second World War, and to provide the elements of a Melanesian feast with the proceeds of contraband cigarettes.) Or Clark Wissler, whose lectures on the Plains Indians carried me right back to eastern Montana and the Crow people, the smell of sagebrush, the wind, the dust, and the buckskin ponies for which I traded with the Crow.

The paying job at the Peabody Museum was matter of fact and down to earth—the sorting out of the basic data of anthropology and archaeology: arrowheads, pots, baskets, Indian buckskins, and Polynesian war clubs. Also, I was expected to organize these things in exhibitions that made sense to casual visitors as well as the students. Museum exhibits in those days were do-it-yourself affairs with no experts but the curators. Dr. Lull, the director, installed his own dinosaurs with the help of his secretary and an artist to paint the background. I began with an exhibition of ghost figures from West Africa, highly indecent little figures of black men, by the standards of that time, and was shocked to find that Dr. Lull's secretary later had tied a neat little white diaper on each one.

To learn something about digging we students dug a rock shelter near New Haven during a few weekends in October. Certainly it was very slim pickings with only a few crude potsherds, a bone awl, or a rough shell tool, but the trees were brilliant in the slanting yellow sunlight of fall, there was the familiar smell of burning leaves and applewood, early frost on the corn shocks, and all the charm of New England in its best season.

There was little fuss about excavation techniques fifty years ago. You read about earlier digging in the region, mapped, dug, and recorded in whatever way seemed reasonable, and that was it. Education and theory involved only book work and interpretation. Thus, with no special training I was soon launched by the museum on an archaeological survey of Connecticut that, during the first two summers at Yale, was to take me all over the state and to result in my first publication, with the ponderous title, "A Compilation of Historical Data Contributing to the Ethnography of Connecticut and Southern New England Indians."

For some reason the Peabody Museum decided upon a Caribbean regional archaeological campaign. Cornelius Osgood and I initiated this with the excavation of several small Indian mounds, which turned out to be burials, in the Okefenokee swamp of northern Florida and southern Georgia. Thereafter, Osgood decided on a system for the campaign: I did the digging and he the writing. Of course it never worked out that way but the system was at least a reflection of our compatibility, a personality conflict that in the end led me to abandon a promising job at Yale for a new frontier at the University of Alaska. In the meantime, however, there was the Caribbean campaign.

Planned excavations of Weedon Island on the west coast of Florida were aborted when the financial "angel," a cinema producer, backed out on us. But that did give me a chance to dig at Crystal River, also on the west coast. In those days Crystal River was unspoiled, an idyllic place in the forest where a huge spring boiled up out of the limestone to fall through a series of crystal pools into a sheltered bay on the gulf. The pools teemed with fish and were a natural place for an Indian village site. Oddly enough, this inconspicuous and quite important little excavation in Florida was to have a special influence on what I think of archaeology in general.

It was the first discovery of something that did not belong there, unexpected and inexplicable. Of the ordinary Indian relics found there I now remember nothing. But deep in the wet sand beside a pool I struck a human skull, dark brown to black, mineralized, and as hard as stone. It was a normal human skull except for one thing. Along the sutures at the back of the skull had grown, been cut, or impressed, a T-shaped groove, during life not after death. Only once had I seen anything like that, precisely the same grooving on a skull from the Stone Age in France. Physical anthropologists at Yale could make nothing of it; there was no explanation and I suppose it remains unpublished somewhere in the collections at the Peabody. A small thing, perhaps, but an accumulation of the unexpected and unexplained in excavations had followed me around the world for many years. It is the accumulation of such things in archaeology that leaves me uneasy about many of our accepted theories.

After a trustees' meeting at the Peabody one day during the winter of my second year at Yale, I met Allison Armour, a man who was to leave the bulk of his fortune to his college at Yale for the sole purpose of supplying dinner port "ad infinitum." He was an Edwardian gentleman (not to be confused with the meat-packing family, he assured me), then in his seventies, with a large, portly build, impeccable English clothing of an earlier generation, and the kindly, thoughtful manner I associated with my maternal grandfather.

That afternoon, walking down Hillhouse Avenue to his college, he proposed that I join him on his research yacht, the *Utowana*, for archaeological exploration of the Bahama Islands. The ship, a converted Dutch freighter, was his contribution to research of all kinds, particularly in the West Indies, where winter cruising is at its best. He explained that we would be joined by Tom Barbour and Jim Greenway from Harvard, who were zoologists bent on collecting birds, butterflies, snakes, lizards, and bats.

In those days the 700 Bahama Islands, extending over 760 miles in the Gulf Stream off Cuba and Florida, were not yet discovered by the mass of urban dwellers along the Atlantic coast of America. Most of the islands are flat, seldom rising more than a few feet above sea level, but there are some hills on Eleuthera, Long, and Cat Islands that reach 100 feet or more. Now tourists swarm over the lovely white beaches and cruise the emerald-green waters, but in the 1930s the few inhabitants (on only twenty-two of the islands) scratched a bare living out of the bootleggers, who used such islands as Grand Bahama as bases for the transshipment of Scotch whiskey by plane and boat into Florida. Most of the population is black, but there are also native whites who are descendants of Tories who fled from the colonies at the time of the American Revolution.

The Native Indian history of the Bahamas still puzzles me. When Columbus made his first landfall in America, on San Salvador Island, he found Indians who spoke a language similar to that of the Arawak Indians of Cuba and Santo Domingo. Like all West Indian natives, those of the Bahamas did not long survive Spanish occupation and were soon replaced by African slaves. But the archaeological remains are strikingly different from those on the neighboring islands to the south. On Cuba, Haiti, Santo Domingo, and Puerto Rico are large village sites marked today by shell middens filled with potsherds, bone, shell, stone tools, and burials. No such middens are found in the Bahamas. The only remains are in the earth of cave floors or entrances to caves, and these are very rare. Also, such deposits contain very few shells. Theodore de Booy of the Heye Foundation in New York, who worked in the islands in 1912, alerted me to this curious circumstance, but neither of us had an explanation. Could the islands have been occupied for only a short time prior to 1492, and were the Lucayan Indians of the Bahamas really the same Arawak people who lived in large numbers on the island of Haiti— Santo Domingo?

Research based on a private yacht in the West Indies certainly was not what I expected in graduate school during the lean years of the Great Depression. A 250-foot vessel manned by a crew of forty and equipped with a library, machine shop, carpenter shop, and laboratories, the *Utowana* was everything one could hope for. Moreover, Mr. Armour was the kind of man who would push his captain to take the ship in among lethal coral reefs so that we could reach a difficult shore with one of the power launches. Often the nervous captain would stand by with engines running and without anchoring for hours while I explored a cave, Tom collected lizards or butterflies, and Jim shot birds. Sometimes we had good sheltered anchorages where we could remain for a few days. Then, if it was one of the big inhabited islands, I could hire a horse and a guide to investigate many possible sites on a large part of the island. In this way we worked over ten of the major islands in a few weeks.

Some of the islands are honeycombed with caves, as in many limestone regions, with great chambers filled with stalactites and stalagmites and with long winding tunnels in an underworld maze that frightened me, particularly when no guide was available. Only near the mouth of the cave could I find any refuse of Indian occupation, but Indian skeletons were tucked away in chambers far underground in total darkness. The search for such burials had my occasional black guides very jumpy indeed. When we were deep underground one day, the beam of my flashlight reflected from the somber green eyes of a goat in a black recess off the channel along which we were crawling on our hands and knees. The guide, a tall, skinny black fellow wearing only a long-tailed shirt, when turning in his attempt to flee, pinned down his forward shirt tail with large bony knees, trapped himself, and moaned, "He got me Boss, He got me!"

The discovery of those human bones, mysteriously hidden away in dark chambers far underground, made me begin to wonder about some of my student preconceptions of history and archaeology. Also, in wandering about one of the uninhabited islands by myself, I think there was a glimmer of future thinking about the futility of trying to fit all those bits of debris from the past into an acceptable history of mankind.

There is something about an uninhabited stretch of land in an open ocean that confuses one's comforting, culturally induced, concept of time as flowing like a river through finite space from a beginning to an end. Perhaps it was the surf breaking on an empty shore, the scuttling of an iguana, smaller but much like an ancient reptile, the flight of birds—all incapsulated in infinite space and time—just as it was for the first man to step ashore there.

Like De Booy I turned up very little of real interest in the Bahamas except for the puzzle as to why those lovely islands, though only a few miles off the Greater Antilles, should be so different archaeologically. Mr. Armour decided to extend our research to Haiti and Santo Domingo, perhaps to give the youngster more results to make his mark. Haiti at that time, 1934, was in its last year of occupation by the American marines, and Santo Domingo, the eastern half of the island, was an independent state run by a dictator. Haiti was predominantly black and French-speaking, Santo Domingo predominantly white and Spanish-speaking. Collections of Indian relics had been made since Colonial times, and some excavation of the great shell middens marking the old Indian villages had been carried out over the past several years. But I was in a new era when "stratigraphy" was all the go in archaeology. We looked for large and deep shell middens that might reveal culture changes or different periods of occupation by aboriginal people.

Marine-occupied Haiti had one great advantage for me: there was a marine air force and a marine pilot willing to fly me all about the island in search of sites. We had many amiable if somewhat hair-raising flights in tiny, primitive fighters with an open cockpit, and in a two-seater amphibian known as the "Duck," exploring Gonave Island off the west coast of Haiti and the northern parts about Cape Haitien and Fort Liberty Bay.

There are many promising caves and large shell middens in Santo Domingo, but it was the Fort Liberty Bay region that interested me the most. There we found the extensive middens with their possibilities for stratified deposits but also, among the artifacts purchased from field workers, some crudely flaked flint blades that I had not seen before in the West Indies. They were so different from the usual implements found in the middens that I was intent upon finding where they came from. Mr. Armour proposed that I return to the Pettigrews' sisal plantation on Fort Liberty Bay during the coming summer to do a systematic search and excavation there.

The cruise of the *Utowana* certainly was an extraordinary way for a student to do his first independent research. Work with experienced scientists like Tom Barbour and Jim Greenway was, of course, the best kind of training in the meaning of research, but, in retrospect, it was the general human environment of that introduction to the West Indies that would have the most lasting effect upon my attitude toward research, the academic world, and professionalism.

Madame Theagene St. Fleur, the tall, raw-boned, commanding black woman, known as "Queen of the La

Gonave Island," led me through the bush of the interior to her caille, a circle of huts much like an African kraal, and with half a dozen prisoners from her jail on the island helped me excavate a midden. Dozing off to sleep by the fire at the center of the kraal among the black prisoners sprawled about the ground, with the muttering of the night birds and the hum of tropical insects, I drifted in three worlds: Africa transported to the New World, a village much like that of Arawak Indians of a thousand years ago; an equally dreamlike world of a dinner party on a yacht with Princess Alice, granddaughter of Queen Victoria; exploring caves with jittery Bahamians or flying over Christoph's castle with Major Moore, playing polo with the marines in Port-au-Prince, or sitting a whole night at a voodoo ceremony with my workmen. This West Indian survey reinforced my experience in the Far East with a new recognition that there are startling differences in belief and behavior wherever you go, even within a small island world. La Gonave, only a few miles across the straits from the bright lights of Port-au-Prince was a different land, unexpected and thought-provoking in terms of my job as a digger.

Major Moore flew me in one of his larger aircraft from Port-au-Prince to San Juan in Puerto Rico via Santo Domingo City—quite a stunt in those days. Refueling in Santo Domingo, we stopped for coffee in a cafe under the walls of the central fortress. We could hear regular bursts of machine gun fire just over the wall. A grim waiter explained that the new dictator was eliminating his opposition.

Prof. Clark Wissler at Yale and the American Museum had arranged with the New York Academy of Sciences for me to undertake a survey of Puerto Rico with the cooperation of the island's Department of Agriculture. There had been sporadic digging in ball courts and middens over many years with helpful publications to give me a lead. Also many collectors, like Adolfo de Hostos, had accumulated impressive collections of elaborate stone collars, carved stone figures known as "zemis," and pottery figurines known as "adornos." Compared to the Bahamas Puerto Rico was a very rich hunting ground. Generally rectangular in shape, the island measures about 50 by 150 kilometers, is mountainous in the interior, and at that time was a major exporter of sugar and coffee. As in all the West Indies, the original Indians were very soon replaced by European whites and African blacks to form a mestizo population with a terrific birthrate. One of the charms of the island is the cool, steady, northeast trade wind.

For two months, accompanied by my brother, Rex, an engineer on vacation, and representatives of the Department of Agriculture, I ranged over the whole island, usually on horseback, recording middens on the coast and ball courts and caves in the interior. Sometimes we were a troop of horsemen made up of local farmers, guides, agents of the Department, soldiers, and police who simply enjoyed the ride and the huge meals with barbecued pig invariably furnished by some plantation owner wherever we went. Once, traveling alone, I was taken desperately ill, with a high fever, in an isolated mountain village and was cared for by all the housewives in the village. Each morning, in half-conscious delirium, I could hear these ladies calling to one another from balcony to balcony to discuss my condition in minute detail and to decide what kind of purge I should be given that day. Puerto Rico remains for me the smell of roasting coffee beans, the pungent odor of crushed sugar cane, brilliant flamboyant trees, the trade wind, horse tracks between villages, and the friendly peasant people in their thatched houses—so very different from the industrial, overcrowded, and tourist-jammed island of today.

Near Ponce on the south coast, Montalvo Guenard, a collector, led me to one of the largest shell middens on the island. In a zone known as Barrio Canas, shells and artifacts could be found scattered over several acres, and in this area were a group of mounds measuring about 65 by 30 meters. I had learned that test pits a few meters square in shell middens could tell you little about the full range of artifacts to be found in them and that such digging was often misleading. To tackle anything as big as Barrio Canas meant a lot of manpower. Fortunately, there was a Puerto Rican Emergency Relief Administration set up to cope with starvation during the depression. Colonel Riggs, a Yale graduate, who was then the chief of police for the island (later to be shot by students at the University of Puerto Rico), provided thirty pick-and-shovel men from the administration. That meant I could dig long, parallel trenches, in 2-meter square sections and 25-centimeter levels right across the whole mound complex.

Barrio Canas, my first major full-scale excavation, was to teach me a lesson in digging that I have never forgotten, and a lesson in humility that was good for a cocksure graduate student. On the hotter, more humid south coast in summer it was customary to begin work very early and to knock off for a siesta in the shade after lunch. One day after weeks of work on the site the foreman roused the workmen and set them to work without waking me. Sometime later I was awakened by our very excited waterboy Andreas shouting, "Something very beautiful, come quick!" In one section of a long trench, nearly 2 meters below the surface, the workmen had reached the bottom of the shell mound and had gone right on down into the subsoil simply because I was not there to move them into another section. And there, in what I had thought was undisturbed earth preceding any human occupation, lay the large part of a red-and-white painted clay vessel startlingly different from anything I had seen in the Greater Antilles.

That turned out to be the "stratigraphy" for which I had been looking, but it was not at all what had been expected. We found that our long trenches through the mound complex intersected a limited area where the familiar shell midden had accumulated over a yellowish substratum that turned out to be composed of sand densely packed with minute particles of disintegrated land crab shells. These curious land dwellers can be seen today in many regions in Puerto Rico, popping in and out of their burrows or scuttling across sandy areas; they are, in fact, a great help in surveying archaeological sites because they tug out buried potsherds when digging their burrows. Whoever made those remarkable red-and-white painted pots must have lived in large part on land crabs. There were also manati, hutia, fish and bird bones, and fragments of the clay platters still used to cook manioc cakes, so their diet was not entirely crab. The following weeks of digging exposed a considerable area of the substratum with painted pottery and land crab shells, contrasting so sharply with the great middens of large marine shells and cruder unpainted ware. In that small island the surprising objects found below the shell middens at Canas led to streams of visitors, newspaper stories, and a certain amount of embarrassment on my part since the credit went to an overlong siesta.

Once the clue was unearthed in a neatly stratified site at Canas, it was not difficult to detect the remains of the two periods and two cultures at Barrio Coto on the northwest coast and Monserrate on the northeast coast. That winter, back at the university, buried in many thousands of potsherds and bone, shell, and stone tools, I wrote a Ph.D. thesis on the sequence of two distinct cultures in Puerto Rico, a thesis that was attacked and buried, then revived by later discoveries, so that it remains a bone of contention to the present, fifty years later.

Irving Rouse, who took over the West Indies research when I moved to the Arctic in 1935, generally excavated only pits in the shell middens because he did not have the funds to employ many workmen, and never found stratified deposits as in the

Canas site. Hence he decided that there was no sharp distinction between the two types of culture but that over time the older simply changed into the later. Then another student of mine, Juan Ortiz Aguilu, much later, discovered another stratified site like Canas, reviving my theory of two cultures representing two distinct peoples, one succeeding the other in certain islands of the West Indies. Now I suspect that this simple conflict of opinion about archaeological interpretation may have had some effect upon my future skepticism concerning the way we reconstruct the past.

The following spring, eager to be back in the West Indies, I managed to avoid graduation ceremonies and arrive at Fort Liberty Bay in Haiti a full-fledged, card-carrying member of the archaeological guild. With me was a young undergraduate, Irving Rouse, who was destined to spend his professional life in West Indian archaeological research and to demolish my theories about the history of the islands. Introducing him as the speaker to a group in Philadelphia, many years later, my clearest memory of him was sitting in a small Haitian jail with me, while the local police chief and his men dug out a large mound at Meillac in north Haiti, where they thought we were digging for pirate treasure. Perhaps that was a good beginning for a very serious and very academic sort of youngster.

Thanks to the cooperative Haitian field workers on the Pettigrew sisal plantation, we did finally run down the source of those puzzling flint blades on ancient sites that were occupied before West Indians made pottery. Theoretically they should be very ancient, and for once this was generally accepted, but only after the development of radiocarbon dating. We also dug a number of shell middens, much like those in Puerto Rico, but found no earlier horizon with hard, well-fired, painted pottery as in Puerto Rico.

Then, later in the summer, I returned to Puerto Rico to teach in the university there and to continue excavating at

Monserrate, which is now one of the great beach resorts for the people of San Juan. At that time it was a lonely, lovely beach backed by coconut groves and occupied only be land crabs. I lived with the foreman of the plantation in the only house in the vicinity and, with workmen, excavated a series of shell middens in the shade of rattling coconut palms and the roar of surf on the reef protecting the beach. That was my farewell to tropical West Indian archaeology. For years, on the Arctic coast of Alaska, I would remember Monserrate beach and wonder why the search for those hypothetical migrants from Asia to America across the Bering Straits could possibly keep me on that forbidding Arctic shore.

Fifty years later I returned, briefly, to work in Haiti with Juan Ortiz Aguilu, who was then excavating the site of Bois Neuf on the west coast of the island. Scores of archaeologists are now working all over the West Indies, and the whole conception of island prehistory has changed.

What I had termed the "Flint Culture" in north Haiti had been found at other sites in Haiti, Santo Domingo, and Cuba, with traces also in Yucatan. With carbon dating it is now thought to date to between 3000 and 1000 B.C. Moreover, it had been observed that the flint-chipping method is remarkably like that of the so-called Levallois technique of Middle Paleolithic times in Europe.

My "Crab Culture," now known as "Saladoid," has been traced through the islands from Puerto Rico to the north coast of South America, and an apparently related culture with similar advanced technique of ceramic manufacture has been found on Vieques Island off the east coast of Puerto Rico. What

I called the "Shell Culture" is now known as the "Ostinoid Series" and is also traced to northern South America. There is still an argument as to whether these two cultures represent different people of different time horizons. Both are now dated within the Christian era.

Recently I have learned that Pepe Ortiz, one of the present "upsetters" in West Indian archaeology, has found a totally unexpected site in the mountains of Puerto Rico where terraced mountain slopes represent an advanced type of cultivation resembling that in the Andes.

Speaking at a recent International Archaeological Conference on the Caribbean Region, in Puerto Rico (where many young people were surprised to find I was still alive), I thought of all these changes and spoke about chance discoveries that were unexpected and inevitably altered our theories of the past. Afterward one young man came up to say he thought my theories of fifty years ago had been proved right after all. But another youngster told me bluntly that he did not believe a word I said. Apparently, even in this rather limited cul-de-sac archaeology is alive, well, and as controversial as ever.

Whaling Captain shares catch with his crew and the villagers. Point Hope
Alaska, 1940. *Photograph courtesy of the author.*

CHAPTER THREE

The Arctic

My first sight of Eskimos was a group of boys swimming in the sea near Nome, Alaska. We were flying in a little bush plane along the shore on one of those rare but very hot days in late summer. The pilot took delight in skimming the beach to prove they really were Eskimos, playing in the surf of the Bering Sea. En route to St. Lawrence Island, I was to meet Captain Pete Paulson and his little schooner, the *Nanuk* (polar bear), at Nome for a crossing to the island. Aircraft were rare in Alaska in 1936, and no one would think of flying across the Bering Sea to St. Lawrence.

Dr. Lull, director of the Peabody Museum, and Mr. Armour, my sponsor for research in the West Indies, both thought I was mad to abandon a promising future for an unlikely gamble in the Arctic. But Professor Wissler in his manipulating role at the American Museum had a job up his sleeve that was tempting. A German naturalist, Otto Geist, had excavated part of a very large Eskimo site at Kukulik on St. Lawrence Island, and, at the newly formed University of Alaska, had a vast collection of artifacts that must be studied and prepared for publication during the months from September to April. With Geist, I was to do this and also to establish a department of anthropology and direct the university's new museum. I left Puerto Rico in late August to arrive in Fairbanks by the middle of September, just in time for the first snowfall.

With the thoroughness of a nineteenth-century naturalist, Geist collected everything. There were scores of crates of walrus bones, stones, very crude potsherds, fragments of tools and weapons collected all over the island, and natural history specimens of all kinds. In the few buildings of the new university at College, Alaska, near Fairbanks, there was not even a room to unpack in, to say nothing of storing such collections. My first step was to sort out those cases of excavated and labelled specimens, then dig a large hole out back of the main building and rebury a large part of the rest. It was one way of clearing the deck so that some sort of publication could be prepared during the winter. Geist suddenly became ill and went to bed for most of the winter with a supply of cigars and muscatel wine.

Dr. Bunnell, president of Yale University, in preparing me for a first winter in central Alaska, described it as a "cozy" country. And he was right. Silent, windless, day-after-day snowfall buried the evergreen forests in a soft, deep, white blanket. Woodsmoke from cabin chimneys rose straight up through the trees and the temperature dropped to 50 and 60 degrees below zero. Inside tight warm cabins people read, listened to music, played poker, and entertained their neighbors, who arrived on snowshoes, skis, or by dog team. The world "outside" seemed unreal and very far away. Most of the time it was dark except for stars and moonlight and when the sun rolled along the horizon for a few hours; the frenetic activity of summer was gone and the world of humans drew in upon itself, waiting for the sun.

Spring, with mosquitoes hatching out under snowbanks and the northward flight of birds, found the Kukulik report finished, Geist back on his feet, and plans made for an expedition into the Upper Tanana River valley. The snow and ice would not be gone from the Arctic coast and St. Lawrence until July, but in late May and June one could work in the interior.

The seasons set a pattern for me that would continue for the next seven years: early summer searching or digging sites with Athapascan Indians of Alaska's forested lands, late summer on the tundra of the Arctic coast with the Eskimos, and winter usually at the university teaching, writing, and sorting out collections in the museum.

Those years with totally different tribes of Arctic people have left me with many unresolved theories about the nature of heredity, the influence of environment, and the chance of history. How does it happen that Alaska's Indians speak a language related to that of the Navajo, so many thousands of miles away, and completely different from that of their close neighbors, the Eskimos. Why should Athapascan men give up when faced with the shattering effect of western civilization, while Eskimos take to it so easily that some become cinema actors, golf pros, army officers, and successful politicians. One summer I found the Athapascan village of Cruskshank at Tanana Crossing very near to starvation. Most of the men were ill in their cabins, and it was the women who managed to keep them all alive. When Moses, one of the few men willing to leave the village, and I left on a ninety-mile walk to Ketchemstock, we came upon a migration of caribou, numbering thousands, only some thirty miles from the village. To my proposal that we return at once to advise the village of an endless supply of meat, Moses only shrugged and said, "The men won't come out anyway." Twenty-five years later I found Andrew, an old friend from Tanana Crossing, living on the Alaska highway. He said there was no point in returning to Tanana Crossing because all the men were gone and there were only women and half-breed children.

During those years I found only one Athapascan group that was healthy, strong, and a going concern. That was in the far north near the headwaters of the Chandalar River, a tributary of the Yukon. With an Eskimo and an Indian from Fort Yukon I ascended the river for perhaps 150 to 200 miles in a small boat with an inboard engine. When we could see the smoke of the village, the Indian said the Eskimo and I should wait until he had gone ahead to arrange for us. "These people do not like Eskimos and are afraid of them," he explained. That village was for me a total surprise. It was as if some Wellsian time machine had transported me into past centuries before white men had discovered Alaska; there were no dilapidated cabins, no junk of civilization, no ragged Indians in cast-off clothing, and no feeling of dejection. They were proud people in clean, new, caribou-skin clothing, living in skin tents that were clean and fresh with evergreen boughs and new skins on the floor. We were received with caution and reserve but with traditional hospitality.

I was to learn that two brothers dominated the settlement and had determined to isolate it from all possible white contact. Occasionally the brothers would travel to Fort Yukon for ammunition, tea, sugar, and new guns, but for the most part the people remained cut off from the modern world in a vast uninhabited forest. The Chandalar Athapascans were my only glimpses of the ancient hunters of the Arctic taiga, a kind of people who, in very small numbers, once occupied the enormous forested region of northern Siberia, Alaska, and Canada. They seemed to me shy, introverted, difficult to know or understand, and totally unlike the Eskimos. In spite of migrating caribou herds, fish in the rivers and lakes, rabbits, and grouse, the taiga can support only a very small population, a condition that explains the very few, difficult to locate, and very small archaeological sites in the forest zones.

Of course, as an anthropologist, I recorded the customs, beliefs, and other cultural traits of the disappearing forest people as well as thóse of the tundra Eskimos, but only the culture in action remains vivid to me. When I asked the two brothers about ancient sites on the Chandalar, they spoke of their permanent winter camp many miles to the south, but were reluctant to take me there. Finally they agreed and at the winter camp I understood their reluctance. On the door of their parents' cabin was a note written in a script that missionaries had long before taught the Indians to use in writing their own native language. It said simply that those two very aged parents had gone off to hunt rabbits. The brothers looked stricken. Then I learned that the parents had been left alone in the winter camp to die, as was the custom for the old people. We did not go in search of them. My own grim sadness at the thought of those lonely old ones hopelessly trying to snare a rabbit was reflected in the eyes of their sons.

The lonely course of the Chandalar River, winding through stunted, near-tree-line forests of alder, birch, and spruce, like the Indian village near its source, is for me symbolic of an ancient world in the Arctic taiga. Its essence is the cry of the loon. That mysterious bird, still casting its supernatural spell over endless lakes in the Arctic, appears in the myths of all the many different Arctic tribes, its meaning elusive, but its cry as lonely, haunting, and sad as it is today in the forest wilderness. Once, in an ancient Arctic grave, I found the skull of a loon with carved ivory eyes in the empty sockets and an ivory band encircling its beak.

That very hasty study of Geist's collections from St. Lawrence Island, and the cultural stratigraphy I worked out for its publication, had left me very uneasy about my conclusions. When the ice had drifted northward out of the

Bering Sea in July that first year, I reached St. Lawrence on the *Nanuk* with Father Raymond Murray of Notre Dame. Earlier in the summer we had floated down a stretch of the Yukon from Rampart Rapids to the mouth of the Tanana on a raft. A priest who taught archaeology at Notre Dame for many years, Father Murray had decided to learn something about archaeology in the field, and proposed to try it out with me. It might seem an exasperating business to work alone in the Arctic with an elderly man who had never used his hands for anything, but I soon learned that the spirit can be more important than physical ability. The raft was the test case. Made of driftwood logs held together with wooden pins and being the first I had ever made, it was anything but reassuring. On the Yukon, a mile wide at some points, with strong currents and stiff winds, it is very important that a raft should hang together. Father Murray, who must have been even more terrified than I, cheerfully worked his hand-held sweep and sang "Mighty Lak a Rose." Later, in the small hold of the Nanuk during the whole of a very rough crossing, he was desperately sick, but when he emerged from the hold off the coast of St. Lawrence, he grinned and said, "I have decided that it is softer to lie on canned peaches than on canned pears."

There are only two Eskimo villages on the island, one called Gambel and the other Savoonga. Five miles to the east of Savoonga, on the north coast, is the huge midden left by the ancient village of Kukulik, which Geist had excavated. To reassure myself on the sequence of cultural remains, it was obvious that we must make a deep cut through the midden from top to bottom. But, of course, it was frozen solid with only a few inches melted on the surface. How does one cut through a frozen mass of bones, wood chips, dog dung, bits of skin, driftwood logs from ruined houses, stones, ancient meat caches, and tools and implements of all kinds? I could see from

Geist's cuts that we must get down nearly ten feet to reach the earliest "Old Bering Sea" remains.

With the Great Depression's "Emergency Relief" funds, Geist had built and equipped a long frame house at Kukulik that was still stocked with quantities of canned foods as well as tools and other digging equipment, all carefully maintained intact by the Savoonga Eskimos for the past three years. Father Murray and I decided to run two eight-hour shifts of Eskimo diggers each day and to feed them and ourselves from the three-year-old stocks of canned food. Then began our experiments in thawing frozen archaeological deposits. For some reason Geist had laid on an astonishing supply of vegetable salad oil. First we tried burning this in panlike sections of oil drums on the frozen ground after the surface few inches of thawed material was removed. It was useless; heat goes up, not down. An inch or two would thaw naturally each day, but at that rate we would never reach bottom in the short summer season left to us. With a water pump from the storeroom and a firehose it was possible to pump sea water up onto the mound to flood the trench we were digging, but the Bering Sea is very cold, and the increased thawing was not great. There was also a large store of twelve-gauge shotgun shells. I tried blasting with a theory that charges of powder set in drilled holes might crack the deposit so that sea water could penetrate deeper. It might have worked except that I could never concoct a satisfactory fuse. We were reduced to reliance on sea water and natural thaw.

The thawed muck from that deposit is indescribable, except that is was very slippery. A plank trestle was built out from the top of the mound so that we could shovel the mess into wheelbarrows and then trundle it out along the trestle to be dumped in the tailing pile on the sea shore. The Eskimos, somehow, in their slippery sealskin-soled boots managed to keep their feet on those exceedingly slippery planks. But

Father Murray, who I'm sure had never before touched a wheelbarrow, was determined to try it. On his first attempt he went right over the end of the trestle with his wheelbarrow into the ooze below. As usual he came up grinning. The Eskimos rolled on the ground in laughter.

When the *Nanuk* returned to take Murray back to the mainland, I missed him very much, and so did the Eskimos. They continued to live in Savoonga, commuting to Kukulik in their "umiaks," walrus-skin boats with outboard engines, while I stayed alone at the site to continue water pumping during the short night hours between shifts. But someone in Savoonga always seemed to have an eye on Kukulik, five miles away across the bay. One night, carrying a hurricane lantern, I went out to gas up the pump engine and foolishly put my finger into the tank to test the level of the gas. The inner edge was peened over so that my finger was trapped. I felt like one of the monkeys we caught in the Philippines with his fist in a chained and perforated coconut ripping the hazel nut we had cached inside. It was cold and wet and a long time until daylight and the next shift. But it was not long before I heard the hum of an outboard and then was surrounded by laughing Eskimos. I told them about trapping monkeys in the Philippines.

When the first snows came we had reached the bottom of the cut, and I was packed up waiting for Captain Zeusler and his Coast Guard cutter, the Northland. Fortunately, the stratigraphy was correct, and defined clearly by a sequence of changing forms of harpoon heads, just as distinct periods are defined by changes in pottery forms in so many sites around the world. From elaborately engraved harpoon heads known as the "Old Bering Sea" type through "Punuk," "Birnirk," and "Thule" to the much plainer "modern" types with iron blades, there were certainly represented here many centuries of occupation. The Savoonga people told me that Kukulik was

not abandoned until white whalers from New England
introduced rum after 1850, and a great many St. Lawrence
people starved because the hunters were too drunk to go out
after walrus. The Eskimo council allowed no liquor of any kind
on St. Lawrence while I was there.

The pressure of time during the short summer season makes
Arctic digging a different matter from the leisurely excavations
of temperate zones. Moreover, it rains through most of that
short season so that one is constantly working in a downpour.
Directing two Eskimo crews for sixteen hours a day, cooking
canned food meals for them and myself, and making notes,
charts, and photos and labelling bagged artifacts six days a
week did not leave me much time to get acquainted with the
people of Savoonga. But there were Sundays, when no
Christianized Eskimo would work, and long hours on the site
learning about Eskimo jokes and laughter, the influence of
successful hunters and responsible men, and their quick
intelligence.

Some individuals I shall never forget. Pillowak was a refugee
from the Eskimo settlement at Cape Chaplino, Siberia, and one
of the most ugly and cheerful men in the group. One eye was
gone and his whole face was distorted. As an outsider with no
family connections on the island he was at the bottom of the
social scale and was relegated to the worst possible dirty jobs.
He was always at the bottom of the cut in the worst of the
muck, but I could usually hear him singing; his favorite tune
was "A-roaming in the Gloaming." To win his place in the
Savoonga village he was working for one of the chief boat
owners for seven years, in order to marry his daughter. Ataka
was a handsome, neat, meticulous, and successful man who
looked as if he were Japanese. His daughter, Ellie, was also a
handsome girl, who succeeded in life. Many years later she sent
me a photo of herself, buxom and radiating vitality, taken with
her four tall, husky sons. I was reminded of her famous

wedding aboard the Northland when I returned to St. Lawrence three years after my first work there. We received a radio message aboard the cutter, sent by a "ham" Eskimo operator, explaining that there was no priest on the island and asking if Captain Zeusler would perform the ceremony. The chief engineer made a wedding ring, the cook prepared a wedding breakfast, and the captain turned out the whole crew to greet the bridal party in dress formation. Up aboard the cutter, Ellie proudly marched down the line, at least eight months pregnant.

At that time in the Bering Sea "outside" contact for the Eskimos was largely limited to missionaries, teachers, a few traders, and the summer patrol of the Coast Guard ship. Zeusler was for several years on that patrol and had grown to like and admire the people to whom he brought medical care, emergency relief, and a tenuous kind of government supervision. He had a profound and informed interest in Eskimo history as well, and thus was glad to pick me up or deposit me at out of the way places like the Diomede Islands in the Bering Straits, isolated King Island, Point Hope on the Arctic shore, or at Nome or Point Barrow. Over the years I became like one of the crew and like them admired the man. Basically a nervous person, operating in a very stormy sea along dangerous coasts, he would still take his ship into precarious positions if an emergency required it, or even if he felt it was part of his duty. Those tight spots were hard on his crew and hard on him.

There is something moving about the esprit de corps on a successfully commanded ship. Somewhere the crew had acquired a wildcat kitten and raised it aboard the Northland. That was strictly against Coast Guard rules, and when the crew learned that the commandant was to come aboard for part of the cruise, there was consternation about the cat. Zeusler simply said, "What cat?" During his first morning on the bridge the cat ambled out of the wheelhouse as usual and the commandant exclaimed, "My God! A wild cat!" Both the watch officer and the helmsman calmly said, "What cat?" Thereafter the commandant as well as the crew failed to see any cat throughout the duration of his inspection cruise.

In 1937 Zeusler cabled me from Seattle to say that he had been ordered to take his ship into Netepalmer Bay, just south of the point at Cape Chaplino in Siberia, and that was my chance to land in forbidden territory. Russian attempts to fly across the Arctic Ocean at that time meant that Washington and Moscow had agreed upon coordination of weather stations, and the U.S. Coast Guard was to initiate this with a call at Cape Chaplen. In late summer again, I was picked up at Nome for the sixty-five-mile crossing from Cape Prince of Wales via the Diomede Islands to the Cape Chaplino. We anchored off a small native village of Eskimos and Chuckchi and were soon surrounded by umiaks. This was my first look at Siberian people, and I could not tell Chuckchi from Eskimo. Not since shortly after the Russian Revolution had any ship crossed from America. The natives were just as excited as we and swarmed aboard with grins and handshakes. But the welcome was short-lived. Red Army officers soon followed. There was no welcome, and they ordered us to leave at once and said they had never heard of any agreement between Moscow and Washington. There was no allowance made for a gale, just beginning, and we steamed out into one of the worst I have ever seen in the north. The Northland managed to keep her head up into the wind, but we were blown down to the Kamchatka coast during the next few days and crossed and recrossed the international date line until it was difficult to know what day it was. Zeusler ordered a meal of walrus meat just to see how immune we were to seasickness. In the worst of it the strains of Debussy's "La Mer" ran through my head, and even today that music reminds me of my worst storm in the Bering Sea.

At that time Levanevskiy, a Soviet flyer, was lost trying to fly across the Arctic Ocean. A great international rescue plan went into effect and several Soviet research planes were based at Fairbanks. Because the Soviet flyers knew little or no English, my wife, Penelope, who had learned Russian in order to translate Soviet reports on archaeological work in Siberia, became their interpreter. That meant that we saw a good deal of the flyers during several weeks, entertained them in our home, and talked a lot about the lack of communication between the Soviet Union and the United States. About a year later, one of the flyers sent us an article that he had written about life in Alaska. In it was the comment that in that backward country even professors lived in log cabins. True, we had built one, much more expensive than a frame house, but in the Soviet Union at that time log houses were the shame of Moscow. Because of the search and the attempted friendly relations, Governor Gruening of Alaska and I hit upon a plan to propose scientific cooperation with the Soviet Union; he spoke with our State Department and the Soviet ambassador. As a result, while the search still continued, my wife and I left New York for a conference in Moscow with the head of the Soviet Academy of Sciences.

That was in the winter of 1937-1938 and the time of the ill-famed Moscow trials. Looking back, it now seems naive to think we could have arranged an exchange of Soviet and American archaeologists for cooperative research in the Bering Strait region when almost any contact of Russians with outsiders could mean the concentration camp and when only a few officials were allowed to leave the country. But I knew of several Soviets working in northeast Siberia who like me were trying to find evidence of the hypothetical ancient migrations from Asia to America. It was obvious that we should collaborate, and there was a certain relaxation of tension with the search for Levanevskiy. At the Soviet Academy we met with the director and a party-member interpreter to present our case. When I had finished, the two of them conferred in Russian, thinking it impossible that two Americans like us could understand them. The gist was that there was nothing they could do about our proposal and yet they must string us along for a polite interval or propose we work with Soviet archaeologists in southwest Asia. Northern Siberia and an exchange of persons was out of the question. The the director explained through the interpreter that the Academy would consider our proposal. In the meantime we should visit museums, meet Soviet archaeologists, and join members of the Academy at official dinner parties. We should return next day to work out a schedule for our Moscow visit.

Upon our return the chief was there with no interpreter. We waited speechless, all of us growing more and more embarrassed until Penelope broke down and addressed the chief in Russian. He looked horrified, remembering the day before. It was awkward, but worse in that pathologically suspicious period, we then came under suspicion. From then on we were under the tight control of a tourist guide at all meetings, museum visits, parties, and tours through the countryside.

Of course, nothing came of it except for meeting several Soviets who were to stay in touch with us for more than a generation—Georgi F. Debets, who came to the United States in 1956 to work on a collection of skeletons from Alaska; Boris Petrovsky, later director of the Hermitage Museum, who also came to visit us in Philadelphia; and M. G. Levin, who died of lung cancer just after the Soviet confrontation over Cuba, but not before we managed through a drug company in Philadelphia to fly pain-killing drugs into Moscow during those few days when the confrontation was at its most critical point.

Ordered to leave the Soviet Union before the first of May, we chose to go by train through Romania. In the long, slow ride to Odessa we lived in a four-bunk compartment with an army officer and an official, who, in the customary traveling pajamas, spent many hours in their bunks arguing with us about the merits of communism versus capitalism, life in the Soviet Union versus that in the United States, and life in general. The trials and the concentration camps were taboo; anything else was fair game for argument.

The essence of the Soviet attitude at the time was, for me, symbolized by the little two-car train that carried us across the border into Romania. Before the border we were removed from the usual old, battered railroad cars and transferred to a coach that belonged with Alice in Wonderland. Like the new engine, it was polished to shine, red plush seats were equipped with lace doilies, fresh flowers were everywhere, and the conductor looked like a German bandleader. Indeed, we steamed into Romania in great style, but did not fool the Romanians. Customs officials were filled with laughter and asked how we liked the "showboat."

Penelope's uncle, Lincoln MacVeagh, was then the U.S. ambassador in Athens, and it was he, upon our return from the Soviet Union, who introduced me to classical archaeology. For an anthropological archaeologist digging in the frozen mounds of the far north, the never-ending American dig at Corinth was a kind of "precious" excavation: stuffy students, classical professors interpreting remains with Greek logic, and a general attitude that only Greek remains and Greek thought were of any significance. I had seen the Acropolis eight years before, with a Greek boy off the *Iphigenia*, after an early morning visit to his uncle's wine cellar, but sitting on the Acropolis in the moonlight with Uncle Lincoln, a Greek scholar, was a totally different experience. As ambassador for twenty years he had become famous for his influence on young Foreign Service officers and their careers, an influence that was to have a far-reaching effect on my own career. Not only did he counteract a first, somewhat impatient reaction to traditional classical archaeology, but some years later he effectively advised me to return to archaeology from the U.S. Foreign Service, which I had joined during the Second World War. At one time he accompanied me on a search for classical sites to excavate in Spain and Portugal, and later lived to see me turn to a search for Archaic Greek Sybaris in southern Italy.

With an ominous shadow of war over Europe and the rising belligerence of the three forms of state socialism, Penelope and I decided to see something of the other two forms before returning to Alaska. That summer of 1938, prowling in Italy and Germany, I came to the conclusion that all three were dangerous forms of dictatorial, regimented state socialism, and the most brutal was the Soviet Union, the next was Germany, and the least Italy. That opinion survived the Soviet-Allied detente of the war, lasted during the Cold War period of the 1950s, then shifted somewhat upon our return to the Soviet Union in 1957, just after the Twentieth Soviet Party Congress. But in 1940, on the pack ice off Point Hope, Alaska, as a member of an Eskimo whaling crew, I found it very difficult to explain to those men just what was happening in Europe.

Chance, surely, is one of the most imponderable elements in any life. One morning in Germany we suddenly decided to attend an International Congress of Anthropology in Denmark, meeting in early September that year. Congresses, like committee meetings, have always bored me to death, but at that one I met Helge Larsen, in a beer hall—a chance meeting that was to change both our lives. A tall, slender, dark-haired Dane, serious in his work but with an infectious sense of fun, Helge was bursting with energy and ideas. That first evening we agreed to set up a Danish-American expedition to Point Hope, Alaska, where his compatriot, Knud Rasmussen, had found in the 1920s what he thought to be the most interesting site in the American Arctic.

Helge joined me the following summer with all the equipment required for a meticulous Danish excavation. Louis Giddings, a biologist studying mosquitoes at the University of Alaska, and I eyed all those tools, survey equipment, long painted poles, and other elaborate gear with misgivings. Louis, an old hand in Arctic research, who was joining us to try tree-ring dating in the Arctic, knew, of course, that we three and a pilot must try to crowd into a tiny bush plane on pontoons and take with us only a minimum of essential gear. The pilot obligingly tried to accommodate us, loading all the Danish gear into an already overloaded plane. It was a rare night for Alaska, hot and still, when we tried to take off from the Chena River outside Fairbanks. Even though all three of us hung over the pilot to get the weight forward, he could not get the plane off the water, even when rocking it up on one pontoon. Much of the gear was unloaded and we finally made it, barely clearing the first hill. Helge was learning about archaeology by air in the Arctic. We landed in a rough sea off the sand spit at Point Hope, and the pilot held the aircraft against the beach with the engine while we unloaded.

Point Hope was then a native village of about 250 persons at the tip of a long sand spit extending eleven miles out into the Arctic Ocean from Cape Thompson, 200 miles north of Bering Strait. With a few new frame houses and several old semi-subterranean traditional Eskimo houses, it still occupied the landward side of the ancient village site of Tigara, a complex group of low grass-covered mounds made up of abandoned houses and debris accumulated over many centuries. It is difficult to comprehend that Point Hope (Tigara) has probably been continually occupied nearly as long as Rome.

We found a very considerable archaeological excavation already underway at the old site. A group of Eskimo women were systematically digging in search of artifacts that could be sold to Coast Guard crews each summer. That created a difficulty. The Eskimo council that controlled the village saw absolutely no reason why we should interfere with the business of their wives. For two days we sat in the council trying to explain why, until Helge finally won the argument with his statement that Knud Rasmussen had recommended such an excavation as ours. All the old men remembered him, that impressive half-Eskimo half-Danish fellow who in 1924 had crossed the whole American Arctic from Greenland to Alaska by dog team and could speak their language.

We agreed to set up an excavation that would not interfere with the wives, and then proceeded with the expert advice of the women. They were most critical of our methods. In our separate excavations a hearty Eskimo laugh was on us. They uncovered an old house floor upon which lay some fifty carved wooden masks and a kikituk; ancient Eskimo dance masks are now a rare collector's item and were even then very valuable in trade with the Coast Guard. But the kikituk was something very special, a grotesque animal with sharp inset teeth that was born of a male shaman and could be used by him to kill people. All during that summer we bargained to buy the collection before the Coast Guard arrived. It was no go until all the tobacco in the village had run out, and our last pound clinched the negotiations. Then, desperate ourselves, we tried to talk the one missionary in the village, an Episcopal priest, out of some of his. Archdeacon Goodman sent us back to camp with three sticks of bubblegum.

Scientifically controlled excavations in the Arctic were rare at that time. They were ordinarily confined to the low grass-covered mounds, marking old Eskimo villages, that could be seen all along the Arctic coast from Eastern Siberia to Greenland. Earlier excavations of such mounds had defined a sequence of periods of cultural development known as Old Bering Sea, Punuk, Birnirk, Thule, and Recent (levels where European trade objects were found). At that time there was no way of dating the early periods, but we surmised from the changes and the extensive deposits of debris that Old Bering Sea must be as old as the beginning of the Christian era (always a convenient date for Western archaeologists). Old Tigara, which showed us just such a sequence, held little interest for Helge or me. After his excavations in Greenland and mine on St. Lawrence Island; the objects and periods represented there were all too familiar. Consequently Helge went off to dig at Jabbertown, a long-abandoned nineteenth-century commercial whaler's village seven miles east of Tigara, where he found buried houses of the Thule period, thought to be about seven or eight hundred years old. Louis prowled the coastline in search of driftwood logs that could give him a long tree-ring growth record. Such logs, drifting down the Yukon and other Arctic rivers to the Bering Sea and the Arctic Ocean, are beached all along the shore. In the Arctic cold they can remain intact for centuries, and they have always supplied the Eskimos with fuel, wood for boat frames and implements, and wood for house construction. I continued to work at Tigara with a small crew of Eskimos.

One evening Helge and Louis, returning together along the beach on the north shore of the spit, noticed some odd rectangular depressions on the surface of the tundra. That night in camp we got into one of our usual argumentative discussions about that those depressions were. Louis, the biologist, thought they might be the remains of ancient houses, but Helge and I, the professional archaeologists, knew that such remains always appeared as mounds, not depressions, and proposed that they were the result of frost action on the tundra. But I remembered that Jimmy Killigivuk, one of the Tigara Eskimos, had brought me a small piece of ivory from that part of the shore carved in a style I had never seen before. Helge and I were bored with our excavations anyway and so decided to dig into some of the depressions to see what they really were.

The next morning each one of the three of us picked his own likely-looking depression and began to dig. Within a few minutes we were all excited. Only a foot or two under the surface, near the center of the depressions, we turned up large numbers of flint chips, and then began to find very small, thin, and beautifully chipped blades, strikingly different from the large, thick, and more crudely chipped blades found in familiar Eskimo sites. We soon realized that we were digging around the central fireplaces of rectangular houses of some sort, where men had been sitting to make their knives and weapon points.

All work at the other sites ceased, and before the Coast Guard arrived to take us off the point we had excavated several of the houses. We then knew that we had found a new and completely unexpected horizon in Arctic history. Moreover, a few fragments of carved bone and ivory were in a style that seemed to be related and yet distinctly different from what was then called "Old Bering Sea Style 1." Also, not a single fragment of pottery or polished slate tools, the most common objects in Alaskan Eskimo sites, had been found. Hence we concluded that the site preceded the Old Bering Sea period and was, then, the oldest known site in the Arctic. Were the inhabitants Eskimos or some other earlier people?

Helge was aboard a ship returning to Denmark when Europe went to war. With Denmark occupied by the Germans his return to Alaska the following summer, 1940, seemed hopeless until Professor Gutmund Hatt in Copenhagen somehow managed, through the German general in command there, to arrange Helge's return to the then-neutral United States via Germany and Portugal. With his wife Gerda and son Ole, he arrived in New York by clipper plane in 1941 and soon all three joined us in Fairbanks. With the United States later at war they could not, of course, return to Denmark until the end of the war, and Helge continued to work in Alaska and at the American Museum in New York for the duration.

In the meantime, with the discovery of an unexpected and enigmatic early horizon in Arctic history, I decided to return to Point Hope in January 1940 to spend the late winter and spring hunting with the Eskimos in order to gain some comprehension of aboriginal life during that most difficult part of the year—the most characteristic season in the life of the Arctic people, which very few archaeologists had ever experienced.

Just after the first of the year Penelope and I arrived with a bush plane on skis to find the Tigara people very near starvation. The whale hunt of the previous spring was poor so that meat caches were empty, and pack ice had closed in so tightly about the Point that seal hunting through the ice was not possible. Even worse was the shortage of fuel, the seal oil then used for light and heat in the semisubterranean houses and the new frame houses covered with sod and snow blocks. With temperatures of 30° below zero and high winds, the village had almost disappeared under drifting and hard-packed snow. And, with little food and almost no fuel, the dark interior of the houses was very grim. All my ideas about life in the high Arctic, acquired like most diggers during the bright summer months, began to change. We moved into a sod- and snow-covered frame house, ten feet square, with a Malinois pup (a gift from an aunt and uncle in Antwerp) and an Eskimo girl who was to teach us how to survive in an Arctic winter. A moderation in the weather made it possible for two Eskimos with a dog team to fetch a load of lignite coal from a surface deposit about fifty miles from Tigara so that we could melt ice for drinking water, cook what little food we had brought with us, and at least melt the ice that had gathered on the inside of the house.

By late January, shifts in the pack ice opened leads that quickly froze over, but made it possible to fish for tom cod and to kill an occasional seal. The women and children sat about holes in the new ice jigging for those very small, almost transparent tom cod, and the men ranged over the pack looking for openings where they could shoot seals rising to breathe. Each morning, when a glow of daylight appeared on the horizon, I dressed in two layers of caribou skin clothing and boots made of caribou leg skin with sealskin soles and, with rifle and ice pick, joined the men on the pack. From the first, they were adamant that I should never hunt alone. Anyone without long training took great risks on the treacherous pack around Point Hope at that time of year. Strong currents and high winds break up and move the pack so that it suddenly opens up in great cracks, piles into high-pressure ridges, or slowly relaxes to form areas of loose ice blocks that can drop the inexperienced into the freezing black water below. Once wet, a man freezes quickly unless he is close enough to race back to the village for warmth. And the weird groans, moaning, sharp cracks, and grinding of the ice in motion can, at first, be terrifying.

We stood, during those short hours of dim daylight, at openings in the ice watching for a black spot on the water that would be the nose of a seal who was suddenly, and very quietly, there to breathe. It was weeks before I killed my first seal. There is very little time to aim and shoot at a minute target, and the light refraction over the water is confusing. Even when you hit you are not sure of meat and fuel. Some are thin and sink, others drift away into the pack where you cannot reach them with the "munaktoon," a drop-shaped wooden object set with hooks and attached to a coil of line, that is hurled out beyond the carcass so that you can snag it and then draw it in to the edge of the ice.

During those winter days on the ice, and the nights spent sitting on the floor of dark, cold houses recording the ancient tales that hold the wisdom of the Eskimos, I came to know them as individuals with whom I worked, not as strange tribal people surviving from an ancient world of the Stone Age. The following year, giving a lecture at Yale University, I found myself describing "the life and culture of the Eskimos" as if I could wrap that all up in a neat summary of an exotic people. What nonsense! It sounded to me like a typical anthropological textbook. Then I realized two things: you cannot translate the ideas, the beliefs, and the nature of one culture into the language symbols of another, and people, whether hunters on the Arctic coast or professors in a university, range through all the basic personalities. I could see before me, among that group of professors and students, Okpik with his cheerful grin, Attunorak with his somber preoccupation with the supernatural, very dignified but rather stupid Kunuknorak, and clever, tough, and energetic Ebrulik. Today, with our new understanding of the interrelation of all living things, one would think that the nature of the relation between all men, living and dead, would be clearer than it is. Perhaps the present growing comprehension of the realities of genetics and biochemistry, as well as the functioning interrelation of time, space, and energy, will eventually clarify what we now speak of vaguely as "a common humanity" to explain similar behavior among people in widely separated time and space frames.

Probably, if there were any sure ways of measuring, we would find the average intelligence of Arctic Eskimos considerably higher than that of our contemporary urban populations. The reason is obvious. Only the most intelligent survive to reproduce themselves. Just as an example comprehensible to moderns, we were able to teach the Tigara people to write their own language, phonetically, in just one week.

Ebrulik, the tough young man who had accumulated a substantial sum of money in Hollywood as an actor, urged me to go with him on a circuit of his trap line in the interior. His stake of money meant that he had the biggest dog team—thirteen fine huskies. We took off in a blinding blizzard in February for the 250-mile circuit of his traps. At Cape Thompson a strong current had opened the pack ice offshore, as Ebrulik had expected, and it was there that he had planned to find food for ourselves and the dogs. We were lucky. After only one day of hunting we had five seal carcasses strapped to the sled and enough food for Ebrulik's outsize team. From the Cape we headed inland across the tundra toward the northeast, directly into a stiff wind. Once away from the coast we were in a world of pure white marble—snow so hard that the sled left almost no mark on the surface—and there was nothing to be seen on the surface but wave ripples made by the prevailing winds, no hills, rocks, brush, or stream beds to guide our way. How could Ebrulik find the reindeer camp at least seventy miles ahead? He pointed to the ripple pattern and then to the lead dog, who was cutting the ripples at an exact angle. In spite of the wind in her face she maintained a steady bearing throughout the day. One of us rode standing on the broad flat runners at the rear of the sled and holding on to the handlebars while the other ran alongside. At that speed we had to shift positions every few minutes. The wind in our faces was unbearable, even with a tightly drawn parka hood with its wolf and wolverine ruffs. It was necessary to take the wolfskin belly bands from two of the dogs and strap them across our faces. Even so Ebrulik developed small white spots on his cheekbones, and when I noticed them we stopped so that he could rub them gently with the fur of a mitt. They would suppurate for weeks to come.

After dark we heard the barking of dogs, and our leader swerved slightly to head for the reindeer camp. A young Eskimo from Tigara, his wife, and their eighteen-month-old son lived in a snow burrow cut into a deep drift where a patch of willow brush was buried in a ravine. It was so small that I could not stretch out between the walls, and yet, stormbound for three days, all four of us could lie curled up and tightly packed together. At first it was not so bad. Little Charlie, as I came to call him, was terrified of the *nalaukmiut* (white man) and left me alone, but as the days passed he lost his fear and began to scramble all over me also. Charlie wore only a brief shirt; he was not housebroken and had no control. When I said I preferred the storm, everyone rocked with laughter, even Charlie.

But the storm broke, and we had one day with our host, learning to break reindeer to the sled—more fun than a toboggan ride. Domestic reindeer had been imported from Siberia to northwest Alaska about fifty years before that time.

Each village in the back country, where there were sufficient lichens to feed them, maintained a small herd. They had to be moved regularly, and that required constant herding. Also the herder must protect them from wolves. They are much smaller than caribou and can be caught, held, and thrown down by one man. We caught and harnessed the young, unbroken deer and then, attached to the sled with double traces, they were turned loose with one man aboard. Like the wind we rushed across the hard-packed show completely out of control, sometimes for a mile or more before the deer stopped, panting, with tongue hanging out, head down, and forelegs spread apart. During the storm I had watched the herder carving a wooden collar for the deer harness. He had chosen a piece of driftwood with a promising shape, and with an adze chipped out the collar with its several intricate and exact curves, made to fit the shoulders precisely, with no model and no guide but his inner eye. It was truly a work of creative art.

Our next target was the hunting camp of Ebrulik's hunting partner, some fifty miles further inland. The weather had moderated, but there was still a stiff wind and extreme cold. That was our worst day. The dogs' noses clogged with ice; I broke a hole in one boot so that we had to stop and sew it up before the snow could enter, dampen the inner reindeer skin sock, and then instantly freeze the foot; both we and the dogs were tired. Somewhere on the tundra we lost our ax, probably where we stopped to chop meat out of the back of a caribou killed by the wolves. Without the ax to chop up frozen seal meat we were like an engine without fuel. Nearly exhausted, we reached the camp in starlight. It was empty and the subterranean sod house was full of drifting snow. We had eaten a few chips of caribou farther back, but the dogs had nothing and were famished. Without the ax to chop rock-hard seals there was nothing for us or the dogs to eat. We and the dogs dug enough snow out of the house so that we could crawl in out of the wind, and slept. In two layers of caribou winter skin clothing you can sleep in the snow in almost any temperature. Why the partner had abandoned the camp we did not know, but without him to supply another ax we knew we must abandon the trap line and head for the nearest inhabited camp. Ebrulik thought there was a family encamped on the shore north of Tigara, and that was our best chance.

I remember very little of that next day, probably because I was hallucinating. Hunger, fear, weariness, and the featureless white desert can turn one into a zombie. Of course, I owe my life to Ebrulik and his dogs, but that is commonplace in the high Arctic mid-winter. I do remember the care with which he watched the dogs, resting them often, but moving them to their utmost effort with a sure knowledge of what they could and could not do. It was a very long day. Again, in the dark, howling dogs led us into camp and the snug warmth of people, dogs, a seal oil lamp, a boiling pot of ptarmigan, and dried salmon for the dogs.

In those endless hours running, or riding on the runners of the sled, I could not help becoming more and more skeptical of all those armchair theories about the original migration of ancient men across Bering Strait and down through Alaska to continental America. On a map it looks obvious. On the frozen tundra in winter it looks ridiculous. Of course, the Eskimos have lived there for many centuries, but they did it with a thorough and highly developed native science. Theirs was a complex technology that must be in place in the human mind before, not after, the invasion of man's most difficult environment. I have no idea how this was achieved, nor where, nor when. Radiocarbon tells us, we think, that men lived in the high Arctic some 10,000 to 12,000 years ago and that men like us were in America perhaps 20,000, and maybe more than 50,000, years ago. But that only tells me that they had the science and technology to master the Arctic 10,000 years ago.

Where did those earlier people in temperate America come from?

When the snow birds return, some time in April or May, the people of Tigara watch the pack ice with a new intensity and prepare the whaling gear, sharpening the harpoons and cutting knives so that they will not hurt so much. I joined the crew of David Frankson, the grandson of Acetchuck, a famous shaman. With the help of Dina, his wife, he performed his secret ceremonies on the beach, sang his charm songs, and also went regularly to services in the Episcopal Church, even though he could not abide the vicar.

Six of us dragged David's skin boat on a small sled across the shore to the first open lead in the sea ice. There we propped it up on an ice block, like a lifeboat ready to be shot into the water, and waited for the sight of a spouting whale. Eight other crews were scattered at the edge of the long stretch of open water. There were no tents, no sleeping bags, no food, and no place to sit except on the small sled or on ice blocks. The crews were not expected to go ashore until a whale was killed—and that might mean several days. Unlike the Eskimos, I did not learn to sleep standing, and three days without sleep or food was my maximum. But like a wild animal one learns to wait patiently, almost unmoving, and in a kind of trance, for the prey.

At last the trance was broken with shouts and frantic activity. Far out a bowhead whale exhausted steam into the cold air; we piled into the boat with the harpooner in the bow, and David the steerer and the captain were left to shove us off the block and then jump into the stern seat.

With our paddles the six of us could almost lift the boat out of the water. All nine boats raced toward the spout. I had the taste of pennies in my mouth before David gave the order to stop and wait. The whale had sounded and the sea was still, unruffled, silent, waiting, like us.

A bowhead whale must rise to blow every fifteen to twenty minutes. When that one rose we were, luckily, the nearest boat and thus the first onto him. To my astonishment, David steered so that we drove the boat right up onto his back, a huge animal, much larger than our boat and weighing, perhaps, twenty tons, with a powerful winglike tail that could smash a whaleboat like a matchbox. But his tail was horizontal, not vertical like a fish, and so when he sounded the boat was thrown clear, not smashed. Our harpooner, standing in the bow, drove his harpoon straight down into the back with all his weight on the shaft. Instantly everything loose in the boat was thrown overboard. We carried an air bag made of a complete sealskin, attached to the harpoon head by a walrus-hide line. In the flesh of the whale the harpoon head was detached from the shaft, and the sounds dragging the line and the float deep into the sea. If the line or float fouls anything in the boat, there is no time to cut the line, so the boat and the crew go down with the whale. At twenty to thirty degrees below zero and no shelter on the ice there is little chance of survival if swamped.

The boat, the gear, and the method of hunting were the same as they had been for centuries, except for explosive bombs discharged from a bronze barrel set in the head of the harpoon shaft. These "darting guns" were adapted from the white whalers in the Arctic after 1890 and had not been changed. A trigger discharged the bomb when the harpoon head was driven into the whale, and the cylindrical, sharp-pointed bombs were supposed to explode deep in the flesh of the animal. But the homemade bombs we used often did not explode. If not, then the kill proceeded very much as it always had.

All the nine boats collected about the place where the whale disappeared, waiting for a sight of the sealskin float that would appear a few seconds ahead of the whale. It rose a few hundred yards distant, and again we all raced to get there first. One of the other boats arrived in time to place a second harpoon with float before the wounded animal could exhaust and sound again. I do not know whether either of the two bombs exploded in the whale, but on his third rise his spout was a crimson mist. Crippled, he could not sound again and lay bleeding, but very much alive, on the surface. The boats swarmed about the injured whale and the lance-men probed with very sharp steel-headed lances searching for a vital spot. Stephen, a young man with great strength but little experience, was left clinging to his lance, embedded in the whale when the boat was thrown clear of the thrashing animal, but only for a few seconds until one of the boats could drive in to take him off.

The carcass of the whale was towed by all the boats together to the edge of the ice and anchored so that it could be cut up while still afloat. We all stood with heads uncovered while Peter Kuniak gave thanks to the Christian God. Then the whole village came out onto the pack ice for the cutting up and the first feast of *muktuk*, whaleskin which, when cut into strips, looks much like the cross-section of a rubber tire, with thick black skin on the outside and thick white blubber on the inside. Boiled it is still tough but tastes something like fresh salmon.

During the two months on the ice we sighted scores of whales, struck about a dozen, but landed only three. Only one Eskimo was killed. He tried to shoot a bowhead from the edge of the ice with an old nineteenth-century bronze shoulder gun; the bomb exploded in the barrel, spreading bronze bits of shrapnel all about us. One piece got him in the stomach. We were unable to reach the doctor in Kotzebue with the one radio in the village and could only stand by until he died three days later. Kunuknorak also had a similar gun explode while trying to kill from the ice (whales sometimes rise in small ponds of open water when the long open leads are closed). Many of us were standing about on watch and could see Kunuknorak double up with his hands over his stomach. He remained that way for perhaps two minutes, then straightened up smiling and said, "I'm all right, but look." He showed us a small hole in the front of his parka and another at the back. Then he pulled up his parka to show us that there was no hole in his stomach or his back. He had been praying and was convinced it was a miracle, as were all the other Eskimos in the village. There was no doubt at all. As the word spread people come from neighboring villages to see the man who had survived by a true miracle.

All of us remembered the celebration in the mission house just before the hunt began. Even though it was in part a Christian prayer meeting, one of the old ceremonies took place in a half-serious, half-joking form. Small models of whaling boats and crews were suspended on lines to imitate the hunt; dancers and singers with drums went through a ritual performance that told of great hunts of the past; one man appeared with a top in which were several seagull feathers. After a song he set the top spinning with a thong. There was a hushed silence and then a gasp as the feathers came loose and the top skidded across the floor. Old Negawana, sitting beside me, explained that that could mean bad luck—a death during the hunt.

Days of waiting on the ice, the constant cold inducing a trancelike state of numbness, a mind filled with tales of whale hunting through the centuries, and the shifting horizon of endless pack ice began to affect my own culturally determined ideas of time, space, and reality. A mail plane that managed to land on the ice off Tigara brought me copies of *Life* magazine describing the German invasion of Western Europe. There were pictures to show what I struggled to explain to my crew mates as we waited on the ice. Even to me the war began to seem less real, more fantastic, and more confused in space and time than the flight of Acetchuk from the dance house to Siberia and back a generation, or perhaps five hundred years ago. All my crew mates could see the "owner" or soul (inusaq) riding on the back of whales we struck; the stripped skull of the whales must be returned to the sea so that the soul "owner" would return again. Bob Oviuk could see his daughter leaving Kivalina, seventy miles to the east, simply by looking backward with his head between his legs; once the people walked on their hands before the raven stole the sun and gave them sunlight; men could turn into bears and bears into men; all this is not sequential, it is there and not there and floats in reversible time and unmeasured space. Now, many years later and absorbed in contemporary theories about the nature of the universe, I think how foolish it is to stuff all this into the conventional pigeonhole of "primitive superstition." At the time it was just confusing.

In late June the boats were drawn up onto a snow-free beach, and we walked across the tundra, now turning into a Persian carpet of tiny flowers, to the place of Nulukatuk by the monument of record-breaking whale jaws set up on end. In the shelter of upturned whale boats old men sang to the beat of their tambourine drums, the young people danced, and we all took our turn being tossed into the air from a walrus hide held by scores of tossers. The skilled ones remained upright and danced in the air as they tossed slabs of whale skin to the audience. But neophytes like me landed on the back of our necks or sprawled face down to shouts of laughter. It was all great fun, but for me it had begun with an agonizing trial. Dina, my boat captain's wife, awakened her husband's crew at five in the morning, then on the beach by our boat, offered us breakfast of raw whale lung, liver, and heart. Penelope faced her trial later with the women when she had to eat raw whale meat from last year's catch all covered with ghastly yellow scum.

With the thaw our thoughts turned from the living Eskimos and their ways to the mysterious ancients of Ipiutak and the remains of their settlement on the north shore about a mile from Tigara. The snow had gone and the tundra grass was turning green. Planning that season's work, I walked across the site one bright sunny morning, turned back to look into the sun, and suddenly saw something unbelievable. All about me and as far as I could see were neat yellow rectangles in the new green grass. There was a plan of a town, not a village as we know them in the Arctic. Soon I realized that the taller grass in the slight depressions marking the house sites still appeared dead and yellow, while the shorter new grass about them appeared green. I knew then that I had only a few days before the color equalized to map all those house depressions.

Within ten days I had mapped about 600 houses. Also I could see from debris washing out along the shores at the western end of the site that there must be at least another 200 house sites in that section, buried too deeply under the sand to be noticed on the surface. That meant that the Ipiutak settlement extended for about three-quarters of a mile eastward and probably numbered over 800 houses. If they were all occupied at once that could mean a population of some 4,000 people, about the size of Fairbanks in 1940, and sixteen times as large as the present Tigara. Theoretically impossible in the Arctic, and yet I could not see one yellow rectangle intersecting another as would happen if one house was built over an earlier one.

Discussions with the Tigara people, and reference to early accounts of the first white contacts with them, led me to believe that the population of Tigara, before the common diseases of whites decimated their population, must have been about 1,000. A village four times that size is difficult to imagine, but in three seasons we excavated more than seventy houses to find no significant change in the cultural remains from one end of the site to the other, no house overlying another, and no certain proof that they were or were not all occupied at the same time. We also learned that they had no seal oil lamps and burned driftwood, perhaps with some oil. Bones in the refuse proved that their most common food was seal and walrus, and that they did not hunt whales. Most puzzling were the many implements made of caribou antlers, vessels made of birch bark, and willow twigs used for flooring, all of which pointed to the interior as their homeland for most of the year. We concluded that they must have spent the spring and summer hunting seal and walrus on the shore, and the balance of the year hunting caribou in the hinterland. The houses were framed with driftwood and covered with sod blocks, not unlike the recent houses of the Nunatarmiut (inland Eskimo).

One of my students at the University of Alaska, Jiggs Marks, and his Eskimo wife joined us at Tigara that summer, and the four of us, with two or three Eskimos, continued the excavation of Ipiutak houses. In each case deposits around the central fireplace were rich in antler, bone, ivory, and wooden artifacts, together with masses of flint chips and a great many small, thin, and beautifully chipped flint blades, engraved, and remarkably delicate as compared with familiar Eskimo implements. By contrast the later craftsmanship seemed crude and primitive. But for me the repetitious discoveries of precisely the same kinds of objects in each house became boring. With an Eskimo I began to explore eastward, away from the sea, in search of burials. There were no signs on the surface and we could only dig one hole after another hoping to hit a burial by luck.

One evening in the Eskimo council I explained what we were doing and the difficulty in a blind search for burials. One old fellow then said that there was nothing to hunt at that time of summer so why not turn out the whole village to help me. I agreed to pay three dollars for every burial found. The next morning was wet, cold, and windy, but at least fifty villagers—men, women, and children—turned out with shovels, bone picks, and even large spoons, to dig holes in the tundra. As the day wore on they spread farther and farther to the east along the north shore. Late in the afternoon little Okpik came running from the east in great excitement. Someone had found a grave more than a mile from the Ipiutak site.

That evening, surely, will be remembered by all the Tigara people. Within a few minutes several graves had been found around the first one, and some contained carved ivory objects like nothing I, or the Eskimos, had ever seen. For all of us the most startling, eerie, and mysterious was the one with the ivory eyes. One of the boys, Okpik, I think, had struck a mass of decayed wood no more than two feet beneath the surface. I moved in with a trowel to cut away the soft brown wood and revealed a perfectly preserved skeleton lying on its back on a decayed wooden frame. Suddenly, when I peeled the wood from the face, I was staring into the face of a skeleton with ivory eyes—white eyeballs with jet pupils. My shout brought all the Eskimos in the vicinity to stare down at something totally unexpected, macabre, and for the Eskimos supernatural. All the bones were complete and articulated so that I could conclude that the body had been buried intact and only the eyes gouged out to be replaced with artificial eyes. One old woman remembered an ancient tale of a man with ivory eyes who frightened the children.

During that and the following summer we found more than 150 graves extending from about one mile east of Ipiutak to Jabbertown, about five miles further east. The Eskimos located them by digging hundreds of holes so that a stretch of tundra four miles long looked like a battlefield after an artillery barrage. While the Eskimos searched for graves we four whites cleared them for drawings, photographs, recording, and numbering.

There was one other skeleton with ivory eyes and also nose plugs in the form of birds' heads. Three skeletons had engraved ivory mouth covers and another had a carved ivory rod jammed down through the neck and along the vertebrae to separate the pubic bones. Another three were fitted with ivory lip plugs. One pair, found in the same grave, had flint arrowheads imbedded in their bones. Among the hundreds of complete arrowheads, harpoons, harpoon sockets, ivory knives, and lance heads inset with flint blades, wrist guards, ornaments, and carved animal figures were the many queer twisted engraved and inset ivory objects that we called "pretzels" or openwork carvings, for lack of a better name. Some were in the form of swivels, others grotesque and unrecognizable.

In two graves we found rectangular masklike sets of ivory carvings, and one of them lay, articulated, on the chest of a male skeleton that had an infant's skeleton between its legs. These were elaborately engraved and inset with jet. They reminded me of similar masklike sets of carved tortoiseshell from the Shang period in China (1766-1123 B.C.). Heine-Geldern, the Austrian expert on ancient art, was later to point out that some of the curved animal figures and engraved elements were like Scythian work, in the widespread "Siberian Animal Style." One important clue to the history of Ipiutak people was an engraving tool set with a minute blade of wrought iron, probably steel, judging by chemical analysis. Steel could have been obtained by trade from China as early as 500 B.C. Was Ipiutak an Asian source of walrus ivory and walrus-hide line? Both were precious materials in Eurasia, walrus ivory because of supernatural qualities (to stop bleeding, for example) and walrus-hide line because it was the strongest cable known to man before steel cable; it was even used to build Gothic cathedrals.

Helge Larsen's return in time for the start of the last season at Ipiutak, 1941, enabled him to excavate a number of the Ipiutak graves and to see for himself what it was like to find each day surprising and complete objects carved in an unknown art style. The graves with their complete and assembled objects were, of course, very different from the houses with their fragmentary artifacts found in the refuse of living. In that respect Ipiutak is unique. No other such cemetery has ever been found with the elaborate artwork of that ancient Arctic period.

Helge's excavations were to lead us into a famous collision with agents from the Federal Bureau of Investigation. Someone, probably the new white teacher at Tigara school, had reported that there were two suspicious men, perhaps Nazi agents, at Point Hope. One had a German Christian name, and the other spoke with an accent and had just come from Europe. The F.B.I. sent two agents with the Coast Guard ship to investigate. As usual, everyone rushed to the beach to welcome the men from the cutter, and in the confusion the agents asked one of the Eskimos where the two white men were working. Told that it was several miles distant across the sand spit, they took off at once for their investigation. Helge happened to see them, far off across the tundra heading for Ipiutak, and became so suspicious that he followed them. At the place of his excavation he found them filling their pockets with ivory carvings that were lying in place about the carefully uncovered burials waiting for drawings and photographs. Helge has never told me what he said or did, but they all returned to the beach together. Helge was furious and exploded with, "Those two bastards have been out there looting the graves and will not return the carvings." Aboard the cutter, Captain Zeusler made short work of the problem—either they returned the carvings or they stayed at Point Hope. We heard no more of the investigation, and, with ham radios all over Alaska, the whole country was soon laughing.

The last year at Point Hope, Helge stayed on the site until late fall (and was very nearly lost at sea on the southward voyage of the *Nanuk*) while I left early on the northward voyage of the *Nanuk* to Point Barrow, and was caught in the ice south of Barrow. Miss Keaton (known as "Buster"), the traveling nurse, and I abandoned Pete Paulson and his schooner to walk ashore over the ice. On shore, we found ourselves farther south of Barrow than we expected and blocked by the outlet of a large inland basin. It was snowing and blocks of ice were already forming in the channel. There was nothing for it but to strip, bundle the fur clothing on our heads, and wade across, hoping we did not have to swim and wet the clothing. Two days later we found some Eskimos who took us on to Barrow in a skin boat. The joker on the Point Barrow radio passed on another good story about how "Buster" Keaton and Professor Rainey were establishing a nudist colony on the Arctic coast.

Helge and I were working on the description of about 10,000 artifacts from Ipiutak, at the University of Alaska, when the Japanese attacked Pearl Harbor. Later they landed in the Aleutian Islands, and the isolated Alaskans were in a state of near hysteria. In the short-lived flap that followed, one of the more officious faculty wives organized us all into militia to guard the small power plant at the university. Only such a flap, and the faculty wives, could dig most of us out of bed at two o'clock in the morning, to take over our shift, with the temperature at 50° or even 60° below zero. Of course, we packed the rifles once around the power plant, then huddled, for the next two hours, about the furnace inside. But the ladies were more determined. They organized a women's rifle team to shoot down Japanese paratroopers, and began shooting practice on the university's rifle range. But that also was of short duration. One morning there was a headline in the Fairbanks News Miner, famous for its cryptic headlines, "Mrs. Butt Shot in the Rump." This was not quite up to the headline on the day of a hanging in Fairbanks, "Billy Jerked to Jesus this Morning."

By the return of summer, the whole collection had been worked over, classified, and absorbed into a theory of what we found, the remains of an unknown people (a study of the skeletons should indicate whether they were or were not related to the Eskimos) who lived perhaps 2,000 years ago on the Arctic coast with a technology equal to that of the Eskimo, but quite different, and more advanced in the sense of skills; a people who must have had trading relations with peoples in eastern Asia and who shared with them an ancient and widespread art form known as the Siberian Animal Style; people who lived in surprising numbers, both inland and on the coast, on walrus, seal, and caribou, and who had developed a culture that, so far as we could see, was limited to northwest Alaska. (Other Ipiutak sites, much smaller and without the cemeteries, were to be found in that region after the war.) This cultural type has now been accommodated in a general theory of cultural development in the American Arctic, but in fact it remains an enigma. The study of nearly 600 skeletons from Point Hope (about 400 of them from later periods that we found in a vast cemetery to the east of Tigara on the south coast) has not been completed even now, and we do not know if the Ipiutak skeletons are of the familiar Eskimo type. No other site comparable in size and richness has been found.

Georgi Debets, the Soviet physical anthropologist, managed to make an examination of the skeletons before his death and concluded that the Ipiutak people must have been related to the Yukaghir in Siberia, rather than to the Eskimos. My own theory is that some Siberian group moved into Alaska before the time of Christ (radiocarbon now gives us dates of A.D. 0-500 for Ipiutak culture) to exploit the herds of walrus that must haul up on the Point Hope spit to rest after the 200-mile northward movement from Bering Strait, and at the same time based their economy on inland caribou as they did in Siberia. Bering Strait and the straits between Novaya Zemlya and the mainland of Siberia are the two regions in the north where walrus can be taken in very large numbers. Ivory and rawhide line have been precious commodities for many centuries. The Coast Guard soundings, and my own aerial observations off Point Hope and Cape Prince of Wales, indicate that the sand spits once extended farther out into the sea. Both points are still being eroded by the surf. How different the whole thing might look if we could excavate the ancient dwellings that now must be beneath the sea.

Seven years of searching in the Arctic proved nothing about those hypothetical Bering Strait migrations that are supposed to have peopled America at an unknown time in the past. That theory is still accepted as fact although no real proof has yet turned up in the Bering Sea region. My guess is that in the future some other theory will replace it to explain the origin of the American Indians. Theories about the ancient past rarely last for long.

Clark Wissler again stepped in to change the course of my affairs. America was then frantically trying to supply the Soviet Union with war materials. A crash program to open a supply route via Alaska and Siberia meant construction of a road, 1,600 miles long, from the Peace River in British

Columbia to the Tanana River in Alaska, through an almost trackless taiga forest—and it was to be completed in one summer. Wissler thought I should scout the whole region while the army engineers built the road. This was arranged through the National Science Foundation, and I went to work with seven regiments, based at different points along the proposed route. They were moved in from access points while the ground was frozen and, with summer, began clearing the way with bulldozers. Strips in the forest were cleared for aircraft, and they became the only contact between the regiments.

Even though I moved up and down the route several times during the summer on aircraft, rode 250 miles on horseback in a survey that was outdistanced by the bulldozers, and covered many miles on foot and in jeeps, I still do not know how it was accomplished in so short a time. By snowfall one could travel the entire 1,600 miles by jeep, crossing many rivers and streams on log bridges, and a great many miles of bog. But the archaeological survey was a "bust;" I found just one flint arrowhead (lost out of my pocket in a jeep ride), and no evidence of that presumed migration of ancients through what was supposed to be an ice-free corridor during the last glaciation. Actually, I spent much of my time reporting to the seven different colonels in command of the regiments on how the other divisions were getting on; no one else was regularly moving up and down the route by air, except for the pilots who rarely left their aircraft.

After the summer of 1938 in Europe, I was convinced that the real war would be between Germany and the Soviet Union, and that the Western countries should not get involved in the fight. But they did get involved, and after Pearl Harbor the United States was also in the fight. War propaganda of the period meant nothing to me, but in a global war it was impossible to avoid some part in it. If I took a commission in the Army, as urged by so many army friends employed with the Alaskan supply routes, I would obviously end up in the cul-de-sac of the Aleutians, where the Army was desperate for men who knew the Arctic. An alternative was the Board of Economic Warfare, where I could serve the country and yet not have to kill men with whom I personally had no quarrel. Looking back at the war years and remembering all the troops I served with as a civilian, I think now that war is for most men the ultimate sport. Bored with the routine of conventional job and eager for the excitement of risking their lives, few can resist the appeal of war. At the front, that small proportion of men in a modern army who do the actual killing are embarrassed if you ask them why they are doing it. It is obvious: they kill so as not to be killed. Those popular theories about the great causes that serve the bulk of the nation are, for the real fighters, just a smoke screen.

Twice, after the war, I was drawn back into Arctic research, first in 1950 when Larsen, Giddings, and I returned to northwest Alaska and again in 1965, after Giddings was killed in a motor accident. Then I flew directly from my excavations in southern Italy to the Kobuk River in Alaska as the official "cover" for Douglas Anderson, a graduate student continuing Giddings' excavations at Onion Portage.

In 1950 Giddings was beginning his work at the now-famous site at Cape Denbigh, Larsen was digging the Trail Creek cave site on Seward Peninsula, and I did a reconnaissance in search of sites in the region of Cape Prince of Wales.

But at that time, as director of The University Museum in Philadelphia backstopping a worldwide series of excavations, I realized it would not be possible for me to continue in a specialized field of research. I did continue to teach Arctic studies at the University of Pennsylvania and in 1971 wrote a brief review of Arctic prehistory—thirty years after the discovery of Ipiutak. From this I quote the following summary:

Thirty Years Later

There were no major archaeological excavations in the Arctic during the War period (1941-1945). Following the War, however, a new interest in the area developed and many young American, Russian, Canadian, and Danish archaeologists began a whole series of surveys and excavations there. Probably all this revived interest was sparked by Louis Giddings' discovery (1964) of what he has termed the "Denbigh Flint Complex" in a cultural stratum lying below fairly typical Eskimo remains in a site on Cape Denbigh on Norton Sound in northwest Alaska.

In this flint industry, the small, thin, beautifully chipped blades were very much like those found at Ipiutak, and it was clear that there must have been some relation between these flint-working industries. But with the Cape Denbigh material were a great many minute micro-blades struck from small prepared cores and a tool, probably used for cutting grooves in bone, ivory, and antler, long known in Europe from Paleolithic collections as a burin. Micro-blades and cores of this "Mesolithic" kind had been found in one site in central Alaska on the University of Alaska campus, but the burins had not been recognized previously in American collections. There were no organic materials preserved in the Denbigh site, and this speculation on age and relationship was based on flint objects alone.

The discovery and description of the Denbigh Flint Complex came at about the time when Willard Libby was working out the radiocarbon method of dating. It happened that I was at that time a member of a small group of archaeologists working with Libby in attempts to confirm the validity of the system. Perhaps because of that I managed to have some of the earliest trials made on a few Arctic samples. Wood form the Ipiutak site at that time gave us dates of about 1000 A.D. instead of our guess date of about 1,000 years earlier. Without organic remains at Cape Denbigh, and with no actual fire pits to give us charcoal, significant C-14 dates were not possible. Some clues to age in the nature of the deposit led [David]Hopkins of the U.S. Geological Survey and Giddings to estimate a date on geological grounds of about 6000-4000 B.C. Both Larsen and I were puzzled by this because of the obvious relation between the types of flint work at Ipiutak and Cape Denbigh, which, by such estimates, would appear to be separated by some 5,000 years.

Giddings' research in Alaska, first for the University of Alaska, then for The University Museum in Philadelphia, and finally for Brown University, eventually led to the discovery of two more critical sites in the American Arctic, one at Cape Krusenstern and the other at Onion Portage (Giddings, 1967) on the Kobuk River. The first contained materials representing a whole series of cultural periods nicely related in time by their position on a series of beach ridges paralleling the present seashore. The second contained materials from an even longer series of cultural levels beautifully stratified in a deep site on an ancient caribou migration route and river crossing.

With these two sites and a much more highly

developed radiocarbon method of dating, we now have a
very long and accurate chronology at at least certain
events and cultural forms in the American Arctic. The
Denbigh Flint Complex at Cape Krusenstern and Onion
Portage dates from 2500 to 2000 B.C. and Ipiutak from 1
to 500 A.D. Both periods are represented at the two sites
in stratigraphic or shoreline relation, and very extensive
C-14 datings of the most accurate kind, with all now-
known corrections, have been made by the laboratories in
Philadelphia and Copenhagen. There is still a long time
span separating the apparently related flint industries.

Also after the War, Larsen discovered a large late-
Ipiutak house at Deering on the south shore of Kotzebue
Sound, and traces of an Ipiutak-like culture at Chagvan
Bay, south of Nunivak Island in the Bering Sea. [John]
Campbell, in addition, discovered in inland Alaska near
Anaktuuk Pass the kind of Ipiutak inland site we had
anticipated with the first discovery at Point Hope. Thus
today we have a sound date for the Ipiutak culture and
the evidence we expected for a coast-inland economic
base. The age corresponds remarkably well with our guess
date and assures me at least that the basis of that guess,
the probably relations with the Animal Style and metal-
using people in Asia, was sound. But the site and culture
of Ipiutak, I think, remains something of an enigma. It
just does not yet fit comfortably into the whole long series
of Arctic cultures discovered, dated, and described during
the past 30 years. Our anomalous "Near-Ipiutak" culture
became "Norton" after a number of sites with similar
remains were excavated. It is earlier than Ipiutak at Cape
Krusenstern and Onion Portage and is at a pottery
manufacturing level, which clearly proves that pottery
had been known at Point Hope before the Ipiutak period
and then abandoned for a time. Still earlier, there is now

a "Choris" period at Kotzebue Sound and on the Kobuk River, also dating from the time when pottery was made, and most puzzling of all, an "Old Whaling Culture" at Cape Krusenstern only about 100 miles from Point Hope and we must now assume that whaling was practiced on this coast in 1800 B.C. and then again after Ipiutak times about 500 A.D.

The kind of flint industry characteristic of both Cape Denbigh and Ipiutak (that is, the small, thin, finely chipped blades) is now often referred to in Arctic literature as the "Arctic Small Tool Tradition." It has been found right across the Arctic from Alaska to Greenland and even on the northern tip of Greenland, where no me have lived in historic times. The micro-blades and cores, reminiscent of the ones found at Denbigh but not Ipiutak, appear at Onion Portage and at Anagula in the Aleutian Islands about 6000 B.C. and at the Trail Creek site on Seward Peninsula about 7000 B.C. Still earlier at Onion Portage is a "Kobuk" period with implements that have a Paleolithic character and date from about 8000 B.C.

On the whole, radiocarbon dates for many sites with the "Small Tool Tradition" are much earlier than Ipiutak, and that is one reason why it does not fit easily into the general sequence. A few of the elaborate Ipiutak (Animal Style) carvings have been found at other places, such as Point Spencer, Cape Krusenstern, and Deering, but no other large town site or cemetery comparable to Ipiutak has been found anywhere. Moreover, all of the later work in eastern Siberia by Russian archaeologists since the War has not turned up a trace of Ipiutak material.

We are left with an archaeological riddle. Here is quite certainly the largest settlement and cemetery known in the Far North, with a flint industry that seems to survive from a much earlier period, an art style that is related to a widespread Eurasian Animal Style, with highly developed gear for hunting sea mammals like that used at the same time in the Bering Sea, but with no pottery or polished slate blades, which had long been known even in northwest Alaska in the same region as Ipiutak. Moreover, what little knowledge we have as yet reported about the physical type of the people points to a relation with the Yukaghir in Siberia rather than with the living Eskimos. Perhaps all this would be less of a riddle if the other sites in a time horizon comparable to Ipiutak contained such well-preserved organic material and a preserved cemetery. Actually none of the really old sites excavated in the Arctic during the past 30 years is comparable in this respect, and we are constantly faced with the problem of comparing Ipiutak with sites where essentially only stone tools remain. There is still the difficulty in explaining the problem of an Ipiutak flint tool technology, which appears to be an anachronism in northwest Alaska as late as the early post-Christian era.

Looking back over these thirty years I am most impressed with the complexity of Arctic history as we now see it after all the recent discoveries and excavations. Certainly I did not agree with the advice to Larsen in 1939 that Alaskan prehistory had finally been worked out, but it did appear to be a much simpler problem in 1939 than it does in 1971. Cultural change in the Arctic clearly has been continual, profound, and sometimes abrupt. One look at those nicely stratified levels at Onion Portage and the evidence of sudden changes from coarse, heavy, stone tools to minute, delicate, and exquisitely chipped implements will convince anyone of this. Arnold Toynbee's conception of Eskimos, based on an earlier idea among archaeologists, as a people who reached a certain plateau and remained there because of the overpowering challenge of a tough environment is, of course, true in the sense that they could not go on to agriculture and the kind of civilization based on it. But that the culture remained static and in a frozen, unchanging state for millennia has now been thoroughly disproved.

Today, looking back over the many years since Larsen and I marshalled our wits in an attempt to understand the Ipiutak site and culture, both during the digging period and later while working over the collections, I still feel there is no truly satisfactory explanation for what we have found. We might have dug somewhat more carefully (and sacrificed something in terms of numbers of houses, graves, and objects), and we might have preserved more organic materials for laboratory study with current advanced techniques, but I do not think the results would have been much different. With the discovery of an Arctic site which was not obvious on the surface of the ground, we launched a whole new approach to Arctic archaeology that led to the discovery of more and more ancient remains in the far north but, as I see it, no clarification of the enigma of Ipiutak. Much more extensive research since the War, in Siberia as well as in America, has not turned up Ipiutak-related sites in Asia as we expected.

At present in North American archaeology, there is a particular enthusiasm for attempts to interpret archaeological remains in terms of cultural anthropology and thus reconstruct customs, behavior patterns, social structure, and cultural change as one would in the study of living people. This inevitably leads to the identification of archaeological remains with historically known tribes, linguistic groups, or racial types—perhaps with less scepticism than in other parts of the world where there is not the same theoretical interest. In any case, I think most archaeologists working in the American Arctic at present believe that those people who made the extraordinarily fine and small flint tools at Cape Denbigh and at many sites across the Arctic, some 2,500-2,000 years before Christ, were Eskimos or their ancestors. Probably there is less agreement about the still older cultures known from Onion Portage, the Aleutian Islands, and other sites.

If it is possible to trust language as a reliable indicator of a people's history, then the distribution of people who now speak Eskimo, from Cape Chaplen, Siberia, to Greenland and south as far as the Aleutians in the west and Labrador in the east—as well as the unique, unrelated nature of the language itself—points to a long period of isolation in the American Arctic. (The language is a distinct stock related to no other but with a possibility of some connection with Uralic languages in western Siberia and eastern Europe.) This period of isolation argues in favor of identifying most archaeological cultures in the Arctic, at least those dating from the past several millennia, as Eskimo remains. In spite of the anomalous position of Ipiutak in relation to other Arctic cultures, the fact that we naturally have no way of knowing what language they spoke, and George Debnetz's opinion that they are not Classic Eskimo in physical type, most Arctic diggers would still consider the Ipiutak people to be Eskimos.

Giddings and Douglas Anderson, interpreting the strange fluctuation of flint tool industries in the deep stratified site at Onion Portage on the Kobuk River in north Alaska, believe that Eskimos and Indians (Athapascans) alternated in possession of the site over a period of many thousands of years. The present distribution of Athapascan-speaking people, from the Arctic in northwest Alaska to the southwestern United

States, argues in favor of great age for the language stock and, as Edward Sapir has shown from linguistic studies, for a very ancient occupation of north Alaska-Athapascan speakers surrounded another linguistic group of languages, Tlingit, Tsimpshian, and Haida of the northwest coast. In northeast Siberia, the Paleo-Siberians, Yukaghir, Chuckchi, Koryak from still another distinct linguistic group, were unrelated to their Ural-Altaic speaking neighbors in Asia.

There are, then, in historic times, at least four different linguistic stocks in the North, three of them in the fairly close vicinity of Point Hope. At Onion Portage the fluctuation between Eskimo and Indian occupation is presumably based on minor climatic changes that determined the advance and retreat of timberline and thus the zones occupied by people adjusted to forest as opposed to those adjusted to tundra. Is it possible that the riddle of Ipiutak lies in the shift in the zones occupied by very different people? In the period 1,500 to 2,000 years ago Point Hope may well have been occupied by a people belonging to any one of three or four existing language stocks or to one that no longer exists anywhere. One day a thorough study of all those skeletons from Point Hope may give us a clue. In the meantime some of the more recent investigations in north Alaska have shifted back to the period of Ipiutak. Probably the puzzle will again rise to plague the younger generation of diggers.

(The Ipiutak Culture: Excavations at Point Hope, Alaska.
Froelich Rainey. *A Module in Anthropology.* Addison-Wesley Modular Publications, 1971.)

During those thirty years as director of The University Museum I continued to keep in touch with Russian friends met in Moscow and Leningrad in 1938. And in 1956, after the first relaxation in Soviet-American relations, when I was the president of an International Anthropological Congress held in Philadelphia, it was possible to entertain three of them in my home there—the first Russian anthropologists to visit the United States after the war.

Probably to repay that hospitality, an invitation to give two lectures at the Soviet Academy of Sciences reached me the next year, oddly enough just when I was on an around-the-world tour for the Department of State investigating Soviet penetration of the developing countries. It was all so very different from our first visit in 1938. This time we were met by friends at the railway station in Moscow, entertained in their homes, and all the fear of contact with foreigners was gone. Debetz, however, warned us that the relaxation would not last. He was sure that there would be ups and downs in the liberation movement. Of course, he has been proved correct. At the academy I talked about archaeology in America and about new scientific techniques, such as radiocarbon dating, then being developed in the United States.

Penelope's Russian was much improved over the years, and thanks to her knowledge of the language we had many long talks about what was happening in Russia under the post-Stalin regime and about the state of the cold war and its effect on the world as a whole. Two of my lectures were published in Russian. Because all such papers were paid for by the academy I was asked what I wanted in place of the rubles, which could not be transferred to foreign currency. I suggested a Russian-made saddle. But months later Debets wrote to say none could be had. He was sending over a bucket of fresh caviar with Madame Zolotarevskaya, who was flying direct from Moscow to Philadelphia. He also proposed another attempt to work out a plan for Soviet-American research in the Bering Strait region, in a conference to be held in Copenhagen the following year.

That conference, composed of Russians, Danes, and Americans, was a very jovial affair—but there was no issue. Shortly after our arrival, Debets, Tolstov (Director of the Institute of Ethnography of the Academy of Sciences of the U.S.S.R.), and Levin proposed to meet Penelope and me privately in the hotel bar. Sadly they explained that the Soviet Foreign Office had instructed them not to agree to any joint archaeological research in Siberia and Alaska, and thus the whole point of the meeting was gone. But to save everyone's face we agreed to proceed through several days of discussions as if there were some point to it.

For me, the high point of that jolly meeting in Copenhagen was an episode in one of the city parks. A group of us were taking air on a bright sunny afternoon, when we noticed a large group of Danes watching some ducks in a pond. As it happened, several ducklings had become separated from their parents on the other side of the wire netting, and all the Danes were debating what to do about it. With hardly a moment's hesitation, three of the Russians, in their heavy woollen suits cut in that unique Soviet style, waded out into the pond, caught up the ducklings, and returned them to the frantic mother. A great cheer went up. There could be no mistaking those Soviet suits. For a moment a warm glow enlightened the cold war.

A Christmas party at The University Museum with staff members dressed in ethnographic costumes from the collection, left to right: Loren Eiseley in Chinese court robe, the author in Tlingit potlatch costume, and Henry Fisher as Arabian sheik. *Photograph courtesy of the author.*

PART II

Interlude

The author with local vaqueros high in the Andes Mountains in Ecuador
awaiting the arrival of mule trains in 1943.
Their purpose was to hijack the cargo of cinchona bark
(the source of quinine) desperately needed to
combat malaria ravaging U.S. troops fighting
in the South Pacific
Photograph courtesy of the author.

CHAPTER FOUR

War and History

A t 15,000 feet in the Andes there is often fog and a bone-shaking chill, even on the equator. Ex-Colonel Rodrigues and I, with ten of his vaqueros from the ranch, on horseback and huddled in heavy woolen ponchos, shivered, and listened for the sound of a mule train coming up the steep track on the Pacific slope of the mountains. There should be about fifty mules, each loaded with 200 pounds of cinchona bark. Our purpose was to hijack the cargo as the mule train emerged through a narrow pass onto the paramo, the high grassland between the Andean peaks.

The U.S. government had an agreement with the government of Equador, a co-belligerent but not a participant in the war, providing for a monopoly on all cinchona bark, and the quinine produced from it, at a fixed price. With the fall of Java to the Japanese, the world supply of quinine was cut off from the Western nations, and in the South Pacific more U.S. soldiers were dying of malaria than from bullets. Atabrine was not then accepted by the Surgeon General's office as a cure for malaria. Cinchona seedlings were brought out of the Philippines by submarine, but the army's need was immediate. The Board of Economic Warfare and the Defense Supplies Corporation decided to build a quinine industry in Columbia, Equador, Peru, and Bolivia, where "Peruvian bark," as a cure for malaria, had been discovered by the Indians. Wild cinchona trees grow in the Andes between 6,000 and 10,000 feet. Our job was to find stands of wild trees, strip them, dry the bark, and ship it to Merck and Company in New Jersey for processing.

As director of the Quinine Mission in Equador, I soon discovered that an Italian company was already producing some quinine from wild bark in Quito and also that it was being shipped, by some clandestine system, to German and Italian troops in North Africa. As in most of the world, official agreements could be avoided with payments in the right quarters. My official protests through our embassy were useless. I knew I must act on my own, and quickly, before the embassy and the office in Washington heard of it and fired me as their representative. Colonel Rodrigues had everything to gain and nothing to lose. He would receive full payment for the Italian bark.

When we heard the clatter of hooves on stone and the jingle of harness through the fog, we deployed in a circle around the opening of the pass with rifles unslung from the saddle holsters. But the armed guards with the caravan, surprised and outnumbered, put up no resistance. Disarmed, they followed us with the mules back to the ranch, where I had two army trucks waiting, then returned over the same track with their mules.

That was the turning point in the Equador mission. Very soon we had several botanists searching the mountains for groves of cinchona, Equadoran companies organized to strip trees and dry the bark in the forest over open fires, chemists to analyze the bark for quinine sulphate content in our own laboratory, trucks to haul the bark down from the plateau to Guayaquil, on the coast, for shipment to the United States, and crews to construct mule trails up from the forests to the plateau. Within a few months cinchona bark was the third-largest export from Equador.

But in Quito I was to sweat out a bad few weeks. The head of the Italian company, a friend with whom my wife and I often dined en famille, brought a suit against me, personally, for $60,000, the black market value of his bark. There was, of course, nothing the embassy of the U.S. government could do about it (in fact, they did not know about the whole operation), and I must necessarily fight the case in Equadoran courts. Fortunately, a pro-Ally attorney who had worked in the old League of Nations took my case. He quashed the whole thing very quickly, simply by advising the Italian company that if they persisted he would bring a case of treason against them for dealing with the enemy.

It was not one jump from Alaska to the Andes. I had joined the Board of Economic warfare, with friends from Harvard, in a scheme to produce vegetables in the South Pacific Islands in order to relieve some of the burden of troop supply. But in Washington the scheme bogged down in bureaucracy to the point where all of us were sitting idle for months on end. By chance I met the army colonel who had brought the cinchona seedlings out of the Philippines, and it was his idea to produce quinine from wild trees. With tongue in cheek, he told my chief at the board that he had learned that anthropologists were the best administrators to be found anywhere. Almost overnight, I was on the way to Quito; months later a cable arrived from Washington saying the office was having difficulty in arranging transport for me from Quito to Noumea, in New Caledonia, and did I have any ideas. Bureaucratic confusion probably is compounded in an all-out war effort, and it was to plague me all through the war years.

Once in the Quito office, I was confronted by a Jivaro Indian from the headwaters of the Amazon on the eastern slope of the Andes. These are the people who shrink human heads over an open fire, at that time for sale to tourists. He had brought to me several hundred pounds of cinchona bark and told me that his people in the jungle could supply us with a steady trade if we paid on delivery at the road head in Banios. By the rules we were supposed to analyze the bark in the Quito laboratory and pay on the basis of quinine sulphate content. In dealing with illiterate and still very primitive Indians, that was not possible. We purchased his bark at an estimated value, and I instructed the office staff to arrange regular pickups in Banios and to pay in cash on delivery at the same price. Unfortunately, a new accountant from Washington arrived at our office while I was in the States, consulting, and, as a good bureaucrat, refused payment to the Indians (who had back-packed the bark for something like 200 miles) without prior analysis. We never saw another Jivaro, and that first cargo turned out to be some of the richest bark in Equador.

It is difficult in the high Andes not to be distracted by archaeological sites and fascinating Indian tribes, who make up the working force of the country (Equador was still 85% pure Indian). Much of my time was spent with the field crews on the forested slopes or traveling across the high plateau between the two Andean ranges, and everywhere we worked with Indians. Ed Ferdon, one of our field men, was an archaeologist who had been digging in the country, and with him I was often sidetracked to a site or a different tribal group.

The one indelible memory of the mountain Indians is their endurance. Like their small horses and mules, they back-pack very heavy loads up and down mountain tracks at elevations that had my heart pounding with the slightest exertion. Living almost like serfs on the vast farms and ranches of that time, many of them were oppressed and humble people. Others, independent and living on their own small farms, remained a proud people. Sometimes, riding along a surviving section of the great Inca road that once extended 2,500 miles along the crest of the Andes, I could imagine those small, tough, enduring people as part of the great empire. I thought of the several succeeding civilizations of the Andes and the coastal desert, beginning at least as early as 800 B.C. and probably long before, of the great monolithic buildings, so much like those of the Bronze Age of the Old World, the elaborate gold work, the pyramids, and the mysterious markings in the desert that were discovered only during the war, from the air. Do people, just because they are human, develop similar social structures and similar technologies in isolation, or have they maintained some sort of contact through the ages? An old argument with no answer. How can we explain pottery of 2500 B.C., found on the coast of Equador, that some experts say is the same as Jomon pottery made in Japan?

Suddenly, the Surgeon General's Office decided that atabrine could be substituted for quinine, and we were instructed to fold up our production in the Andes at once. Then I discovered it is often more difficult to stop something than to start it. A whole chain of men, companies, and activities involved in an ongoing business must be stopped without ruining the people who got into it. Ambassador Scotten was one of those truly conscientious men who went to bat with me, insisting that the board must pay our way out. Funds were appropriated, and we thought I could liquidate the operation without serious financial damage to anyone. But some niggling bureaucrat in the Washington office hit upon the idea of paying off with surplus equipment rather than the appropriated funds. By that time such equipment was a drug on the market and of no use to Equadorans with their money invested in quinine production. Backed by Scotten I returned to Washington to work with men in the State Department in their efforts to put pressure on the board.

The affair continued for months, finally coming into the hands of attorneys and accountants supervised by the embassy in Quito. It was time for me to move on. Scotten and friends in the State Department urged me to join the Foreign Service. I chose the European theater and was assigned to Robert Murphy's staff, then stationed in London.

Our convoy of more than ninety ships assembled off Halifax for the crossing to England in February 1944. By that time submarine defenses were much more effective than in the early years of the war and sinkings were considerably reduced, although German subs were still active in the North Atlantic and the Irish Sea. Terrific winter storms followed us for fourteen days and were more effective defense than the aircraft carriers, since in such high seas submarines could not fire. In the wardroom of a battered freighter I spent much of the time listening to German-language records, interrupted often when a particularly heavy sea sent the pickup needle screeching across the record disc. As a child I had spoken German with my maternal grandparents, but with the First World War this was abruptly broken off. In the university I relearned just enough German to qualify for a degree but could not speak it. The staff in London was scheduled to become the political office for the American element in the Allied Control Commission for Occupied Germany.

In mid-Atlantic, in some of the worst weather, the steering control of our ship went wrong and we were abandoned, dead in the water, waiting for repairs, while the convoy steamed off eastward. Those were the most anxious two or three days while

Froelich Rainey, 85, A Museum Director And an Archeologist

By BRUCE LAMBERT

Froelich G. Rainey, an archeologist, museum director and creator of an award-winning television program, died on Sunday at a hospital in Cornwall, England. He was 85 years old and lived in Cornwall.

He died of cancer, his family said.

As a young field researcher, Dr. Rainey found major artifacts supporting the theory that early humans migrated across the Bering Strait to America. He was among the first to find bone shafts, used as lances to kill animals hunted for food

In his youth he worked his way around the world doing odd jobs. He received a bachelor's degree from the University of Chicago, and doctorates in English from the American School in France and in anthropology from Yale University.

In World War II, Dr. Rainey served on the Board of Economic Warfare, ran a mission in Ecuador to highjack bark gathered for the Germans for use as quinine and worked for the State Department.

His marriage to the former Penelope Lewis ended in divorce.

Surviving are his wife of 17 years, Marina; a daughter, Penelope Rainey of Philadelphia; a sister, Viva Rainey of California, and two grandchildren.

Subscribe and see the full article in TimesMachine

New York Times subscribers* enjoy full access to TimesMachine—view over 150 years of New York Times journalism, as it originally appeared.

*Does not include Crossword-only or Cooking-only subscribers.

We are continually improving the quality of our text archives. Please send feedback, error reports, and suggestions to archive_feedback@nytimes.com.

A version of this biography: obituary appears in print on October 14, 1992, on Page B00010 of the National

them.

From 1947 to 1976 Dr. Rainey headed the Museum of Archaeology and Anthropology at the University of Pennsylvania. He revived the museum from its Depression era and World War II doldrums, expanding its budget and collections. Under his leadership, the museum sponsored 230 expeditions in six continents, including the ancient Greek community of Sybaris; Ban Chiang, Thailand, and its Bronze Age discoveries, and Tikal, Guatemala, with its Mayan treasures. Award-Winning TV Program

Adapting the museum world to modern communications to reach larger audiences, Dr. Rainey developed Expedition magazine and a Peabody Award-winning television program, "What in the World." In the program he moderated a panel of experts trying to identity artifacts, while viewers were given clues to the answer.

Dr. Rainey was a past president of the American Association of Museums and the International Congress of Anthropology.
He was born in Black River Falls, Wis., and grew up on a cattle ranch in Montana.

repairs were made, and we then steamed all out to catch the convoy, except for the brief period in pitch darkness after the breakdown, when sister ships in the convoy rode up on our small blue stern light and slipped past us in breathtaking misses. There were alarms but no serious attacks until we reached the calm Irish Sea. Off Bristol the convoy was hit hard. We never learned how many ships were lost. That first taste of serious warfare was, somehow, not so upsetting as my first experience with V-2 rocket bombs in the streets of London. At first I could not understand how Londoners took them so calmly, but, as weeks passed, I too learned to take early morning tea in bed while the rockets came in during the usual early morning bombardment.

When I reported to Bob Murphy at the embassy in London and he quizzed me about my experience and training in European affairs, his only comment was, "My God, now they are even sending me experts on Eskimos and quinine!" Thereafter, my past and profession were never mentioned, except when there was a flap, months later, about my security clearance.

In the FBI files was a statement from one of my students in Alaska to the effect that I had "taught race" (the usual beginning of an anthropology course, having to do with the races of the world), but even a mention of race at that time was suspicious.

There was a powerful element in the embryo American contingent at that time, advocating that millions of German war criminals, once they were in the hands of the Allies, should be exterminated in the concentration camps then being used to exterminate so many people in Germany. But the good sense of the British element and the majority of the Americans soon quashed the idea. Oddly enough, in all the books about the war, I have never seen a mention of that fantastic argument waged at Bushy Park during that period. Some echo was to remain in the war trials and the famous military order "1067," which, at first, was meant to destroy Germany's industrial potential, but vengeance did not long survive the first months of occupation.

The last year of war and the first year of occupation remain with me as a shattering experience in the imponderable behavior of human beings. During the advance through western Germany, when some foolish person in a village fired on American troops, the commanding officer would pull them back and order an artillery or tank barrage to destroy the village with all the people in it; then a few months later the same officer would be living with a German woman, supporting all her family, and strongly advocating the reconstruction of Germany. We met our "great democratic allies," the Russians, in Berlin and a few weeks later received a secret memo from headquarters instructing us not to call them "those Russian bastards." Americans fought to free France from the Germans, then a few months later admired the Germans and disliked the French. We blew up nitrogen-producing plants one year and rebuilt them the next to supply a Europe desperately in need of fertilizer. While the American press still wrote about good old Uncle Joe Stalin and our brave Russian allies, I sat in the turret of a B-25 flying into Vienna and watched for flak bursts from Russian anti-aircraft guns stationed along the narrow air corridor into the city.

In Berlin we were stuffed with food that choked us when the noses of pale, starved, blonde kids, like my own, were stuck against the window panes to watch us eat. Of course, most of us broke the strict military rules and carried food out the back door to the kids. We were all sent to see the ghastly remains of the death chambers in the concentration camps but somehow could not connect them with the friendly Germans who seemed so much like Americans. We tried to isolate Nazis from Germans, like the goodies from the baddies in a western film, but it was not easy: black shaded into white. Who is the enemy and who is the friend? It is all very simple in war with front lines, but very confusing when they disappear. No wonder I had had a bad time trying to explain the war to the Point Hope Eskimos.

One evening in Berlin, shortly after the Western allies joined the Russians there, a troop of entertainers in our officers' mess sang a new and very popular song, "Berlin will rise again." There was utter confusion—did we stop it, boo, or applaud? That confusion remained throughout the first winter, then slowly resolved into a fundamentally human reaction: let's get on with reconstruction.

As the war drew to its bloody and confused end, the political office was besieged by surrendering German officers with proposals on how to end the thing. After the "Battle of the Bulge" everyone knew it was finished, but with that curious policy of "unconditional surrender" there was no machinery to stop it.

Eventually, in April, U.S. forces met the Russians on the Elbe south of Berlin, then withdrew to the agreed-on U.S. zone of occupation, leaving the Russians alone to occupy Berlin—a U.S. decision strongly opposed by Churchill. Probably with that decision the "cold war" was born.

VE Day found me in the Place de la Concorde for a wild night of celebration. All the good wine was gone with the German troops, and the new wine was very sour. Probably never before were there so many hangovers in Paris. And to make things worse, victory did not at once restore French food supplies. Only on the black market could one find a meal worthy of the celebration. Luckily, one of our staff, recently transferred from Central America, had brought with him 200 pounds of coffee beans. With that, we had Parisian dinners as I remembered them. He also bought an automobile and set himself up in a grand apartment. The black market and the financial and economic chaos of newly printed occupation currency was just beginning.

One of my special assignments was to advise the political office on fuel supply in Europe, an odd job for a political officer, but still political in the sense that a touchy question of massive imports of U.S. coal must be decided in a hurry. The search for information began in Denmark, still occupied by German troops because no allied forces had reached Copenhagen to take their surrender. In a military plane with two army officers I had the curious experience of landing on an airfield near Copenhagen still under the command of the Luftwaffe. Neither they nor we knew how to handle the situation. Did we salute? Clearly we were not the expected Allied occupying force, but who commanded? Actually, it was all quite simple and friendly. We just took a taxi to the Danish Government Office concerned with fuel supplies.

To the great surprise of my army companions, once our assignment was completed I proposed that we visit the Danish National Museum, not explaining why. Helge Larsen, of course, was still in the United States, but all his colleagues in the American section were old friends. Kaj Birket-Smith, chief of the division, looked startled and completely uncomprehending when three Allied army officers walked into his office. (I was a civilian, but in army uniform to make travel easier.) He did not recognize me until I removed the military cap; then he exclaimed, "It can't be you, in army uniform in Copenhagen!" We were the first Allied soldiers seen by the Danes since the beginning of their occupation, and hence the symbol of liberation. None of us will forget the celebration in the National Museum. Schnapps, beer, and food appeared from somewhere. The staff gathered in one of the largest working laboratories, where tables were soon littered with bottles together with skulls, war clubs, pots, stone tools, and fur parkas. We brought news, and cigarettes, from the outside world; the Danes brought tales of what it was like to be occupied for years. When we left late in the day, one of my reeling companions asked, "Are you really one of those Academic Johnnies?"

The key to the fuel problem in Western Europe was the Ruhr, where heavy bombing and bitter fighting on the ground had destroyed a large part of the industrial plants. But the Allied armies had been instructed to avoid mine heads because power plants at the mine heads supplied current to Western Europe, and we found that few were out of action. My companion in the investigation of coal mines was an army engineer experienced in American coal fields. We talked with mine managers and mine owners and also descended with working crews to the coal face, sometimes as much as one mile deep. His conclusion was that Ruhr production could be stepped up quickly to supply most of the urgent demand in Europe. But I began to realize that the problem was manpower at the coal face. All forced labor had been liberated. Not only during the war but long before, men working underground on the coal seams were generally Poles and none were left. Mine managers were dubious about the amount of coal that could be produced with unskilled labor. We watched new workmen, some still in German army uniforms, attempting to replace the experienced Poles.

Back in Versailles, I wrote a report for Bob Murphy that urged immediate and massive shipments from the U.S. The army engineer reported to his unit in a much more optimistic vein. Bob, quite naturally, accepted the opinion of the expert and my report for the State was shelved. Months later when large shipments from the State were on the way, Bob stopped by my office to apologize, something very rare and heartwarming in government and the army. Assignments for me thereafter were more significant and fully backed.

The Rhine river was blocked by sunken tugs and barges.

Like roads and railroads, clearance and reconstruction claimed high priority in the restoration of industry. The old Rhine Commission of Riparian States was called together for a meeting in Strasbourg, and Murphy was instructed to send an American representative. I was named as that representative only two days before the meeting and ordered to Strasbourg by military aircraft. But the weather fouled up the flight for some time so that I arrived late, after many resolutions had been agreed on by the commission. The French ambassador, who was presiding, proposed that the secretary read through all those resolutions so that I could approve or disapprove for the United States, and asked if I wished to have them translated into English. My French was almost nonexistent, but, embarrassed, I said it was not necessary. Each commissioner had a staff of experts seated behind him, except for me. All waited as each resolution was read through and I formally agreed. Then, in a pause between resolutions, Sir Osborn Mance, the British commissioner seated next to me, grasped my arm and whispered, "Hold on, young fellow, this is the money resolution, you had better have it translated." Thanks to Mance, I did not agree to U.S. expenditures for which I was not authorized. (Some years later, when I was brought back into temporary government service as the U.S. Commissioner for the Rhine, most of the 1946 representatives were still serving, and they all remembered that one resolution translated into English.)

Opening the Danube to navigation was a different problem. In Germany all of us were aware of the ominous clouds gathering in Eastern Europe long before the people at home had focused on a new enemy. Soviet ideas about occupation were certainly not those of the West, neither in the four-power control of Germany nor in the Soviet control of Eastern states liberated by the Russian Army. Norman Padelford, an advisor to the Secretary of State, thought that the Danube and its international commission might be used to force the issue of free, international communication among the riparian states, exclusively Soviet-occupied below Vienna. Together we convinced the State Department to request the U.S. Army to seize all tugboats and barges above Vienna (where most of them had gathered, away from the Russian drive through Eastern Europe). That would be a powerful lever in forcing agreement on free and open travel along the Danube.

When I returned from Vienna, after the seizure, friends in the political office laughingly accused me of firing the first shot in the Third World War. If so, it was a dud. The Secretary of State and President Truman held out for some months, then reached a pious agreement with the Soviets officially proclaiming free and open navigation. Boats moved downriver, and the Iron Curtain clamped down east of Vienna.

Another member of Murphy's staff, Jack Tuthill, and I hit it off from the beginning, and after we moved up from Versailles to Frankfurt and then to Berlin, we took on together many assignments having to do with the political aspects of increasing economic problems in occupied Germany. Jack, his wife Erna (also working in the Control Commission), Brewster Norris, and I were billeted in a house in a suburb of Berlin. The house, and an old couple who lived there, had survived intact both the bombing and the wild weeks of Russian occupation before the Western Allies were allowed to enter the city. Even after we arrived, we saw many horse-drawn wagons laden with furniture, clothing, and personal effects, heading off toward Russia along the autobahn. The old gentleman who owned our house told us how Siberian soldiers, billeted in their house, used the flush toilets to wash their heads. When he explained their purpose, they were very angry and shouted "Sabotage!" At least they let the old people continue to stay on in the house. Our housekeeping unit ordered them out. We found them in a bare attic room in the next house, and late at night when no army guards were about, Jack, Brewster, and I packed a collection of furniture out the back door and up to their third-floor attic. Even at that hour the stairs were lined with astonished Germans watching what were to them three army officers sweating under bedsteads and overstuffed chairs.

That bitter cold winter in Berlin, a shambles of destruction, with no fuel, very little food, and total disagreement among the occupying powers, left all four of us with a conviction that we either had to find something to laugh about or go crazy. We grew up in a hurry. Living through the brutality of an occupation is a condenser of life experience and a shortcut to a mature recognition of the human anomaly. Laughter and tears are very close together. The only thing the Western Allies and the Russians could agree upon was the reopening of the ballet, the opera, and the orchestra. We were all there for the opening of Eugene Onegin, even though we froze. When an American G.I. shot the Berlin Orchestra conductor, all troops were disarmed.

The daily Four-Power meetings in Berlin became a joke. Nothing ever happened. The less experienced, and rougher, Russians and Americans were bored to the point of explosion. One afternoon, in a transportation division discussion, the French and British representatives kept going the polite forms of international discussion while the Russians and Americans brooded. When the American spokesman was half asleep, I suddenly remembered an issue (just what I have now forgotten) that had the British and French at swords' points. I whispered to our man, suggesting an irrelevant statement that would spark that issue. It did, and we were all awakened by a brilliant and bitter, but irrelevant, fight between the British and the French. When the meeting ended, General Kvashnin came around the table, threw his arms about me in a great bear hug, and cried "Tovarich!"

To lighten the grimness, Jack and I developed our own little game. When one of us was sent out of the country on some job in London, Vienna, or Poland, he would leave a note for the other simply saying, "Take over what I have been doing," with no details at all. The results were sometimes hilarious. Like all of us who have had a measure of success by the time we are forty, Jack had his stuffy period, but at that time he was irrepressible. When a cable arrived from King Farouk in Cairo demanding the immediate return of Nefertiti by military aircraft, Jack smelled something funny and referred it to me. The young army officer with the cable rushed into our office and shouted, "Who the hell is this babe Nefertiti?" Later, Professor Hermann Ranke, who was involved in the transfer of that famous bust to Germany, and had then returned to Philadelphia in charge of the Egyptian section at The University Museum, hugely enjoyed my account of the episode—as much as Jack.

By the spring of that year it became increasingly obvious to all of us that a restored stable currency in Germany was essential to get people back to work, to revive industry, and to clear communications along the all-important Rhine River. As the U.S. representative on the Rhine Commission, Murphy asked me to explain the situation there to General Clay, the top-ranking U.S. officer in Germany. Perhaps my account was too abrupt, too opinionated, and undiplomatic. In any case, Clay blew his top and dressed me down as if I were a lieutenant in the army. That was too much for me and I exploded. After a swearing match, I resigned and walked out, to the great embarrassment of Murphy the diplomat. Back in our office, I had just called General Clay a son-of-a-bitch when I turned around to find him at my elbow, grinning. His soothing words did not alter anything, and I packed up to leave for England, where my wife and children were then living. Later, Murphy sent word that Clay had proposed that I take over as military governor in Munich, but by that time I was in the Foreign Ministers' Paris Conference working with Norman Padelford.

For someone with a family to support, out of a job, and known to be undiplomatic with a commanding officer, it was a relief to be reemployed in the Department of State as chief of a division on European Transportation Affairs. Soon I was to learn that General Clay fully agreed with me on the need for the reform of currency in Germany; what I did not realize in Germany was that he was tied by formal military orders, and himself had to lead a basic change in policy.

In England at that time it was not easy to arrange transport for five of us to the United States. At last orders arrived to embark at Southampton on a military transport carrying European wives with their babies to join their G.I. husbands in America. On board ship it was a nightmare. Over 900 women and children were stowed in four-tier bunks everywhere. My wife and two children with their nurse were bunked in the empty psychiatric ward, and I was huddled on deck trying to keep clear of the bedlam. But the ship's captain took pity and hid me in the pilot's cabin far above the wails, fights, and curses. Working my way down through that mass of displaced humanity to keep in touch with my family, I was often struck by the variety—everything from prostitute to English aristocracy, dumped into a kind of madhouse, and all fearful of what they would find on the other side. It was pathetic to watch them search through the mass of civilian men who met the ship, looking for husbands no longer in uniform, and often quite unrecognizable. Sometimes disappointment was written all over their faces. In civilian clothes some of them did not look so good, and romance was gone. I wonder how many of them stuck it out.

The anti-Nazi war was finished and the anti-Communist "cold war" would not crystallize for three years. In the United States people still spoke of "our great democratic ally." No one wanted to hear about the next conflict. In England, radio broadcasters poured out pride and sentiment—how England had stood alone against the great power of Germany. They apparently forgot the whole British Empire, the Russians, the Americans, and a Germany no bigger than the state of Texas, with few resources and a population not much greater than that of England alone. With the power of human emotions, sentiments, and fixed ideas, the history of events is inevitably distorted. But the war, and the aftermath, left me with a strong conviction that myth and history are indistinguishable. It was not what I read about it. That is not to say that historical accounts are consciously distorted, but simply that many unpleasant and shameful things are left out, and what remains as factual history is highly colored by the emotions and beliefs of those who write it. One can only imagine how different a history of the Second World War would have been if the victorious Germans had written it.

Ten years of digging had left me skeptical about the way we reconstruct man's past with what we find in the earth and what we have learned about primitive people still living in remote regions. Active engagement in a world war that surely will remain a highly significant event in history now leaves me equally skeptical about how history is recorded for future generations. So much of what I experienced is glossed over, left out, colored by convictions, redrawn to fit theories imposed by fanatic propaganda, and designed to make our side heroes, the others monsters. Even though this generation looks at the Germans and the Japanese as our great friends and allies and the Russians our enemy, the biased accounts of the war remain history. It is often said that the rewriting of history by future generations will sort it all out so that it comes right in the end. I think, however, that history, like archaeology, is reinterpreted by each generation with its own theories and bias so that there are no absolutes in the flow of time and events. Just as the revolutionary current research in biology, chemistry, and physics now changes our whole concept of the nature of the world we live in, so history and prehistory are an ever-changing process in human thought.

The Lucy Wharton Drexel medal of The University Museum being presented
to Sir Leonard Wooley (center) by the author (left) and Percy Madeira
(right) at The University Museum in 1955.
Photograph courtesy of The University Museum Archives.

CHAPTER FIVE
Skeptical Return to Academia

Percy Madeira, president of The University Museum in Philadelphia and a banker, wrote a history of the Museum entitled Men in Search of Man* —a title that is the essence of a tradition and an institution. It began in the late nineteenth century with a banker and a minister discussing English and French archaeological discoveries in Mesopotamia. A. H. Layard and P. E. Botta, excavating Assyrian palaces near Mosul, had set in motion a great popular interest in digging that was to sweep the Western world. That discussion at a summer camp led to a small group of Philadelphians launching the first American excavations in Mesopotamia at the ancient site of Nippur in what is now Iraq. It was an age of massive digging, with hundreds of workmen under the direction of only two or three scholars, that established the outline and the theory of ancient history in the Near East that are still dominant. And at Nippur, with the discovery of a library of more than 50,000 clay tablets, Philadelphia's University

* Published by the University of Pennsylvania in 1964.

[121]

Museum was born as a center for the interpretation of the ancient world behind the Bible.

But it was also an age of massive digging and startling discoveries in many other parts of the world. Before the turn of the century the Museum was also working in Peru, excavating Indian graves where the preservation of objects like woven fabrics, wooden implements, and other fragile things was even more surprising than in the tombs of Egypt. Advanced civilizations in Central and South America that were obviously ancient did not then inspire the popular excitement of Mesopotamian tablets recording Noah's flood, but their discovery opened up a world of prehistory that became part of the tradition of The University Museum. Shortly after the turn of the century its expeditions were in Central America, the Arctic, West Africa, the Mediterranean, Egypt, Siberia, and the Middle East. The "Men in Search of Man" sought for significant archaeological sites around the world that could explain human history and open men's minds to a new conception of what happened everywhere. First called the "Free Museum of Science and the Arts," it was built and funded by "Public-spirited gentlemen of Philadelphia" with the idea that digging into the past was done for the interested public and not for scholars alone.

I first became aware of The University Museum in the 1920s, when Sir Leonard Woolley discovered the Royal Tombs at Ur in a joint expedition of the British Museum and The University Museum. In England and America, newspapers carried regular accounts of what was happening there, and like the excavation of Tutankhamen's tomb, the Royal Cemetery at Ur became headline news. But I did not visit the Museum until the 1930s, first when Frank Speck was advising me in a study of New England Indians, and later when Edgar Howard at a conference there tried to convince doubting American archaeologists that men and mammoths were contemporary in

America. The year the war ended, George Valliant, the director, committed suicide, and some time later, in search for his replacement, Percy Madeira, the president of the Board of Managers, asked me to come to the Museum for a lecture on Alaska. The war years had reduced the staff to a kind of holding operation, and it was clear that nothing much would be done until there was a new director and a new staff.

I was interested in the job as defined by Percy, but nothing happened. (Later he told me that one of the old fellows on the board thought that at thirty-eight I was too young for the position.) A year passed at the Department of State with problems such as the disposal of freight ships built during the war, mostly to the Greeks, who were to found shipping dynasties, political maneuvers to open communications between East and West, and finally aid to Greece and Turkey in the first moves of the cold war.

I had just bought a house and tract of land in Vienna, Virginia, when Percy called to say they had made a decision about a new director. Probably I would have stayed with the Foreign Service if it had not been for Lincoln MacVeagh. It happened that he had just then been called back to Washington for consultation from his post as ambassador in Spain. His long career in the Foreign Service, and his experience in advising so many young men, tipped the balance. He reminded me of all the frustrations in working through the bureaucratic machinery of government, the endless committee meetings, the indecisions, the difficulty of acting on one's own decision, and the satisfaction of managing a private institution where you could get things done. But also he had been bitten by the archaeological bug and thought back to his early years at the Boston Museum of Fine Arts. He was very convincing and he was right.

If one expects to become an expert on Ruhr coal mining, it is wise to learn what goes on at the heart of the matter—the coal seam thousands of feet deep—not only what happens in the boardroom or the manager's office. Probing for the heart of the matter in Philadelphia, I found Mrs. Charles C. Harrison. She was straight out of the nineteenth century—as one of the museum guards put it, "That old lady came in with the bricks"—and she had all the charming downright quality of old Philadelphia that knew exactly where it was going. Her father-in-law was the man with the "little black book" in which he wrote down the names of Philadelphians and the amount of money he decided they should give to the Museum—usually matched by himself. About once a month I was summoned to tea at "Chuckwood" on the Main Line. It began with tea with bread and butter, then progressed to bourbon whiskey. Each time the exposure of Philadelphia and Philadelphians progressed in the same way, from the bland to the pungent. The key to most jobs, I suppose, is people, and it was a tremendous help to find someone who was not addicted to the delicate euphemisms of contemporary times, but rather spelled out bluntly who was who, what did what, and why—including affairs both overt and covert. For a man raised on a ranch in Montana by a crew of cowboys, it was a fascinating education in a world I never knew.

During the depression in the 1930s, the financial affairs of the Museum had been taken over by the University of Pennsylvania, and the Museum became an integral part of the University. However, it remained a public museum, with part of the original cost supplied by the city and part of the operating costs by the state. Hence the director was in an ambivalent situation. He was chosen and appointed by the Board of Managers of the Museum with the approval of the university administration, since the university supplied about half the operating cost. Under the Museum's constitution, agreed on with the Trustees of the University, the director was responsible to the board, which met once a month, but I soon learned it was wise to get unofficial agreement with the University administration before proposing innovations at a board meeting. In 1947 that was easy. William Dubarry ran the university with the guidance of Thomas Gates, the ex-president of the university and chairman of the Museum Board. There was then none of the complexity of faculty committees, senate, or the present bureaucracy. It was highly undemocratic, but if you were persona grata it was certainly efficient. Many times the important decisions were made at the opera. Mr. and Mrs. Gates often shared their box with my wife and me, and Bill Dubarry had his box nearby. Those long arias bored both Tom and me, and we were glad to slip out for a discussion and decision with Bill.

After some months of learning the ropes, rehabilitation of the traditional University Museum was deemed possible. Original research, worldwide, interpreted for the educated public was a tradition to be maintained at all cost. Many in the university wanted to see the Museum become a catch-all for the odds and ends collected in the University, and early on there was a proposal that it take over the Barnes Collection of paintings as well as other fine-art objects. But the Museum had always been an anthropological-archaeological institution with a unique collection of ancient and primitive art. It was world famous for its archaeological research, particularly in the Old World, and had survived the general decline of university museums in America and England. Its future lay in what had always been its strength.

In America, Percy Madeira proposed we tackle one of the largest, oldest, and most important sites in the Mayan field, Tikal in Guatemala. Trouble between Guatemala and British Honduras had meant the construction of a military air strip in the jungle at Tikal. That would make it possible to support an expedition by air rather than by mule train. But our plan was short-lived. The Ubico government was succeeded by a leftist, anti-U.S. government, and no agreement for research there was possible. In the Old World, it seemed advisable to return to Nippur in Iraq, where the Museum had begun, and where so many literary clay tablets in Sumerian had been found. Abbé Legrain remained as head of the Babylonian section in the Museum, but he had reached an age when he no longer wished to return to the field. To get things going again we joined up with the Institute for Oriental Studies at the University of Chicago and sent out a combined expedition in 1949. In the Mediterranean section, J.F. Daniels was young and ambitious. He proposed Sardis, where the Museum had once worked with the Boston Museum of Fine Arts, or Gordion, both in Turkey. In Greece he picked up Rodney S. Young, then working at Corinth, for a look at both sites. They agreed on Gordion, traditionally the capital of the Phrygian kingdom where Alexander cut the Gordion Knot.

At home the problems were recruiting new and vigorous young blood for the research staff, money to finance large-scale excavations, and my own education in regions of the world that I did not know. Tom Gates and Bill Dubarry approved the staff build-up and my search for creative field researchers who would understand and support the Museum's traditional role. Pete Daniels died suddenly in Turkey from unknown causes and was replaced by Rodney S. Young with the addition of G. Roger Edwards. William R. Coe joined Linton Satterthwaite, Jr. in the American section, Francis Steel joined Samuel Noah Kramer in the Babylonian section, Schuyler Cammann was brought in for field research in China (then open to the West), Alfred Kidder, Jr. for South America, Robert H. Dyson, Jr. for the Near East, and also Carleton Coon for a proposed Near Eastern Area Study Center in collaboration with the Oriental Studies Department of the University. Somewhat later Bill Davenport joined us to take over the Pacific field.

Carl Coon's transfer from Harvard to The University

Museum led to some of the Museum's most creative research but also to an explosion. Perhaps it was naive of me to think that Carl could work with Fred Speiser when the Arab-Israeli conflict was just beginning. With one pro-Arab and one pro-Israel, collaboration in Near Eastern research could only end in vituperations. To make things worse, Harold Stassen was then President of the University and a front-runner for President of the United States. That was one conflict he must avoid, and we agreed that the Study Center should be quietly eliminated.

The Board of Managers maneuvered a financial windfall by recovering $100,000, quite a lot of money in those days, from the University Treasurer, which had been taken from the Museum's endowed and restricted funds during the war years. That was enough to launch the field research and to give some respite, before outside fund raising began in earnest. Patrons of the Museum in the pre-income tax era had bequeathed certain funds, the income from which was restricted to active field research, and thus could not be used for maintenance. It was those wise old Philadelphians who were responsible for the traditions and the future reputation of the Museum.

When I was being interviewed by the Appointments Committee of the Museum Board, Brandon Barringer assured me that as director I would not be expected to raise money; that was the responsibility of the board. After nearly thirty years of fund raising, both Brandon and I still chuckle about that come-on. But it is so easy to become an "expert" in a world that wants to believe in experts. Years later Sam Carpenter and I flew from Philadelphia to New Haven in his small plane to discuss proposed research in Mexico with Michael Coe. There was some trouble with the plane in New Haven, repaired by Sam, and then a bad snowstorm on the way back. When we landed in Philadelphia, a bit battered, and just before Sam took off for Wilmington, he reached into his pocket to pull out a grubby check, wrinkled and grease-

stained. It was made out to The University Museum for
$150,000. Later I noticed the cancelled check posted on the
wall in the University's Development Office with a note on the
expertise of the Museum director's fund raising. After long
experience, that "expertise" consisted in never asking for
money.

Scholarship, apparently, depends on building up on earlier
scholarship and thus following a prescribed line of thought. In
archaeology, as in most things, there are modes, styles, perhaps
fads, that lead down a worn path. Naturally, those paths
seldom lead to significant discoveries. It is surprisingly difficult
to keep people searching until they find a new lead to
something that is truly creative, unknown, unexplored. It is so
much easier to begin digging at a known site where you know
you will find something that will be approved by your
colleagues and fit in with the current mode.

My own education in the Museum's traditional world view of
archaeology began in Guatemala and Iraq. Luckily, in Iraq, I
fell in with Fuad Safar, a quiet, wise, experienced, and
competent man who had recorded 7,000 major archaeological
sites in southern Iraq alone. He was to take over the actual
management of our joint expedition at Nippur when it reached
a confused state, but before that, in his quiet way, he had
alerted me to a trend that would affect all work by foreigners
in Iraq. New discoveries at new and significant sites would be
made by Iraqis. Foreign expeditions would work at well-known
sites where they had excavated in prewar times.

The vast ruins of Nippur, appearing like a range of hills on
the flat desert of southern Iraq, are a desolate reminder of what

happened to those rich, irrigated plains when the Mongols swept over them, destroying an irrigation system thousands of years old and an Islamic empire. Real deserts, like the Sahara, are for me regions of great beauty and charm—but not relict deserts as in Iraq, where fine dust from ancient fields can fairly smother you, penetrating everything.

Wandering over Babylon and many other derelict cites in the dust with Fuad stirred up many unconventional thoughts about the future of Mesopotamian archaeology and the Museum's part in it. Already the reduction in the scale of digging that was to characterize postwar archaeology was taking effect. After the massive excavations at Nippur in the late nineteenth century, reduced twentieth-century digging over the same site held little promise of anything more that a bit of additional embroidery. Iraqi archaeologists were just as competent as those of us from the West and would in any case hold the most important sites for their own research. There were huge areas in the world, such as Central Asia and the Far East, that were little known. The most creative contributions to ancient world history would surely be made there.

In Guatemala and Mexico the Mayan ruins were not what I had expected from my reading. Perhaps I should have known by then, particularly after the experience of the war years, that all written accounts are filtered through patterns of thought that conform to the ideas and theories of any given time. In the United States, after all the years influenced by the Monroe Doctrine, isolationism still dominated archaeology. Ancient American civilizations were autochthonous—created in isolation by those hypothetical people who had somehow wandered across the Bering Straits at some unknown time in the past. All theories of transatlantic or transpacific movements of civilized people were popular bunk. Even the writings of recognized scholars like Gordon Ekholm and Heine-Geldern about transpacific movements were embarrassing.

Prowling about those massive stone monuments at Quirigua, Copan, and Chichen-Itza, I felt that I was back in India. If all those remarkable similarities were unrelated, then clearly there is something in human genes that creates the same kinds of figures and structures in stone when men reach a certain stage of development wherever they are. I prefer to think of oceans as high roads for man's wandering rather than as isolating barriers. After all, we know that a New England fisherman, with crippled hands (frozen on the Newfoundland Banks), rowed a Maine dory across the whole North Atlantic to Ireland in the late nineteenth century; and somehow Asians discovered almost all the Pacific Islands in outrigger canoes. I, myself, weathered a severe storm in the Bering Sea in a skin boat not unlike the Irish coracle. Barriers are more in men's minds than in the world's oceans.

Tikal, although a conventional choice of site for excavation, looked good to me. Perhaps there we could learn something about those mysterious Mayans, who were truly literate, remarkable astronomers, pyramid builders, and mathmaticians who, like the Sumerians, had discovered the concept of zero. But I knew then that the problem was going to be the scale of digging. How could one get twentieth-century diggers to explore eight square miles of central city alone, not to mention suburbs of unknown extent?

Not only I, but the Board of Managers, needed education if the Museum's research was to be revived. The president, Percy Madeira, his new wife, Eugenia, Sam and Mildred Eckert, and Brandon and Sonia Barringer joined me for a look at archaeological sites in the Near East. To facilitate travel I passed on a word to friends in the American Foreign Service, and for some unknown reason our little troop became known as "Fro and his traveling schoolteachers." Actually, it was Sam Eckert of the Sun Oil Company, with all his friends in that industry, who smoothed our way, particularly in Iraq and

Turkey. He and Mildred were old hands at traveling in out-of-the-way places, neat and very efficient with baggage, tickets, arrangements, and transport. It was the hatbox that got under his skin. Sonia had bought an elaborate hat in Paris and carried it in a large cardboard box done up with string together with a large collection of other baggage. Somehow it was always under Sam's feet. At last, crossing the desert from Baghdad to Mosul in four cars, we noticed that Sonia's hatbox on the top of the car ahead of us was blowing loose. Despite Mildred's pleas to warn her, Sam watched with joy as the string gave way and that marvelous hat whirled away across the desert.

It was at Nippur that our Board members got their roughest lesson on life in a field camp. The staff had taken over an old Arab house in Afek, near the site, where the only water was a canal used to water and bathe the camels and the burros as well as supply the drinking water for the village and our expedition. The only toilet facility was a pitch-dark closet with an open trench and an old bottomless chair. When you carried in the kerosene lamp (to indicate it was occupied), the walls became alive with cockroaches. I thought of Eugenia's lovely country house on Crum Creek outside Philadelphia and wondered how she could possibly manage. Not a whimper. All of them were very impressive people.

But at Nimrud, in northern Iraq, they saw a field camp that was as it should be. Max Mallowan and his wife, Agatha Christie (the famed writer of murder mysteries), had built an inexpensive mud-brick field house, furnished it with native materials, and lived in simple but complete comfort. At a glance we could see it was not money but experience that could make all the difference in how people lived on a site. Max and Agatha, as well as their staff of youngsters, did a great deal to educate our group not only in Near Eastern archaeology but in efficient management of an expedition. Also, at Gordion,

Rodney Young ran an exceptionally well-organized excavation that impressed me as well as the Board members. It was there that we decided to terminate work at Nippur, in part because of bad management, but primarily because it was adding little to what was learned there in ten years of large-scale excavation near the turn of the century. It was agreed that I should turn eastward through Iran and Afghanistan in search of more promising fields where we could work in unexplored sites with the promise of original discovery. We parted in Istanbul, and I took the old Orient Express back to Baghdad, a leisurely three-day trip on a train then reduced to two comfortable old wagons-lit and a restaurant car, with only three or four people on board, like a private train. Even then I had almost forgotten what air travel has done to destroy the pleasures of traveling by train and ship as they used to be.

Following, roughly, the route of Alexander from Baghdad to the Indus did something to my shifting sense of time and space. That whole route is littered with so many ancient sites, undug and unknown, that the minute number explored and the minute sections of those actually excavated left me skeptical of the whole theoretical scheme of ancient history in the Near East and the time-space relations of human events that cluster about that highway of Eurasian wanderers. You ask a herdsman in some isolated valley what he calls the mound of a ruined city nearby and he will usually give you a name meaning Alexandria, or its equivalent in his tongue. It is as if Alexander's armies had passed that way in the last century, not more than 2,000 years ago.

We drove hard—fourteen-hour days—in a jeep for ten days

between Teheran and Kabul, and I thought of the famous ride of Sir Henry Rawlinson over the same route in seven days on horseback, of the millions of people over thousands of years, on foot, on burros, camels, and horses, who had passed that way; of the armies, known and unknown, of the stream of ideas moving east and west, and of how little we really know of what happened there.

As an ex-Foreign Service Officer and a consultant to the Department of State, I was engaged by the C.I.A. to recruit personnel in Philadelphia for the new clandestine branch of the organization, and also to plant some of its operatives abroad under the cover of Museum research. Looking back, I wonder at my own stupidity. Of course, many of us then were exceedingly concerned about the developing cold war, and few of us could know just how that branch of the C.I.A. would emerge. But I was well aware of the association in the popular mind of archaeologists with spying, and should have known that any link between our research and intelligence agents was not only silly but badly damaging. In any case, with me was a young C.I.A. operative who was to be left behind in Kabul. In Teheran, our ambassador decided to send his interpreter, an Armenian, with us as far as the Afghan border, because neither of us spoke Persian and at that time travelers between the two countries were very rare and unexpected. In Meshed, one morning in the bazaar, we three ran into another Armenian, a friend of our interpreter, who asked him what he was doing there. In English, and in a loud voice, he said, "Oh! I'm only taking a couple of spies up to the frontier." Meshed at that time was crawling with operatives from both sides of the Iron Curtain.

Experience on that journey, and in the home office, quickly terminated all associations between The University Museum and the C.I.A. Back in the United States, I was summoned to the Washington office to face a Board of Enquiry for breach of security. After some dire warnings, the grim-faced chairman informed me that they had learned how in my recruiting in Philadelphia I had told candidates something about what they were employed to do. My laughter did nothing to improve our relations. We parted company, but I was alerted to watch for any other covert arrangements with Museum personnel abroad.

Travel between Iran and Afghanistan in 1952 had some unexpected difficulties. We needed exit papers from Iran to enter Afghanistan, and at the Foreign Office the officials looked worried. Of course, we could have the exit permits, but it was exceedingly dangerous to cross Afghanistan with bandits along the road. At the Afghan Embassy they were pleased to give us entrance visas, but they were worried. It was very dangerous to cross Iran to the Afghan border. At that point our worries ceased, and we took off in a battered jeep, a relic of U.S. Army support for the Mossadegh government, after arranging with the Afghan Embassy to have supplies of Russian gasoline laid down for us at various points in the country. At that time much of the road between Teheran and Kabul was only a track, and all the bridges crossing the principal rivers in Afghanistan had been washed out. Between Teheran and Meshed we hit rainstorms, culminating in deep mud and a nearly impassable track for the last few hours into Meshed. We had picked up a French boy on a motorcycle wandering eastward through Asia, and in the deep mud, rain, and darkness we towed him behind the jeep's trailer into Meshed, arriving about 2 a.m. With much difficulty we found the American consul's residence in the old city and were welcomed at the door by the major domo asking briskly if we would like a martini.

Some miles from the Afghan border the road degenerated into a faint track in the desert, and it was difficult to follow, again at night, in the path of our headlights. Suddenly in our lights was a small dark man in a turban and a long white gown waving a rifle. We had no words to communicate, there was no frontier building, and no other people in the empty desert. The small ghost examined our papers, upside down, and waved us past. Several miles further on we entered a small dark town with no one about. Finally, we raised a body who led us to the government rest house, long unused, but still habitable. Such guest houses, and the bridges, had been built years before in an ambitious plan to open communications with the West, but the rare traveler in the early nineteen-fifties did not justify their maintenance.

Herat in western Afghanistan was a curious journey into the past. Herat is ancient Arya, traditionally the birthplace of the Aryan people. In 1952 it was probably no larger than it was when Alexander passed that way 330 years before the birth of Christ. The ruins of the ancient city lay on one side of the river, and the "new" city on the opposite bank was unlike any city I had ever seen—a city almost unaffected by modern technology and the Western world. An occasional bus or truck got through from Kabul, but for the most part traffic was two-wheeled carts, camels, horses, and burros. With no electricity the evenings were magic. At sunset, blue and scented woodsmoke began to rise above the city from cooking fires, and as the twilight deepened, the glow of yellow lamplight began to flicker like thousands of fireflies in the streets and houses. Water gushed through channels in the grass-grown, stone-paved streets. Craftsmen sat in a circle of yellow lamplight in tiny shops fashioning harness, furniture, saddles, shoes, clothing, pots, and metal vessels. Food shops were filled with fruit, nuts, grains, meat, and pungent herbs and spices that are still rare in the West.

But for one used to westernized Asiatic cities, the startling thing was cleanliness. Neat, well-dressed people, no ragged and troublesome beggars, not even cripples—not crowded or littered with the debris of modern civilization. For once I was seeing a stable population, one that had not yet exploded as in the rest of the world, or yet felt the urban swarming. Some days later in Khandahar the contrast was sharp and clear. There, road construction and the beginning of an irrigation project had quite suddenly transformed the place into a normal twentieth-century Asiatic city—people crowding in for industrial jobs, heavy motor traffic churning the streets into mud and dust, ragged people in overcrowded houses, beggars, glaring electric lights, plastic containers, and the familiar scramble for "things." In Herat we learned that a power plant was to be built so that medical services with X-rays could be introduced by the United Nations. That, of course, meant roads, motor traffic, and all the rest of it. It is, of course, foolish to lament the passing of the last unchanged, stable city population. Who would want to pass up modern medical care? Only in Herat have I truly been aware of the price we pay in the modern world.

Fortunately, we found a young man who could speak English, and when he learned that I was a professor he arranged a meeting with the mullahs, the teachers, poets, and philosophers, who would be glad to meet a Western teacher. We met a group in the tower rooms of the oldest mosque, for tea and discussion, small, neat men in immaculate white gowns and blue turbans, all with white or gray beards. At that time my knowledge of Persian-Afghan poets and philosophers was abysmal. Our conversation limped along, and I felt they thought I was an imposter. Then one bright-eyed graybeard, in a hopeful attempt, asked if I were familiar with Dale Carnegie and his How to Win Friends and Influence People. Language and culture are hopeless barriers between people who instinctively feel there must be a common ground—somewhere. We watched the smoke rising and the lamps beginnings to glow, with the evening breeze off the mountains, while the centuries drifted through our minds, uniting and separating.

They were seeing a "Frank" who was as stupid as the barbarians who fought Saladin and yet had created a magic world of technology that would sweep away their world. I was seeing the holy men who led a jihad to create the world's most advanced civilization in the tenth century, descendants of the same Indo-European people whose other heirs had built San Francisco and Melbourne .

Between Herat and Khandahar things got really tough. The battered old jeep sprang a leak in its radiator in the worst of the desert. We could not carry enough water in the trailer to keep it cool with such a leak and so were stranded in one of the most lonely corners of the world, sitting ducks for all those bandits of the Iranian's imagination. When one finally arrived, alone on a camel, he turned out to be a traveling tinker with all the equipment necessary to fix our radiator. It was not a permanent job, but, thereafter, when it leaked, we just waited for another tinker.

The rivers were in flood and looked impassable, but invariably a camel caravan would eventually arrive and one of those huge camels would tow us across, the Frenchman's motorcycle loaded on top of fuel and water tanks in the trailer, and the exhaust pipe plugged to keep water out of the jeep's engine. I had hoped to take the mountain route from Herat east, but it was too long abandoned to be passable. We were forced to swing south, skirting the northern edge of the vast Helmand Desert, through magnificent desert mountain land, to Khandahar and then north again to Kabul.

The C.I.A. youngster became desperately ill as we worked our way northward into the mountains, and it became a race against time to reach Kabul and, we hoped, a doctor. The embassy there was then a small, bedraggled affair with a staff that seemed curiously demoralized, but Khosad, the head of the Kabul Museum, had been a houseguest of mine in Philadelphia and felt that we were much like relatives. He was our mentor, guide, adviser, and friend. All that in spite of the fact that as a guest of the State Department he arrived in a taxi to Father Divine's Heaven, that odd center of a famous black cult. Khosad, as a proud Aryan with no nonsense about racial tolerance, was furious. He did not cool down until he became part of my family.

The family feeling, however, did not extend to my companion. At that time we never saw a woman's face in Kabul. Women were all veiled in the streets, and no one but the family went to the inner sanctum of the house where women were unveiled. I went alone, on "the night of fire," to celebrate the festival with Khosad's family of brothers and their wives and children, in separate houses grouped about a closed compound. His wife was a tall, strikingly handsome woman, with see-through pantaloons and a ruby in her nose. There was no doubt about who was boss in that household. Khosad, somehow, shrank in size and became an extraordinarily meek kind of person. His daughters also were boisterous and unsuppressed in a manner I did not expect to find in cloistered Muslim ladies. We sat on deep-piled Afghan rugs and ate from great brass trays glistening in candle- and lamplight that was a special blaze for the night of fire. After dinner Madam Khosad formally presented me with a gold-embroidered pair of slippers, with a little speech that Khosad did not translate. He looked embarrassed and somewhat put out. His brothers and their wives laughed among themselves, and made many clearly ribald remarks. I never knew just what that was all about but suspected a symbol of intimate hospitality. The festive clothing of those women, beautifully made of gossamer silk, and for exotic effect, left me wondering why Western designers have missed the point, at least from a man's point of view. Perhaps it is true that in the West women's clothing is designed to impress women.

Bactria, that region in Central Asia north of the Hindu

Kush, was a Greco-Bactrian kingdom established after the conquest of Alexander but, long before that, the site of legendary Balkh, the "mother of cities." Like a lodestone, the legend and a lifelong fascination with Central Asia drew me northward from Kabul. At that time there was only a track through the Ghorband Pass and down through the Bululah Gorge into the valley of the Amu Darya (the Oxus). A cold rain, dark ominous clouds, sheer rock walls, and a narrow cut along a mountain stream made our passage into the heart of Central Asia a grim affair. That passage into another world was sharply emphasized when we met, in the pass, a chief of one of the nomadic tribes and his bodyguard of four young horsemen. He was a handsome man with a pure white beard, an elaborate turban, a beautifully clean and rich-looking gown of bright blue, a handsomely carved and inlaid rifle, and a saber. All were mounted on Ferghana horses, those thoroughbreds that are known from the frozen tombs at Pazyryk in the Altai dating from about 500 B.C. We had also passed, on the way up, a regiment of Afghan cavalry all mounted on the same famous breed of horses. Such men had fought Alexander's disciplined troops, Turks, Mongols, British expeditionary forces, and each other, for many centuries. They are still not suppressed or "civilized" in our sense. I liked their proud, damn-your-eyes expression, friendly but certainly not humble.

Once through the pass we turned up the Bamian Valley, deep green on the valley floor, shut in by steep red stone cliffs, to brilliant snow-covered peaks. At Bamian those cliffs are riddled with chambers, cut into the rock, many with Buddhist wall paintings of great charm. Carved out of alcoves in the rock are two giant stone Buddhas, now faceless. Once these 1,200 rock chambers housed Buddhist priests, scholars, artists, traders of the silk route, and Buddhist pilgrims seeking retreat and meditation. Then, centuries later, Muslims destroyed the sanctuary, cut away the faces of the giant Buddhas, and built the fortress city of Ghalghala nearby. Today Ghalghala is also a ghost city where the wind screams through vacant tower windows and dust whirls about crumbling arches—a victim of the Mongol invasion that swept across Western Asia to destroy the Muslim world. The governor of the province lent me his prized saddle horse to roam about the valley and the ruins, deep green meadows along the river shot with brilliant spring flowers, desert tracks into barren foothills where broken walls emerged from ancient city mounds, snow-covered peaks soaring into an azure sky, a mud-walled village sheltering under the red cliffs of Buddhist Bamian, turbanned riders, children, goats, sheep, and woodsmoke rising from the cooking fires.

Herat, Bamian, and the migrating Pathans whom we met ascending the mountains on their way up from the Khyber Pass were for me a journey into a dim and mysterious past, so ancient and so removed from my scientific industrial world that my ideas, beliefs, and convictions began to slip again into a limbo of time and space confusion. Riding through the shadows of Bamian and Ghalghala and, later, on the mountains above the Khyber Pass, watching thousands of Pathans and their animals move up the slopes, I became part of he stable, cyclic life of the seasons. The nomads with their horses, camels, sheep, and goats follow the spring and the grass up into the peaks, and with the fall and winter retreat to the lowlands where the cities are. And just as the seasons move the nomads, so endless invasions sweep over and move the urban folk, who like the nomads have always been there. The ruins of urban life are everywhere to mark another kind of cycle, like the seasons but irregular, catastrophic, known and unknown—the surge of tribal groups. The urban, literate people have recorded at least some of those cyclic movements over the last 5,000 years, but who knows when or why they began?

The author and a friend searching for isolated hill tribes in Luzon,
Philippine Islands, 1930.
Photograph courtesy of the author.

The author (standing left) and Bob Stockton (second from right in back row)
with school teachers from Legaspi in the Philippine Islands on the *S.S. Trier*
in the Indian Ocean, 1930. *Photograph courtesy of the author.*

Hunting ball courts in the mountains of central Puerto Rico in 1934.
The author is at the far left. *Photograph courtesy of the author.*

Barrio Canas, Puerto Rico in 1934, the author is sitting
examining a complete pot from the site.
Photograph courtesy of the author.

Excavations at Barrio Canas,
Puerto Rico, 1934, showing
the two layers of occupation
called "Crab Level" (the
lower) and "Shell Level"
(the upper).
*Photograph courtesy
of the author.*

Haiti fifty years later—in 1983 the author(right)
returned to the site of Bais Neuf and examined
with a stratified deposit representing several
thousand years of human occupation excavated
by Pepe Ortiz (left).
Photograph courtesy of the author.

The schooner *Nanuk* in the Bering Sea enroute to St. Lawrence Island, Alaska, 1936. *Photograph courtesy of the author.*

Governor Ernest Gruening arriving at St. Lawrence Island in 1940. *Photograph courtesy of the author.*

The author, his wife, and his parents (from left) in Alaska in 1939. *Photograph courtesy of the author.*

Burning seal oil in drums to thaw the frozen archaeological deposits at Kikulik, St. Lawrence Island, Alaska in 1936.
Photograph courtesy of the author.

Workmen from the excavations at Kukulik on St. Lawrence Island in 1935. At left is Pillowak, the Siberian who was serving seven years of labor to win a wife.
Photograph courtesy of the author.

Author at the bottom of 14 feet of frozen refuse from ca. 2000 years of settlement on the Kukulik Mound; Kukulik, St. Lawrence Island, Alaska, 1937.
Photograph courtesy of the author.

Helge Larsen at Point Hope, Alaska in 1939.
Photograph courtesy of the author.

The author (left) and Ebrulik Roc at Cafe Thomson beginning 250-mile inspection tour of trap lines in northwestern Alaska in 1940. *Photograph courtesy of the author.*

One of the more than 150 Ipiutak burials found during the summer of 1940 near Point Hope, Alaska. The skeleton lies in the remains of a log coffin; its eye sockets hold ivory eyes. *Photograph courtesy of the author.*

Villagers being tossed from a walrus hide as part of celebration of whale feast. Point Hope, Alaska, 1940. *Photograph courtesy of The University Museum Archives.*

Lancing a dying whale after harpooning. Point Hope, Alaska, 1940.
Photograph courtesy of the author.

In the shadow of upturned whaling boats, the elders of the village
of Tigara beat on their tambourine drums as part of whale feast to
celebrate the return of the hunters from their months of chasing
whales. Point Hope, Alaska, 1940.
Photograph courtesy of the author.

Return to Point Hope 25 years later, the author at far left.
Photograph courtesy of the author.

Jack Tuthill (left) and the author serving as political officers with the U.S. Central Commission in Berlin in 1945. On a broken German tank are their dachsunds George and Phoebe.
Photograph courtesy of the author.

The administrative staff of The University Museum in conference in the Museum's Brazilian Cafe in 1962; from left: David Crownover, the author, Gloria Swift.
Photograph courtesy of The University Museum Archives.

Gloria Swift wearing the famous gold jewelry of Lady Pu-abi. Her burial and treasure were excavated by the Museum at the site of ancient Ur in Iraq. *Photograph courtesy of The University Museum Archives.*

Dr. Carleton Coon examining an exhibition panel in the Hall of Man at The University Museum in 1953.
Photograph courtesy of The University Museum Archives.

New excavations at the ancient site of Nippur in Iraq, 1952
Photograph courtesy of The University Museum Archives.

James Pritchard excavating at the site of
El Jib in Palestine.
*Photograph courtesy of The University
Museum Archives.*

Bob Dyson plastering over a wall for
restoration. *Photograph courtesy of
The Hasanlu Project of The
University Museum.Hasanlu, Iran
1960*

Land Rovers and trucks lined up for departure from Sebha in the Fezzan, Libya, January, 1968. *Photograph courtesy of the author.*

Oasis of Zuila, Libyan desert, 1968. Far left, Mohamed Ayoub, second from right, American Ambassador to Libya, David Newstone. *Photograph courtesy of the author.*

Wau el Namus, Libyan desert, 1968. Volcanic "blow-out," the black ash shows our footprints. *Photograph courtesy of the author.*

The author (left) with Ahmed Fakhry in Egypt in 1957. *Photography courtesy of the author.*

Tebesti Mountains, Libya, 1968. Tibu guide who helped search
for the Zuma quarry. *Photograph courtesy of the author.*

Tebesti Mountains, Libya, 1968. the author examining some
Neolithic rock carvings. *Photograph courtesy of the author.*

Staff at Tikal, Guatemala in March of 1961. Top row from left: John Rick, Anne Rick,
Hattula Moholy-Nagy, Peter Probst, Anita Haviland; front row from left: William Haviland,
Aubrey Trik, Edwin Shook, Alfred Kidder, William Coe.
Photograph courtesy of the Tikal Project of The University Museum.

At the Etruscan cemetery of Tarquinia in Italy in the summer of
1961, left to right: Professor Mario Moretti, the American
Ambassador to Italy, Fred Reinhardt, Carlo Lerici, and the author.
Photograph courtesy of the author.

Excavations at Sybaris, Italy in the fall of 1961. Elizabeth Ralph (seated)
takes readings on the electron proton magnetometer
while the author holds the detector bottle.
Photograph courtesy of The University Museum Archives.

Excavations at Sybaris, Italy in the fall of 1961. Elizabeth Ralph
(seated at center) with magnetometer is surrounded by (from left)
Miggano, Orville Bullitt, the author, Mrs. Bullitt,
Carlo Lerici, and Giuseppe. Foti.
Photograph courtesy of The University Museum Archives.

Excavations at Sybaris, Italy in the fall of 1961.
Workman and author working on
surveying the site.
*Photograph courtesy of The University
Museum Archives.*

Excavations at Sybaris, Italy in the fall of 1961. Domenico and
Giuseppe Falcone using auger drill.
Photograph courtesy of The University Museum Archives.

Chet Gorman "walking out" from near the Burmese border to meet with the author at
Ban Chiang to discuss the possibility of Museum excavations at that site.
Photograph courtesy of the Ban Chiang Project of The University Museum.

Lionel Chiong of the Phillippines, excavating at
Ban Chiang during the 1975 season.
*Photograph courtesy of the Ban Chiang Project of
The University Museum.*

Searching for archaeological sites in northern Sumatra, 1973. A host of police and army
guides assist the expedition during a ferry crossing. *Photograph courtesy of the author.*

Opening of the Ban Chiang exhibit at The University Museum on November 10, 1982. With
the author (far left), from left: Pisit Charoenwongsa, co-director of the Ban Chiang Project;
Dr. Wilhelm Sondheim of the University of Hawaii, pioneer of Southeast Asian archaeology
and co-director of the Ban Chiang Project; Stephen Young, as son of the American
ambassador to Thailand in 1966, he made a chance discovery of Ban Chiang pots; and
Elizabeth Lyons, research associate for The University Museum, formerly an Asian
consultant for the Ford Foundation.
Photograph by David Gladstone, courtesy of The University Museum Archives.

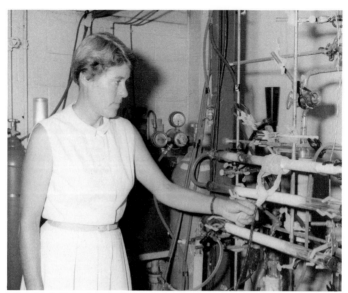

Elizabeth K. Ralph and combustion tube for converting charcoal to Carbon dioxide in Carbon-14 Lab. *Photograph courtesy of MASCA.*

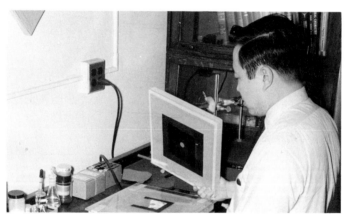

Mark Han sectioning samples for thermoluminescence tests. *Photograph courtesy of MASCA.*

"What in the World" broadcast in the 1950s; from left: Carleton Coon, Jacques Lipschutz (the famous sculptor), and Alfred Kidder examine an artifact while the author (seated at far right) offers encouragement.
Photograph courtesy of The University Museum Archives.

C.F. Rainey (the author's father), holds the author (far right); to their left is Anna Holzhausen, the author's maternal grandmother, 1909.
Photograph courtesy of author.

From left; Dr. Madowar (President of the Institut d'Egypt), the author, Ahmed Fakhry, the author's wife, Marina, and Gamal Monlitar.
Photograph courtesy of author.

The author's home, Oldhay, in Cornwall, England. *Photograph courtesy of author.*

The author ready for a morning ride at Oldhay.
Photograph courtesy of author.

Mounted and well-armed men guard the herds. Women and girls follow with the young, both animal and human. I watched an old and steady camel pass by bearing an infant, a lamb, and a baby camel lashed to the normal pack of tent and rugs. There can be no stragglers. Like their animals, women drop out of the march to bear their young but quickly rejoin their families in the relentless march to new grass barely ahead of the withering winds of summer. Why do such people build up like an electric charge in the stratosphere and then discharge like a bolt of lightning into the urban, settled, agricultural lands to destroy, control, command, and then retreat again? Energy, in balanced electrical charges, is now, in our current philosophy, the fundamental element of our universe. Is it also the ultimate explanation of all human history?

Professor Schlumberger was excavating a city mound north of the mountains and south of the Amu Darya River. We searched for his camp for half of a dark night in another cold downpour. Wet, frozen, and plastered with mud, we finally spotted his dark and sodden tents in our headlights and woke him out of a sound sleep. To this day I have a penchant for Mosul white wines, I know, because that night it was the best wine in the world. As with all members of a guild, there is a camaraderie among archaeologists in the field that is taken for granted and needs no explanation. Of course, there is competition, particularly among Westerners exploring the lands of other people, but there is also a common purpose and point of view. Lying before the fire I learned about his site and of the hundreds of mounds in the region, any one of which could be the capital of the Greco-Bactrian kingdom or the much more ancient, legendary Balkh. Since then the French have found a settlement of the post-Alexandrian Greeks, but what will future generations of diggers find in that maze of ruins accumulated over unknown millennia? With the help of the French and Khosad, I established a base in Kabul for systematic excavations to follow. That country, like Iran, struck me as a most promising place in the Near and Middle East for University Museum research.

We left Afghanistan at the Khyber Pass into Pakistan, heading for Peshawar. There, in what seemed to us the great luxury of an old British-built inn, we were discovered by the local chief of Pakistan Intelligence. I was braced for questions about Russian activity in northern Afghanistan, then of great concern to Western nations, but was astonished to learn that he was only interested in the activities of nomadic people in Badakshan, through which we had passed north and west of the Khyber Pass. The Pakistanis have clearly inherited the old problem of the British on the northwest frontier. Their problems were not our problems. I wondered if he had spotted my young C.I.A. fellow who was to drop me at Peshawar and then return to Kabul. Probably he did because at that time they were all so obvious.

The Museum had worked at Harappa and later would work at Mohenjo-daro. Those ruins were a necessary part of my education, but at the time did not seem promising for us. The Antiquities Service in Pakistan, set up by Rik Wheeler, would certainly take over the major digging in that country. I returned to Philadelphia with long-range plans for Iran and Afghanistan. Even then it was becoming clear that postwar archaeology in most of the world would be very different from prewar digging. The many new nations were stridently anti-colonial and anxious to take over the excavation of the most significant sites. My job would be to find those regions where we could still do major research and to work out a new relationship with local archaeologists, a job that would require a shift in the attitude of our own Western diggers. Perhaps old Tom Gates and Percy Madeira realized that when they hired an ex-Foreign Service officer to run the Museum.

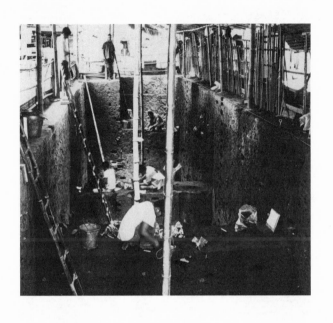

Removing the balks in Ban Chiang at the end of
the second excavation season, 1975.
Photograph courtesy of the Ban Chiang Project.

PART III

In Search of Man's Past

Rodney Young watching Turkish workmen consolidate one of the wooden tables from the Great Tumulus at Gordion, Turkey in 1958. In the foreground are stacks of bronze bowls and pieces of other wooden furniture. *Photograph courtesy of The Gordion Archives of The University Museum.*

CHAPTER SIX

The Near and Middle East

After it was decided in Philadelphia in 1948 that we should begin the revival of the Museum's worldwide research in Central America and the Near East, and had put the excavation of Tikal in Guatemala on the back burner to wait for a new government in that country, I turned to explore the possibilities in the Near East in 1949. One prewar excavation, at Kourion on the island of Cyprus, still existed. It had been directed and financed by George MacFadden, an independently wealthy young man from Philadelphia, who returned there after the war to continue his excavation of the Greek city. The Museum had worked at several sites on Cyprus over many years, and it was there, visiting those sites and traveling over the island with George, that I began to learn something about the philosophy of the classical archaeologists and the long commitment in that field that the Museum had maintained since the beginning of the century. I continued to look in on the Kourion excavation during the next few years, until George was drowned in a sailing accident off the coast of Cyprus and the work there was abandoned. But in 1949 Pete Daniel and Rodney Young had decided to concentrate the Mediterranean Section's excavations in Turkey at the site of Gordion, and that was the next stop on my first venture into the Near East field.

In Ankara, I found that the American ambassador was an archaeological bug, like so many of our diplomatic representatives in that part of the world, and anxious to assist in making arrangements for the excavation with the Turkish authorities. At that time, there was a U.S. military mission training Turkish troops at Polatli, near the site of Gordion. The ambassador thought we should enlist their help and proposed that I join him and the commanding officer for a game of golf.

The first visit to Gordion, about sixty-five miles from Ankara, became a full-scale military operation. First, a helicopter was sent on a reconnaissance to locate the site from the air, then an expeditionary force from the base was sent out with me, including a truckload of soldiers, a command car, and a fully equipped radio vehicle. We found that Gordion lay within sight of the main road between Ankara and Istanbul and a short walk from the railroad station.

But we all enjoyed the picnic. We Americans were in a familiar landscape, much like the rolling grass-covered hills of western South Dakota, ideal horse country for the hundreds of generations of men who had run their herds there and maintained a cavalry that often controlled Anatolia and much of the Near East. It was easy to imagine Alexander and his horsemen sweeping over the prairie around the city more than 2,000 years ago, or the Persians riding in from the east to besiege and take the walled city on its great mound overlooking the river, ancient Sangarios (modern Sakarya). Later we were to find their bronze arrowheads embedded in the walls of Küçük Hüyük, an outpost to the city. For the Americans, however, it was almost incredible to realize that many of the hills surrounding us were man-made—conical hills built over the tombs of Phrygian kings, like Midas, the legendary man with the golden touch. On the long, green mound (500 x 300 m) that contained the ruins of several cities built there over a period of some 3,000 years, only an occasional cut-stone block could be seen protruding above the grass. Below it on a hillside was Yassihüyük, a tiny Turkish village of farmers and herdsmen, who were then still threshing their grain on stone platforms with wooden sledges, spiked with flint chips and drawn by horses. The famous paved highroad of the Persians, running from east to west, lies beneath the turf between ancient Gordion and the present village.

Today there is a little museum in the village, housing treasures from Gordion. The walls of the ancient city are exposed, with many of the Phrygian and Persian buildings surrounded by them, and a tunnel leads in to the intact tomb of King Gordius deep inside the largest of the man-made conical hills. Many visitors still picnic under a clump of trees near the river. But twenty-three years of digging were to pass before some coherent story of what happened there could be pieced together. In those years Rodney Young became "the old man," a kind but authoritative dictator stalking about the series of excavations in his old leather puttees (a survival of his summer job as a motorcycle cop during his years at Princeton) and driving his cadres of graduate students and Turkish women with relentless energy to long hours in the blazing sun. He had no time for committees or democratic decisions. His was the tradition of prewar archaeology in the Mediterranean and the Near East.

During the early years of organizing a number of excavations in the Near and Middle East, I was often at Gordion, not to settle any management problems, as at Tikal, for there were none, but to watch the progress and to backstop Rodney with the support of the Museum and the Board of Managers. But there were times when I could nudge "the old man" into something that did not really interest him, like supporting Macteld Mellink in her need for a bulldozer to clear the outlying mound of Küçük Hüyük. The most difficult nudge was to commit him to the search for the tomb in the largest of the mound burials. He was distressed to find some gold jewelry in the first few weeks of digging—too sensational and not interesting—and basically opposed to anything as sensational as the search for burial treasure. But I had been working with the Sun Oil Company people on the development of new scientific search techniques, and that huge mound, over 600 feet across the base and about 165 feet high, was an irresistible challenge.

The new electronic instruments were of no use on that mound. Howard Pew, head of Sun Oil in Philadelphia and the supporter of all our work in biblical archaeology in Jordan, suggested we try drilling to locate the tomb in the mound before we attempted a search by blind digging. G. Roger Edwards was sent to Beaumont, Texas, to learn how to use a small prospecting drill, and then to Gordion with it to direct the drilling there. Tombs excavated in some of the small burial mounds were found to be covered by rock and not generally at the center of the mound, perhaps placed off center to foil tomb robbers. Hence the drilling was in search of solid rock in what was invariably a mass of surface soil piled up to form the burial mound. Several months later the drill struck rock in the southwest sector of the mound, near the base and lying under thousands of tons of earth.

Rodney and I spent some time calculating the cost of excavating a deep trench into what we believed to be the burial, then went to Howard Pew to ask him for the money to do it. At that time he was in his eighties and absolute boss of Sun Oil. He listened carefully, then asked for some facts and figures about the depth, distance, labor costs, and estimated time required. With those details, as best we could calculate them, he worked with a pencil and paper for a few minutes and announced that we were wrong. It would cost much more and was impractical. The best way was to hire experienced Turkish coal miners and to tunnel into the mound using pit-props to support the tunnel. He estimated the cost and agreed to contribute it. Rodney and I felt like schoolboys dressed down by the headmaster after a bad examination in arithmetic.

The long tunnel reached the tomb while I was in Moscow lecturing at the Academy of Sciences, and I reached Gordion only after Rodney had broken through into the burial chamber. However, it was only a few days, nothing had been removed, and with the others I could experience that eerie feeling of entering a large, untouched chamber that had been sealed under masses of earth 2,700 years ago. Everything was covered with a thin film of wood dust, which stained our clothes, hands, and faces light brown, but the huge finished beams of juniper forming the walls, floor, and ceiling were solid, seemingly freshly cut, and fitted together by master carpenters so that the joins were almost imperceptible. That wooden chamber (17 x 30 feet), the size of a master bedroom, was entirely surrounded by another enclosing structure of uncut logs, then coarse gravel, and outside this another enclosure of cut-stone blocks. Over all was packed clay, which maintained a constant humidity inside the tomb. There was no entrance. It was necessary to cut through the stone wall, gravel, logs, and inner chamber of finished beams. The cut happened to break through right at the foot of the king's bed.

The skeleton of a small man, only five feet three inches tall and about sixty years old, lay on the royal four-poster bed above and below layers of bedclothes that were compacted into a solid brown mass. Filling the chamber were nine wooden tables, now collapsed, which had been set with 166 bronze bowls, as if for a funeral feast. There were also three huge bronze cauldrons set upon iron tripods, two beautifully inlaid wooden screens, a bronze ritual bucket of an Assyrian type in the shape of a lion's head, wall ornaments of embossed leather, and a bag filled with 145 bronze safety pins. There were no weapons and not a single piece of gold or silver. Rodney could not believe that such a tomb was built after the conquest of Phrygia by the Kimmerians when King Midas is said to have committed suicide, and thought that it was the tomb of an earlier King Gordius, believed to have died between 725 and 720 B.C; later research now indicates that this is indeed the resting place of the legendary Midas. Rodney was so sure of his dates, deduced from written records and archaeological evidence, that he announced he would believe in radiocarbon dates only if they proved to correspond with his dating. They did, but I am not sure he ever accepted radiocarbon dating as dependable.

An intact royal tomb of that age is a very rare discovery in archaeology. Like that of Tutankhamen, and the Royal Tombs at Ur, such discoveries appeal to the public in general and become headline news around the world. They are often denigrated by professional diggers as too sensational, but I have a strong feeling that professionals as well as laymen are deeply impressed, probably because an intact tomb of an individual known dimly in half-legendary records of the past lends a sharp reality to our conception of time flowing through a sequence of unique events from a beginning to an end. They fit neatly into our scheme of things and reassure the diggers that they are dealing with real, solid, and predictable historic episodes. Rodney always preferred digging fragmentary walls in the central mound, but the tomb made him famous.

Too much is written about the sequence of pottery types, the measurement of walls, often imaginary stratigraphy in the earth, and in general about the minutiae of digging—and not enough about the very human side of the archaeological research. Scores of professional diggers were trained at Gordion over a period of twenty-three years. Their memories, like mine, must be thoroughly interlaced with many things that happened there that have little to do with archaeology but much to do with how they see the world in which they seek to reconstruct the past.

Early one morning I was standing with Oscar White Muscarella, a student in classical archaeology, at the top of the mound looking down over the Sangarios River, now a small stream, and the encampment of a group of gypsies on its bank. Suddenly we saw two men dash out of a tent and begin to fight with daggers. In little more than seconds one man fell and the other ran to a saddled horse and galloped off across the prairie. Oscar and I ran down to the camp to find a young man lying in the blood of several knife wounds, obviously dead or dying. All the men, women, and children were gathered about the body muttering, crying, or violently arguing in a language we could not understand. One old man detached himself from the crowd, walked slowly to his horse, and then rode quietly off in pursuit of the killer. Oscar was very excited and kept saying we must do something—but what? We walked back to our camp, described the episode to Rodney, and proposed that he send the jeep into Polatli to inform the Turkish police. They arrived at Gordion in less than an hour, talked briefly with the gypsies, then drove off across country along the railroad line in their jeeps. Just as we were sitting down to our breakfast at about nine-thirty, the usual time after two or three hours work on the site, the police returned with the young fugitive in handcuffs.

All of us were thoughtful, subdued, and uneasy. A fight, a death, and a capture, all between sunrise and breakfast. The gypsy camp quieted down, work on the mound went on as usual, the sun blazed down, and two more young men on the prairies of central Anatolia disappeared into oblivion.

Peasant farmers everywhere in our modern world retain the timeless quality of their land and their animals. In central Turkey, their threshing floors, horses, oxen, primitive ploughs, and small, primitive villages are particularly ageless in the industrial and mass-produced environment to which all the diggers at Gordion had become accustomed. But this quality, for me and I suppose for most of the Westerners who worked there, was most evident during those evenings when the men gathered in some firelit courtyard to dance and to drink raki. Many of the diggers, like Ellen L. Kohler in her habitual long, loose, Turkish pantaloons, danced with them and, I believe, in some obscure way became part of the timeless village life. Perhaps that identification with the living history of Anatolia, more than the actual excavations, kept Rodney at Gordion, year after year, when most of us thought that he should stop digging and publish his results. In some curious way the flow of human energy through the ages in any distinctive environment sweeps up those who live long enough with it, no matter how foreign they may be at the beginning. Watching the diggers and the peasant farmers rhythmically circling in the firelight, I remembered those years with the Eskimos, dancing to the beat of tambourine drums, waiting on the ice at a seal's breathing hole, and sitting by our whaling boats trying to explain the war in Europe. Perhaps I too stayed on because I was caught up in a different rhythm, a different time-space relationship, and a flow of energy that was strange, timeless, phased in a frequency that is tuned to a unique environment. That is a real part of the search, and it probably affects all of us more than we would like to admit.

During the first year of exploration, in 1949, I went on from Turkey to Iraq to join our crew for the first season of renewed digging at Nippur, and then to Iran. Before the war Eric Schmidt had excavated several sites there for The University Museum and had carried out one of the earliest aerial surveys in archaeology. His fundamentally significant discoveries surely indicated that the Museum should continue in Iran in the postwar period. My problem was to work out agreements with Iranian officials for such research. Professor Ghirshman had returned by that time to renew the long-standing French research and, as an old friend of Samuel Noah, our curator of the tablet collections, was pleased to introduce me to those officials. But more than that he laid himself out to help me understand the Iranian field and to help in deciding upon a particular site for excavation. His recommendations focused on the site of Hamadan.

In my introduction to Iran I remember most clearly the curious custom of official discussions. For an appointment with the Director of Antiquities, Ghirshman and I would enter his office to find it filled with people also waiting for a chance to bring up their particular problem. Cups of coffee were served to all, repeatedly. When our chance came, we were often interrupted by more urgent business, and then took up where we had left off. It was astonishing to learn that the director could keep all those balls in the air at once, not losing track of the main threads. It was all very congenial and there seemed to be no problem of arranging a concession to excavate at our choice of site. However, after visiting Hamadan I had a shock and some very long thoughts. There is, after all, a large modern city built over ancient Hamadan. Areas not under present buildings were usually vast cemeteries, still utilized. I was familiar with the archaeological problem of dealing with recent Muslim graves. The significance of the ancient site was tempting, but the costs and the difficulties of tackling such a place argued strongly against it. Anyway, at that time we had no one in the Museum who could undertake the direction.

Eventually, I found Robert H. Dyson, Jr., a Harvard Fellow who had experienced excavating in the Near East while he was a student and was ready to take over a site of his own choosing. He selected Hasanlu, a great tell on the south shore of Lake Urimiya in northwest Iran, and I joined him there for his first season. Three of us, Bob, Brewster Grace, an eighteen-year-old son of a friend of mine in Philadelphia, and I, drove from Teheran to Lake Urmiya in an old army jeep. The thing I remember best about that trip was the discovery of some non-Islamic sect in a village near Hasanlu that made a heavy red wine not unlike that in Hungary, which we could buy for about twenty-five cents a bottle. That made our summer on the hot, dry plain bordering the lake where we set up headquarters in an old village schoolhouse, hired a crew of locals from the village, and began a sounding of the tell. But I also remember our arrival, late at night, when we sent Brewster off with a village boy in the jeep to find some food. Brewster, with no knowledge of Persian, in a very strange land, in the middle of the night, returned with a jeep-load of groceries.

In that first sounding I remember a wealth of artifacts, of which the most interesting were molds for casting bronze tools, and the remains of mud-brick-and-stone buildings that indicated an advanced urban culture. Also it was then quite clear that the whole tell, some seventy-five feet high, would represent a series of ancient cities built one over the other during a long period of time. Bob continued at Hasanlu during the 1950s and '60s with a growing staff, so that like Gordion it became a training ground for students and one of the Museum's major excavations in the Near East. In one level he struck the remains of a city that had been attacked and burned. For archaeologists that was a great break because a city burned and collapsed preserved many things intact, and one can more easily reconstruct one moment in history.

Later Bob expanded his digging to older and more primitive sites in the region so that a very long history of northwest Iran could be worked out. I did not return to Hasanlu for several years, simply because there were no problems. The dig was very well managed and ran smoothly for all those years.

Perhaps the most famous episode of those years was the discovery of the golden bowl with fascinating repoussé figures reminiscent of Sumerian art and Sumerian gods produced nearly 2,000 years earlier. With the great popular interest in archaeology during the 1950s, Life magazine sent a photographer to produce a picture story in Iran. However, Bob and his digging crew had left the site for that season before the photographer arrived there, and I had an agitated phone call from his editors asking what he should do. Fortunately, he caught up with Bob and the bowl in Teheran. The full spread of beautiful color illustrations in Life that followed placed ancient Iranian gold art in the public eye. Looting of Iranian sites by Iranians and international trade in such things reached a new high. But from an international relations point of view archaeology had again made a coup. American diggers were persona grata even though American Aid personnel and military advisors were often not.

Thanks to James Pritchard and Howard Pew the Museum was able to launch a series of excavations in the field of biblical archaeology. It had begun with Howard Pew, head of the family-owned Sun Oil Company of Philadelphia. A fundamentalist Christian, straight out of the nineteenth century, he wanted to know if archaeology could prove or disprove the historic validity of the Old Testament. One evening, at the home of Sam and Mildred Eckert in the country outside Philadelphia, when the ladies and the men separated after dinner, while he smoked one of his beloved cigars, he proposed that we at The University Museum try to find out. We had no biblical scholar at that time. Jim Pritchard was at Berkeley in California, but he had worked with us at The University Museum and I knew him as a capable individual as well as a scholar. In Berkeley we discussed his move to Philadelphia and into a long-range series of excavations in biblical archaeology. The difficult decision was about how to do objective research financed by a man with a bias. We agreed that I would explain very bluntly to Mr. Pew that we could not undertake to prove any particular point of view and that biblical archaeology so far tended to show that elements of the Old Testament appeared to be historic while other parts were clearly myth, legend, and special pleading or religious propaganda.

The old gentleman tended to see things in black or white (like the Communist threat). Things were either true or false. But he was highly intelligent, downright, and willing to accept our proposition of doing straightforward archaeology, whatever the results.

The first site Jim dug was to make Mr. Pew happy. Jim's research in Jordan had convinced him that a certain site was the ancient town of Gibeon, mentioned in the Old Testament, associated with King David, and famous for its well. In the excavation he discovered the well near the center of the tell, a great circular stone-cut structure with a circular stone staircase descending eighty-five feet down to a spring. When the whole eighty-five feet of rubble that had accumulated in the well had been cleared away, he found the well still flowing. And in the rubble were fragments of pottery inscribed with the name of Gibeon. The town in its heyday, however, must have been most famous for its wine. There was innumerable stone-cut vats for wine storage and a great many clay bottle stoppers with the trademark of Gibeon wine dealers.

Howard Pew continued to finance the Museum's biblical archaeology for many years as well as excavation of the Gordion tomb and our attempts to develop ground radar for archaeological research. We became friends insofar as the nineteenth and twentieth centuries can comprehend each other. Once he called me into his office to ask me, since I had been on Eisenhower's political staff during the latter part of the war, if I thought the general was really a Communist. When we were building a new wing for the Museum, I asked him for $3.5 million to finance it in memory of the Pew family. He and Mrs. Pew took my wife and me to the opera and there informed me very bluntly that I had not made a good case for the wing. With him I found the blunt, direct, no-nonsense attitude of the nineteenth century most refreshing.

Over the years I often stopped by to visit Jim's excavations both in Lebanon and later in Jordan at Tell es Saidiyeh, once to make a television news film, but usually just for the pleasure of seeing a well-run dig with a good-natured staff, and to learn what was turning up. Once, I remember, he had a Jordanian woman digging Bronze Age tombs and proposed that I get down to business and dig one with her. The tomb was a rock-cut chamber about the size of two bathtubs. We crawled in a small hole and had to work on our stomachs to uncover pots and bones in dry, choking dust. It was as hot as a Turkish bath. Still it was all very congenial, and fun to get back to real digging again.

Jim's wife, Ann, had never wanted to risk a visit to the Near East with the rather dicey political situation there that was endemic. But finally she was convinced it was all quite safe and joined him for a season in Lebanon. That was the year the 1967 war broke out, and they were forced to flee to the

American Embassy and then make their way overland with the
American refugees to a safe country in an unforgettable period
of panic. Ann never returned to the field. Perhaps it was just as
well. At one point, after the Israelis made an attack on the
Lebanese coast, Jim found his site there full of unexploded
shells. I offered to send out one of our men from the Museum
Applied Science Center for Archaeology (MASCA) with
magnetic equipment to locate the shells, but Jim could not wait
for him to arrive and managed to locate them with one of those
toy mine detectors then being used by treasure hunters.

One of the impressive things about Jim's work was his rapid
publication of each excavation as soon as it was finished. Too
many of the Museum's digs took more than twenty years or
more to publish.

Northern Afghanistan, beyond the Hindu Kush, was our one
possible entry into Central Asia in the 1950s. Even though it
was only the southern edge of what seemed to me to be one of
the most promising fields for new and significant discoveries in
archaeology, after my explorations in 1952 I had set up
headquarters in Kabul, arranged for extended research with
Khosad, the Director of Antiquities, and planned for the
delivery of a robust station wagon the next year. With some
reservations, Rodney Young, Schuyler Camman, and Carleton
Coon agreed to take the job. Rodney and Schuyler, with the
addition of Dorothy Hannah Cox, tackled a tell on the plain
south of the Amu Darya, and Carl found a Paleolithic cave site,
also in the north.

One season for all of them was enough. Just why they took
such a strong dislike to Afghanistan I do not know. Perhaps it

was all too strange and beyond their fields of interest or outside the conventional region of Near Eastern research. In any case the whole plan was a bust. Only some years later was George Dales ready and eager to make another investigation in the country for The University Museum.

Carl Coon had not been happy with his first season at Nippur and returned to his old love, cave excavation, begun in Morocco many years before. His work in Iran, Syria, and Afghanistan was to make outstanding contributions to our knowledge of Old Stone Age times in that part of the world and resulted in a highly readable popular book on cave exploration. He was the last of the group to leave Afghanistan in 1953, and I was somewhat stunned to get his cable saying he had sold all the field equipment, closed the headquarters, and gone off to hunt tigers in Burma. Probably that was no surprise to many of his old friends in Boston and Philadelphia.

Ahmed Fakhry, in Cairo, was in a particularly agitated frame of mind in 1957. The abortive attempt by Great Britain, France, and Israel to prevent the Egyptian takeover of the Suez Canal had stirred up a patriotic frenzy in Egypt. Ahmed, with his black eyes snapping and his ponderous belly heaving, gave the impression that he was about to march out into the street and shoot down any Englishman or Frenchman he could find. A Bedouin from the desert who, thanks to his grandfather, the chief of his band, had been sent to school and later to Germany to study Egyptology, he was, of course, not a typical Egyptian. But there could be no doubt of his burning belief in the Egyptian state, free, independent, revived, and destined to become great again.

Israel was anathema, but I had the impression that for Ahmed it was more because the Israelis represented an invasion from the West with overtones of the European colonial attitude. He was the first to point out that there never had been a pogrom in the Arab world even though large numbers

of Jews had lived there for centuries. Ahmedd and I were to
continue our political discussions through all those years of the
construction of the high dam, the Soviet-Egyptian detente, the
expulsion of the Russians, and the recurring wars with the
Israelis. We often disagreed, but I think the views of each of us
were more affected by the other than we ever realized.

By then Rudolf Anthes had replaced Hermann Ranke as the
head of our Egyptian section and had begun to excavate at
ancient Memphis. With no extensive experience as a field
director, he was reluctant to take over a dig at his advanced
age. But he was most congenial and anxious to return the
Museum to its original eminent position in Egyptian research,
begun first after the turn of the century by Sir Leonard
Woolley. Visiting the site in 1957, I soon learned that the Old
Kingdom levels, which are the most important at that site,
were then lying beneath the water table. With the rise of the
Nile water level in the several millennia since Memphis was
founded, any excavation of the lower levels was a complex
engineering job requiring pumps and the expenditure of large
sums of money. After much debate we decided to close down.

Ahmed Fakhry and I discussed many possibilities for work
in Egypt and finally agreed to try for the pyramid at Dashur,
with Fakhry in charge for The University Museum.
Negotiations with the Department of Antiquities continued for
the next two or three years under difficult political
circumstances because American support of Israel made our
relations with many Egyptians a touchy and uneasy business.
Finally, the establishment of an Egyptian military base in the
area around Dashur made our research there impossible. In the
meantime Egyptian and Soviet engineers began their
preparations for the construction of the high dam above
Aswan, and many of us began to think of the important sites
that would be flooded by the reservoir.

In Philadelphia, Sam Smith, then active in United Nations

affairs, proposed that we try to interest the U.S. government in financial support for an archaeological salvage program in Nubia through the United Nations, although at that time no official campaign had begun. Our approach was through senators from the States along the eastern seaboard. None of them would take the initiative. Egyptian-Israeli conflict at that time was a highly sensitive issue in the United States. Both of us had practically given up when, by pure chance, at a lunch in Washington, I mentioned the problem and our discouragement. Mrs. Gates Lloyd, another Philadelphian, proposed that we try Senator Mike Monroney from Oklahoma, and at once phoned him to arrange a meeting the next day.

To my surprise, Monroney was seriously interested—enough to take us that afternoon to the Senate Office Building and with his aides draft a bill for the Senate requesting the President to take under consideration an American-aid program to assist in preserving archaeological sites along the Nile above the future high dam. Not long after that the United Nations campaign for Nubia was set up, President Kennedy was elected, and the Senate took up debate on Senator Monroney's bill. Testifying before the Senate Foreign Relations Committee, I met Senator Fulbright for the first time and was impressed not only by the way he handled the investigation but with his conception of political motivations in the postwar world. The bill passed the Senate with a tight margin, as I remember it, only three or four votes. Eventually, President Kennedy made available $12 million for the movement of Abu Simbel to high ground above the reservoir and several hundred thousand dollars for American excavation of sites to be flooded.

At that time there was no one in the Egyptian section of the Museum to take charge of excavations in Nubia, but I arranged for William Kelly Simpson, at Yale, to set up a Pennsylvania-Yale research program. He and I went to Egypt to survey sites in the salvage area.

In Cairo I found that the German Institute of Archaeology had a diesel-powered launch at Aswan that was ideal for our survey of sites between Aswan and Abu Simbel. The director agreed to lend us the launch but warned me that it was not insured and urged us to take great care with it. Lollie Lloyd, whose brilliant idea of involving Senator Monroney had done so much for the Nubian campaign, and our mutual friend Nancy Grace proposed that they join Kelly and me on the journey up the Nile. Both women, I think, were a bit shocked to see the launch at Aswan. There was one tiny cabin with two bunks and a galley and a crew of two Nubians—a cook and a steersman. Moreover, the drive shaft ran right through a well in the cabin and had to be greased every few hours, night and day. Kelly and I lived on deck and the roof of the cabin while the cabin was occupied by the cook and our guests.

Progress up river was slow, with stops at many sites along the way where Kelly and I tramped over many miles in the desert trying to decide which could be excavated before the flooding and which were the most important. At one point, while we were ashore, the steersman left the engine running with the boat held against the bank. When we returned and moved off again upriver, the engine suddenly burst into flames and black smoke poured out of the hatch. We realized that the cooling-water intake had been plugged with sand while the engine idled on shore. Kelly and I dived down the engine hatch to beat out the flames from burning oil on the overheated diesel, thinking only of the German Institute and their uninsured boat. As we disappeared into the smoke I heard one woman say to the other, "What do we do now?" And the other replied, "I think we phone the cultural attache at the embassy."

Fortunately, we succeeded in beating out the fire before any serious damage was done, and were vastly relieved to find that the engine would start and run properly after it had cooled down. All our problems, the heat, and the discomfort were forgotten that evening when we finally arrived at Abu Simbel. The light of the setting sun cast long shadows on the great seated stone figures at the entrance of the cliff temple. There was no one at all on the riverbank before the temple, and a stillness that seemed to be a part of the timeless quality of that vast monument to ancient gods and god-kings, somehow enhanced by the graffiti of Greeks and Romans, who like us had disembarked there more than a thousand years after the figures were carved from the rock cliff, and two thousand years before our time.

Encamped on the sandy beach when the twilight faded and those brilliant stars of the desert appeared above the river, I felt that time does not flow like the river from then until now, but like the stars, as seen from the desert, it circles the world we know in cyclic surges of energy, creating, and re-creating life forces that we can never understand because our perceptions are only an integral part of it. We may calculate dates for the construction of Egyptian monuments, dig them out of the heaps of blown sand, and read the names of the men who made them, but their meaning and their relation to us in our time escapes us. In those years, traveling between Buddhist wats in Thailand (in some manner so much like a Maya religious center a thousand years ago), Sumerian ziggurats, Greek temples, Egyptian pyramids, and Maya city ruins in the Central American jungles, my whole conception of the past as we know it from relics in the earth continued to shift. One deeply involved in the details of archaeology in one region or one period can fit his or her theories into a rational scheme. But when one moves about, in the jet age so quickly, from one ancient civilization to another, their interrelation and their connection with "now" becomes a greater mystery. There is so much we do not know and can never know.

To build up support in the United States for the Nubian campaign to save the monuments, it occurred to me that a loan of objects from the tomb of Tutankhamen in the Cairo Museum, to travel in the United States, could create a general public interest that would bear upon government appropriation of funds. At that time I was the president of the American Association of Museums and as such believed that I could arrange for it in Cairo even though no such exhibition had ever gone abroad from the museum there. Ambassador John Badeau saw the point, and together we convinced the Minister of Culture that it could make all the difference in launching the salvage campaign.

One problem was insurance. The cost was beyond anything I had imagined. Fortunately, the director of the Rockefeller Brothers fund also saw the point and agreed to foot the bill. David Crownover, my executive officer at the Museum, managed to bring into Cairo the whole amount in cash for the Egyptian insurance company, and the collection of some thirty-five objects was packed for air shipment to the United States. At the last moment the Minister of Culture decided that the American Association of Museums was not a government body, and he needed an official U.S. agency to sponsor it. The State Department decided it had no such authority, there was no Minister of Culture in the U.S., and in the end Ambassador Badeau agreed to take responsibility personally. Such men in government bureaucracies are rare, and for me highly impressive.

The exhibition was opened at the National Gallery in Washington by Jacqueline Kennedy in 1961. Ahmed Fakhry was there to walk about the exhibition with her and the TV camera crew, and to explain the different objects as well as the importance of the Nubian salvage plan. The combination of the President's wife, the fame of Tutankhamen, Ahmed's enthusiastic vitality, and the controversial high dam itself, certainly caught on with the American public. I had, however, made one of the most spectacular mistakes in my career as a Museum director. The Minister of Culture in Cairo, Sarwat Okasha, proposed that admission charges to the exhibition, at the sixteen museums in the United States where it would be shown, should go toward funding the salvage campaign. But I did not think that the name of Tutankhamen would still be so famous and that the number of objects (thirty-four, just about ten less than the traveling exhibition which toured in the U.S. in the late 1970s, which made millions!) was not sufficient to justify admission charges. I have never been more wrong. When it opened at The University Museum in Philadelphia just after leaving the National Gallery, there were lines of people extending for several city blocks patiently waiting to get in. Like the recent exhibit, it was fantastically popular, and I still shudder at the loss we all took because of my decision.

Like Babe Ruth in baseball, Red Grange in American football, Caruso in opera, and Nijinsky in ballet, some individual's name becomes forever attached to a particular activity and is known to almost everyone. Tutankhamen is certainly "the name" in archaeology. Years later Dillon Ripley at the Smithsonian asked me to vet a television program on the Egyptian pyramids, made in California presumably under Smithsonian sponsorship. It turned out to be about "pyramid power" and the idea that the pyramidal shape could do anything from sharpen razor blades to cure disease. It was inspired by the second Tutankhamen exhibition, then touring the U.S. In California I learned what "the name" in archaeology could do. Egypt and Tutankhamen were "in"—the manufacture of small paper and plastic pyramids had become big business, everything from T-shirts to women's dresses to copies of objects from the famous tomb were sold by the millions, and the Egyptian style was again influencing commercial artistic designs. Remembering the block-long queues waiting in the wind and biting cold during that severe winter in Washington to get a glimpse of the treasure in that second small exhibition, I was appalled at the power of a name.

After completing the salvage operations along the upper Nile the Penn-Yale team began a long-range excavation at Abydos, with money remaining from the U.S. funds deposited with the embassy in Cairo. David O'Connor and Kelly had local workmen construct an enclosed compound in the desert near the site of ancient Abydos, with high conical roofs for the separate rooms forming the enclosure, a form of native building beautifully designed for coolness, and one of the most efficient headquarters of the many built by our field directors. A regular guest there was a little old lady, known as "the mother of Seti," who had lived at Abydos for many years believing that she was the reincarnation of the Pharaoh's mother. An English ex-schoolteacher, she became a voluntary guide to the ruins and spoke of the vast ruins as if they were her ancient home. I found her an interesting and charming old person but could imagine that her advice to the members of the crew would become a bit tiresome. Work at Abydos still continues. Also at that time another site in the Valley of the Kings across the river from Luxor was undertaken as well as a curious project proposed by Ray Winfield Smith.

Ray was a distinguished retired diplomat in his middle seventies who came to The University Museum with the idea that we might reconstruct the relief carvings from an ancient temple of the Pharaoh Ahkenaten, using a computer and photographs, with the 40,000 blocks of stone in eight storehouses at Luxor. These were small sandstone blocks, with relief carvings on one face only, that were found in the rubble or used in later buildings, during many years of excavation at Luxor. The distinctive stone and the relief carvings had long been recognized as coming from a temple or temples built by

Ahkenaten (ca. 1375-1358 BC) dedicated to the sun god. (The curious appearance of this monarch, in the many known representations, is thought by some to be the result of Froelich's Syndrome, an abnormality of the pituitary gland.)

I was impressed by Ray's enthusiasm, the idea, and the possibilities. With his astonishing energy we set up a center in Cairo, employed a number of young Egyptian archaeologists, and set Jim Delmege to the job of photographing all those stones in the storerooms. In Cairo the staff attempted to match up the photos of individual stones by computer. However, as time went on and the staff became more familiar with the style and content of the carvings, they dispensed with the computers and took to matching the photos from memory alone.

Some time later, Donald Redford, of the University of Toronto, joined David in the Museum's Egyptian research and completed the matching of stored stones so that whole series of scenes from the facade of the Ahkenaten temple complex could be reconstructed on paper. He then turned to excavation and unearthed the foundations of the temple deeply buried beneath the rubble from many years of previous digging. It turns out that many of the scenes depict a jubilee ceremony celebrating his reign. One part of the temple palace complex contained scenes of Nefertiti, his famous consort, officiating in the celebration. Apparently, she was something of a power behind the throne in that first attempt to set up one God, the sun, as the oldest known monotheism in the Western world.

All of this research in Egypt had me returning there almost every year from 1960 until 1975. There were continuing problems with the Department of Antiquities, with the staff in charge of the several research projects, and in maintaining sufficient funds for each operation. Usually, returning, I made it a point to stop off at the pyramid at Giza on the way to the airport and then at the Acropolis, the same day, in Athens, before going to the Middle East or Philadelphia. It became a kind of ritual. Those monuments, so famous in the history of Western civilization, were for me symbols of two interrelated but highly different cultures that still live in the minds, the theories, and the beliefs of our contemporary world and yet are wholly foreign to all of our contemporary experience. They represent the paradox in our comprehension of man's past, as I now understand it. We unravel the historic connections and see before us the fossil bones of a way of life, but the realities of living two thousand or five thousand years ago and the relation between that way and our way are really beyond our powers of imagination. In some measure archaeology resembles the study of genetics. We can comprehend the function of genes, their constituent amino acids, and dimly the way they operate to continue the life force, but the actual relation between the teeming life in a pond, reptiles, birds, the first primate, and us, is something so mysterious, so intangible, and yet so powerful that we still struggle with the imponderable thoughts of our primitive ancestors.

Once during those Egyptian years I enjoyed a memorable voyage with Tutankhamen. As part of a Sunday news program of the National Broadcasting Company, I agreed to do one of the usual archaeological news stories on the conservation of Abu Simbel, on site with a cameraman from London. And as I was leaving Philadelphia direct for Cairo, the Egyptians asked me to take with me a gold-covered statue of Tutankhamen, from that first traveling exhibition, which had begun to flake off and needed repair. The figure was carefully packed in a large wooden box delivered to me by hand with instructions that I was to keep it in my own hands all the way to the museum in Cairo for delivery to the director only. Because of a snowstorm in Philadelphia, planes were cancelled and I was told to take the train to New York for connections with a European-bound plane from Idlewild (now Kennedy). But in New York the snow was just as bad. Almost no traffic was moving—no taxis. I stood in the street at Penn Station up to my knees in snow, holding Tutankhamen in my arms—all thirty pounds of him. At last a lonely station wagon driven by a black man appeared out of the blinding snow. I hailed him, he stopped, and after some discussion agreed to attempt the journey to the airport. We made it only to learn that the Lufthansa plane for Frankfurt would be delayed four hours. I waited in the lounge with the golden god-king on my lap. But when the plane was finally called, a Lufthansa representative came over to me to say I should wait until everyone else was on board. After some time he returned to escort me into the first-class section, explaining with a broad grin that I held an economy-class ticket but Lufthansa could not have Tutankhamen traveling second class.

The airline had a separate seat for him, next to me, so that he should not be out of sight. The large box was not labeled, of course, and I never learned how the airline had discovered what was in it. We made royal progress to Frankfurt and an escorted change to the plane for Rome. There I was joined by my daughter, Penelope, so that the two of us with my charge arrived at the Cairo airport about two o'clock in the morning. A sleepy customs man asked what I carried in the large wooden box so carefully sealed. When he learned that it was a gold figure of Tutankhamen he became very excited indeed, phoned the Chief Inspector to get him out of bed, and insisted we wait until he arrived at the airport. Before long all the passengers had gone and all the customs men were clustered about us discussing what should be done. I explained that I could deliver it only to the director of the Cairo Museum and that it must remain sealed until he received it. But by four o'clock I was worn out and agreed to leave it sealed in the customs office.

Penelope and I joined the cameraman and his wife in Cairo, arranged for the Antiquities Service boat to take us from

Aswan to Abu Simbel, and spent an extraordinarily pleasant
five days on the river, saddened only by the signs of impending
forced abandonment of all the villages along the river to be
flooded with the construction of the high dam. Back in Cairo
the museum's director explained with embarrassment that
Tutankhamen remained in customs awaiting agreement
between two different ministeries of the government.

When I had first arrived at The University Museum as its
director in 1947 and had begun to revive the prewar,
worldwide field research program, many members of the Board
of Managers and staff were convinced that we must wait for a
more peaceful world, when all those complex international
conflicts of that time had been settled. Luckily we could not
guess that those conflicts would grow much worse. If we had
known, I suppose the Museum would still be waiting to revive
the Near Eastern research.

Ahmed taught me about the Arabs' sophisticated sense of
humor which eliminated my fears about mentioning sensitive
subjects. During the Nubian salvage campaign, after the
Russians had long been involved in the construction of the high
dam and in Egyptian affairs, and had learned just how
unpopular the interfering outsider can be in a newly
independent state, I met Boris Petrovsky, director of the
Hermitage in Leningrad, at the entrance to the office of the
Minister of Culture. We were both there to make arrangements
for salvage excavations above the high dam. The Egyptians
were anxious to avoid confrontation between Russians and
Americans during that hotter phase of the cold war. But as an
old friend Boris grasped me in the usual Russian bearhug and
urged me to meet him for lunch as soon as I was finished with
the minister. We were barely seated at the lunch table in the
hotel when Boris exclaimed, "We should all get along fine here
if it were not for those damned Egyptians!"

Ahmed was delighted when I told him of the Russian

comment. Like me he could appreciate the galling frictions that both the Americans and the Russians were undergoing in our attempts to bribe the fanatically independent Egyptians.

Rebiana Oasis. Author kneeling at center, bartering for spears and knives.
Photograph courtesy of the author.

CHAPTER SEVEN

North Africa

A bomb went off just a few minutes before Bill Kintner and I arrived at the entrance to the French Intelligence Headquarters in Algiers. There was not much damage and no flap among the officers with whom we conferred. At the time—1957—explosions were so common in Algeria that no one paid much attention unless there was considerable loss of life. The bar at the St. George Hotel was crowded with security troops in battle dress who patrolled the gardens, grounds, and entrances, and we all felt in a state of siege.

Bill and I had begun our investigation in North Africa via Algiers, Tunis, and Tripoli. As a member of the Foreign Policy Institute at the University of Pennsylvania and an ex-Foreign Service officer, I had agreed to make a flying investigation of Communist activities in the developing countries in North Africa, the Near and Middle East, and the Far East, together with Colonel Kintner, also a member of the Foreign Policy Institute. He was reporting to the Defense Department and I to the State Department. The bomb at French Intelligence Headquarters in Algiers was our introduction to war in North Africa and the turmoil in that part of the world that was to continue for the next generation.

Our investigations, carried out through discussions with our embassy staffs, intelligence services, and local intelligence officials in each country, continuing through Lebanon, Iraq, Iran, India, Thailand, and the Philippines, terminating in Hawaii with the U.S. Naval Command. But in most countries I had archaeological friends who, off the record, gave us some of the most interesting information about Russian penetration in their country. Even though Bill and I recorded the same data on tape recorders and in notes, we ended with Bill reporting to the Defense Department that the Russians were doing very well with their propaganda and the Americans badly, while I reported to the State Department that the Russians were doing even worse than the Americans. To me it seemed that the burning issue everywhere was complete independence from the prewar colonial system and from dominance by either of the two world powers.

In any case that trip was my introduction to North Africa. In Tripoli I had met Abdul-Aziz Jabril, the Director of Antiquities, and one of his assistants, Mohamed Ayoub, a Sudanese employed by the Libyans. Most of the digging in Libya, under the direction of Italians and French, had been in the remarkably well-preserved Roman cities like Leptis Magna. Ayoub, however, was then working in Sebha in the Fezzan, and I became interested in the possibility of finding in the Sahara ancient sites that could be identified with the ancient, partly legendary, and powerful Libyan people who had fought the Egyptians and were often referred to by the earliest Egyptian and Greek historians. I agreed to return the next year for an archaeological reconnaissance in the deserts of southern Libya.

With a Land Rover Ayoub and I traveled across the western

desert to the Algerian border and south of the Fezzan into the Murzuk sand sea. We often spent a night with Tuareg chieftains as guests in their houses and stretched out to sleep on rug-covered earthen floors after a huge meal of mutton and rice served on brass trays. With Ayoub as an interpreter we talked late into the night about the life of nomads in the desert, the caravans that crossed to the Mediterranean from black Africa, raids, wars, customs, and history. Tifinag, that mysterious ancient script of the Tuaregs, is still in use, and all were pleased to teach me how it was written and to speculate on its origins.

At Ghat, a medieval mudbrick town neat the Algerian border, there were many Tuareg with camel caravans resting after the long desert crossing from Lake Chad as well as the dark men from Niger with their own caravans. It was good to see these aboriginal people still wearing their traditional clothing (which we also wore as the most comfortable for desert travel), and still using hand-crafted saddles, weapons, and tools. At Ghat craftsmen working in the souk (market) were working for "real," not for the tourist trade as in so many modern Arab towns. In spite of a few trucks and Land Rovers, the town and its people were much as I had imagined oases in the Sahara from reading nineteenth-century accounts. But there was nothing quaint or particularly picturesque. It is a harsh land, a harsh people, and probably somewhat terrifying to the modern city dweller. As in Afghanistan a decade earlier, I found the land and the people vital, impressive, and somehow nostalgic—perhaps because of my boyhood spent with cowboys, horses, and cattle in the empty land of the high plains. Again, the intangible links between people and lands so far apart, customs, races, and behavior, puzzled and intrigued me in our wanderings about the desert.

We found deep in the Murzuk sand sea, where almost no life exists today, the ruins of a large walled town surrounded by hills that were dotted with the mounds of tombs. It is nameless, unknown, and ghostly. Fragments of pottery and relief carvings of horses' heads gave me a clue that the surface was of late Roman age and that in that period there must have been enough vegetation to support livestock. Who were all those people, lying in the desolate tombs, who once raised horses and probably also sheep, cattle, and camels in what is now a wilderness of lifeless sand? I toyed with the idea of mounting a major dig to find out, but then realized it was not for us. The Museum had never been interested in sites as late as the Romans, and also the cost of excavation so far from any settlement and a water supply would be ridiculously high.

At that point in the North African saga, the governor of Pennsylvania, who had been sent by President Kennedy to represent the United States at a trade fair in Libya, proposed that The University Museum take over the restoration of Leptis Magna. The U.S. at that time maintained a major Air Force base in Libya and was under pressure from King Idris of Libya to remove it. The commanding officer and the governor thought that some major gesture in the cultural field might help to relieve political pressure. The Museum had never done any extensive restoration, and I had resisted getting involved in such expensive gestures in all the other countries where we worked. However, the Italians had worked restoring Leptis for many years, and after their expulsion from Libya following the Second World War, continuation of the work could have a significant effect on our relation with the Libyans. Moreover, there was a good possibility that the American oil companies, then prospecting in Libya, and King Idris would supply the funds.

Six years of negotiations followed. At last David Newsome became our ambassador there, and with his forceful aid we did finally reach agreement with the oil companies and the Libyan government. Something over $1 million from the companies and the Libyan government were deposited in the Libyan Bank, and I assembled a crew of archaeologists, engineers, and architects to do at least five years of restoration. Just one week before they were to arrive in Libya King Idris was overthrown by a revolutionary group. Everything was lost to us.

Over the years I was to make several more attempts in the North African field—in Libya, Algiers, Tunis, and Morocco— once in a general search for a promising Bronze Age site with Rodney Young, the head of the Museum's Mediterranean Section, and again with Ayoub in Libya and Morocco. We did eventually begin excavations at the site of ancient Lixus in Morocco but were unable to work out a long-range excavation there with the Department of Antiquities. Looking back over all those years of probing in that part of the world, I think of it as an archaeological fiasco. However, from a personal point of view, it was a moving experience in a rapidly changing region and in a desert land that deeply affects my view of human history.

That effect took shape during my last long trip in the Sahara in southern Libya in 1968—a kind of farewell to the desert organized by David Newsome, then our ambassador in Libya, for a group of men who were about to leave the country. We were twenty-five men including a contingent of Libyan desert police who were, in part, in training and also, in part, an escort. We joined up in Sebha in the Fezzan early in January and during the next two week traveled an estimated 1,400 kilometers in eight Land Rovers and two trucks. All the Land Rovers carried intercom radios, and two had radios that could communicate with Tripoli. At one point early in the journey we ran across a stand of ancient dead trees in the desert that were cut up and loaded into the trucks for firewood—a rare treat in that land that gave us campfires for cooking as well as warmth at night and, particularly, in the frigid mornings when the temperature dropped to the freezing point.

At first we followed a track east toward Zuila, a village built on the site of an old Islamic ruin, and then south and east to the village and oasis of Temessi. From there southward across the northeast arm of the Murzuk sand sea there was no track, and we took off over a beautiful flat yellow sand with no riffles where we could drive at sixty or seventy miles an hour and feel as if we were floating. I was reminded of the flat snowfields on the winter tundra in the Arctic. But the next day it was very tough going across a series of black-rock ridges to the last isolated oasis of Wau el Kebir. There for the first time I saw some of the small, dark Tibu tribesmen who still wander in parts of the desert around the Tebesti Mountains, and also a Zuma stone (a semiprecious green gem), known to the Romans as Carthaginian stones, which were more precious than diamonds. We engaged a Tibu man as a guide hoping we could find the Zuma quarry when we eventually reached the mountains.

With us we had an enlarged photo taken from the satellite "Gemini" upon which we could see the remains of a volcanic explosion known as Wau el Namus. After another day of fast travel across an empty and trackless desert we suddenly crossed a sharp line between yellow sand and a black surface that appeared as if we had passed under the shadow of a dark cloud, then realized we were driving over a thin layer of black cinders that was to extend over an area of fifteen to twenty kilometers. At the center the volcanic crater, several hundred feet deep, and some one or two kilometers wide, contained a lake in the center of which was a small cone formed by a later and smaller eruption. A weird and eerie place, it seemed to me natural that it was sacred to King Idris's Senussi tribe.

From Wau el Namus to the Tebesti Mountains there was a sand sea that appeared to be absolutely devoid of life—no birds, insects, or vegetation of any kind and no tracks of animals. Probably there is some form of life there, but we did not see it. Only when we approached the mountains were we aware of scattered camel thorne, clumps of grass, and birds in the wadis leading into the abrupt range of black rugged peaks rising steeply out of a plain of yellow sand.

When we drew up in the shadow of a great peak that we dubbed "the cathedral," I stepped out of the car directly upon a fragment of Neolithic pottery, and as we made camp, several of the party spread out in search of artifacts. In no time we found many sherds of the Stone Age pottery as well as some milling stones and flint chips, then later, in rock shelters, rock engravings of cattle, gazelles, and some unidentified animals. Clearly, some ancient Stone Age people once raised grain and cattle in the Tebesti region. Angelo Pesce, the Italian geologist, spent a day with the Tibu guide searching for the Zuma quarry without success. He was convinced that the Tibu knew where it was but did not wish us to find it.

After some difficulty we managed to cross the Tibesti range through a pass and made camp near a range of hills, a gloomy place with volcanic ash and many bones of camels and goats, where an old track took off from the Tebesti to the oasis of Kufra. Angelo found the first Paleolithic hand ax as we made camp, and then, as we all spread out looking, flint tools began to show up in the hundreds—points, scrapers, and other Paleolithic types as well as many hand axes. Four of the crowd were so fascinated that they hunted until midnight with flashlights.

The next day we realized that was just a beginning. Heading north across the Rebiana sand sea we began to notice patches of glistening stones at intervals all over the shifting sands. They were concentrations of stone tools polished by blowing sand to mirror brightness. For 300 kilometers we were seldom out of sight of one of such concentrations. There must be millions of artifacts in that region, covered and uncovered by the shifting sand dunes over some hundreds of thousands of years. I was puzzled to find potsherds and milling stones together with Paleolithic hand axes on the surface of the sand. Angelo, equally puzzled, came to the conclusion that during and after the Ice Age there were many lakes in this part of the Sahara where first hunters and then farmers and herders lived for many thousands of years in concentrated settlements; then, as the land dried up and the sands began to shift in dunes, the remains of the settlements were denuded of earth, concentrating the artifacts in one level on the surface of the sand.

In any case this astonishing phenomenon in the Rebiana sand sea, as well as earlier wanderings in the Sahara, was for me a synopsis of human events, struggles, dreams, and theories, cast against a backdrop so huge, so empty, and so old that the crises of our particular moment seemed trivial and evanescent. The flashing, wind-polished stone tools lying on the sand in the millions speak of thousands of generations of men, nameless, unknown, totally forgotten. There are the traces of the Romans who lost their legions in the empty land of sand, the tank tracks of Italians and Germans of the Second World War that appear almost fresh in some areas, and surviving them all, the small black men of the Tibesti who still wander with their camels through the wadis and shelter under the rocks with painted scenes of ancient men who might even be their ancestors.

We passed through a region where there was no life—not even an insect—and for me the habitable world came into focus for the first time. I could see it teeming with life in an almost infinite variety of forms, interrelated, reproducing, struggling to survive in competition and cooperation with all other forms, some succeeding, some disappearing, but all depending upon the land, the wind, and the rain. Their destinies are interlocked. Human conflicts of any particular moment dominate men's minds, but in the desert's perspective they pale before the much greater problem of man's survival as a species. Rapidly now, I think, that question moves into the thoughts of men everywhere and will become the essential political issue for all nations.

Overview of the site of Tikal.
Photograph courtesy of the Tikal Project of The University Museum.

CHAPTER EIGHT

The New World

M oses, as usual, awakened me at dawn with morning coffee, and I lay in a hammock looking up at a lizard hunting insects in the palm frond roof. A pet baby ocelot played about the earth floor, and I could hear the chattering of a young monkey on his perch just outside. With that first cigarette, all the worries returned.

We were launched on one of the most extensive and difficult excavations ever undertaken by The University Museum since its foundation in the late nineteenth century. A $20,000 grant from the American Philosophical Society made the beginning possible, but it would cost many hundreds of thousands, and to raise that kind of money the diggers must produce significant discoveries in a hurry. Vast stone pyramids could be seen from the air thrusting their glistening white peaks up above 200-foot-high trees in the Peten's virgin forest; on the ground the tangle of tropical jungle was so thick that one could get thoroughly lost fifty feet off the trail. Where did we begin and how could we even map the site in that tangle?

After several years of waiting for a favorable government in Guatemala, our ambassador there, Norman Armour, who was American Minister in Haiti when we were there in 1934, wrote to tell me that the new government was in favor of our proposal and he could arrange an agreement.

The minute airstrip, cut through the jungle for fighter planes, was still there, and both the Guatemalan air force and Aviateca, the civilian air service, would give us access to Tikal by air. There was no other access at that time except on foot or mule-back. Everything had to be flown in, workmen, food, equipment, and even water. There were only a few sinkholes in the forest near Tikal, and they would disappear in the dry season.

A field director for such a large and complex operation was another worry. In the American section of the Museum Alden Mason was near retirement and Linton Satterthwaite was still working on the publication of his excavations at Piedras Negras. We had to find someone outside our own staff with experience in the Guatemalan field. Ed Shook was the obvious choice, and he agreed to take it on with a five-year contract. A calm, slow-speaking, practical sort of fellow, very much at home in Latin America, he gave me a feeling of confidence. Over the years we became close friends. He was also an old friend of John Dimick and had worked with him on a Maya site excavated for the American Fruit Company. John and his wife, Teena, were deeply interested in Maya archaeology, and he joined us at the very beginning in the onerous job of financing the enterprise. Their own contributions and foundation funds found by John were critical to its success. But I could foresee that in the early days when Ed and his crew made their first attack on the jungle.

Cutting trails from the airstrip into the heart of the vast ruined city of Tikal and construction of shelters for staff and workmen were the first steps. Workmen were Maya Indians from the region about Tikal, a rainforest known as the Peten, who looked very much like their ancestors, the original builders of Tikal. It was a joy to watch them work with their standard tool, the machete, a long sabrelike knife used for clearing as well as construction. And the houses they made of wattle, roofed with palm fronds, were remarkably like sketches of houses scratched on the plaster inside the standing stone structures of the Tikal ruins. The hamlet they built near one end of the airstrip would have been familiar to their ancestors of a thousand years ago.

Luckily another experienced Maya archaeologist and excavator was also an architect, Aubrey Trik. He joined us early enough to mastermind the plan of the finished Tikal village, including staff quarters, workmen's quarters, a married workmen's separate village with school, clinic, power plant, sawmill, and gardens, and a "jungle inn" for visitors.

The period, roughly from 1955 to 1965, now seems to me the time when popular enthusiasm for archaeology reached high tide. Television, popular books, and news stories about archaeology coincided with the beginning of jet travel and the mass movement of tourists by air. The old, battered DC3's (Dakotas) flown by Aviateca landed at Tikal with loads of tourists, at first once or twice a week, later almost daily. Even at the beginning, in 1956, when we had only two or three palm frond shelters at the site and the crew slept in hammocks under roofs with no walls, planeloads of thirty to thirty-five visitors began to arrive, carrying their own drinking water because they had been advised by the tourist agencies that there was none to be had in the jungle. We did not wish to discourage them because we hoped that some would become interested enough to contribute to the cost of what we were doing—and we were right. In the late fifties, visitors contributed more than $50,000 in one year, about half the annual budget at that time.

Then one day an Aviateca pilot dropped off a load of tourists and promised to come back in a few hours for a return to Guatemala City. Bad weather blew in and no landing was possible for three days. All thirty of the visitors tried to crowd into the few shelters, with the elderly ones occupying the crews' hammocks. Drinking water and food ran out. And, to top it all, one broke a leg. Something had to be done to avoid such crises and to protect our own crew. Aubrey designed the Jungle Inn in the ancient Maya style and supervised its construction during the next several weeks. With one long building divided into sleeping compartments, a dining hall and kitchen, and a lounge bar, all made from lumber sawed at our own mill, and palm frond thatched roofs made by Maya as they had made roofs for hundreds of years, the result was charming. Moreover, Helen Webster (later Helen Trik), who had a house in Antigua, came out to Tikal to supervise the furnishing and operation of the inn. Under Aubrey's direction, Moses, the Honduran houseboy, landscaped the clearing about the inn and the staff camp, planting fruit trees, flowering shrubs, orchids, and banana plants. This settlement, with the married workers' village, the sawmill, power plant, school, and clinic a few hundred yards away in a separate clearing, gradually became a model for growing settlements in the whole Peten region. Tourist traffic, not only excavation watchers but people who wished to see the wildlife and vegetation of the unique and isolated Peten tropical rain forest, soon reached several thousand per year. New shops, bars, and hotels in Guatemala City took the name "Tikal," and tourist brochures touting Tikal were soon distributed throughout the world. It was not unusual to hear Swiss tourists yodeling to each other from the temples on top of the Tikal pyramids.

The Tikal jungle is powder-dry during the summer months and soaking wet in the winter. Water during the summer working season remained a critical problem. Tracks for the trucks were cut through the jungle to all the nearby waterholes, basins where some clay on top of the underlying limestone would hold water from the winter rains, but the water soon became foul in summer and ran out before the end of the dry season. The ancient Maya had built huge reservoirs, lined with clay, to catch the runoff, but all had long since been destroyed.

At a Museum board meeting in Philadelphia I was describing our dilemma at Tikal when one of the members spoke up about his experience on his farm outside Philadelphia. There he had hired Henry Gross, the famous water dowser from Maine, to locate a well, most successfully. He suggested we employ Gross to do the same thing at Tikal. I observed that it would be difficult to use research funds contributed to a "scientific" institution for the application of sorcery. At once several board members offered to contribute the necessary money, and I was trapped into flying to Tikal with Henry and his dowsing stick, dreading the reaction of the staff members on the site.

We arrived at Tikal to find Alfred Kidder Senior, the "father" of archaeology in the southwestern United States and then the grand old man of American archaeology in general, together with several engineers from a consortium of oil companies then searching for oil fields in the Peten. Privately, I received a thorough ragging from everyone for attempting to apply magic, but the absolute assurance of Henry Gross began to have its effect even upon the oil company engineers. He had no doubt at all that he could find water. He explained how he had found wells on the island of Bermuda, at Guatemala City, and many other places all over the world.

But when he stood on a mound in the camp clearing with a palm leaf bent into a triangle and pointed out into the jungle, turning about slowly to locate the direction toward the water deposit, there were many suppressed snickers. Suddenly the bent palm leaf flipped downward and he announced that water lay in that direction. He repeated his 360-degree turn several times, and each time the leaf flipped on the same bearing. Then I suggested that Ted Kidder try it. The expression on Ted's face when the leaf buckled and flipped down on precisely that same bearing is something forever memorable—shock, surprise, and a kind of horror. The same thing happened to me and to one of the engineers. The leaf was suddenly alive, active and uncontrollable. It was an eerie feeling. Then we all followed Henry and his leaf off into the jungle in search of the precise spot for the well. A few hundred yards from the camp he stopped and announced that the water lay directly below us. Standing with his leaf erect he counted five, ten, fifteen, twenty, and so on, until the leaf flipped again at, as I remember, 120 feet. He then began again counting ten gallons, fifteen gallons, and so on, until the leaf flipped again at forty gallons per hour. One of the engineers looked down pensively and muttered, "By God, if there is water there at 120 feet with a flow of 40 gallons per hour, I'll become a Buddhist!"

One of the Guatemalan air force freight planes had already flown in a well-drilling rig in preparation for drilling, so there was no delay in testing Henry' claim. No one would think of leaving Tikal until it reached 120 feet. As the days passed, tension grew. Everyone was at the well-head when it reached 100 feet, and waited. It passed 120 feet, then 150, and at 200 we quit. No water. Henry was almost in a state of shock. He just could not believe it. He spent the next two days in the guest house with two bottles of whiskey and then flew back to the United States in a devastated state of mind.

The venture was not wasted. Intrigued by the water problem at Tikal, and jolted by Henry's infectious certainty, the oil company engineers brought in two of their great bulldozers used to cut exploration trails through the forest, and with those machines dug out one of the ancient Maya reservoirs adjoining our camp. Tikal then had its own small lake to enhance the charm of the settlement as well as a supply of water for the camp and the inn. Tanks made of cedar planks were constructed on the spot to catch and hold winter rainwater collected from the tin roof of the newly constructed storage- and workrooms building. Moreover, the engineers, indoctrinated in Maya archaeology at Tikal, began to search for still undiscovered ruins as a part of their oil survey. And when one was found, they sent one of their helicopters to transport a Tikal archaeologist to the site for exploration and recording.

The old Maya reservoir made possible the introduction of flush toilets at the inn—a convenience much appreciated by guests who, until that was installed, were forced to make their way along a track in the jungle to an outhouse of the nineteenth-century variety—a debilitating experience for twentieth-century tourists in a black tropical night with myriads of flying insects and roaring howler monkeys. When my old friend and mentor, Mrs. Harrison, then well on in her eighties, decided she must see Tikal at an early stage, I decided I must send her down by air a sanitary toilet to be installed in the guest house for her special use. But when I again arrived there after her visit, I discovered the inn manager, a Peten workman, had that large, white, and imposing object installed smack in the middle of Mrs. Harrison's bedroom, leaving little room for her to get in or out of bed. It was not a success.

Tikal was not only the most extensive and complicated research operation ever launched in more than 75 years of Museum research around the world, but the most difficult for me in nearly thirty years of backstopping the Museum's expeditions. The problem, as it often is, was management. American archaeologists working in Indian mounds, rock shelters, caves, and in general relatively small sites persisted in tackling a vast city ruin in the same limited, meticulous manner. Ed Shook had worked at a very large site on the outskirts of Guatemala City, but the pressure of American excavating techniques was strong, and I could not convince him to approach Tikal with the scale of excavation and exploration customary in Egypt and the Near East, even after we sent him abroad to visit our own and other excavations in that part of the world. After all that money, effort, and equipment expended to explore an area of several square miles with more than 100 pyramids, acres of so-called palaces, and many hundreds of other ruined buildings, plus several thousand house mounds, it was heartbreaking to see one digger with two workmen digging in a tiny trench across the main plaza to locate separate occupation levels, and another with two or three workmen digging small exploratory pits. The most effective research was Ed and Aubrey's work in locating chamber burials in the great central pyramids by tunneling through the solid earth and stone construction. Those chambers contained magnificent jade, ceramic, and stone objects as well as wall paintings and glyphs that gave some idea of the life of the classic Maya at Tikal, but they did not solve the many riddles about the nature of what is one of the oldest and surely the largest of the great Maya cities.

Finally, in an attempt to change the entire scale of the operation, I transferred Bob Dyson from Hanaslu in Iran to take charge at Tikal for one season, after which the research was directed by William R. Coe, curator of the American section of the Museum. There was much objection from the specialized American diggers, but in the end it was effective. The number of workmen was multiplied several times, excavations of the size customary in the Near East were opened up, and gradually even the Americanists began to look at the site as a whole. At the end of the season Bob's father, a doctor, told me he had never seen his son so close to a nervous breakdown.

Out of that shock treatment grew the very extensive

excavation of the central acropolis with its complex of palaces on the opposite side of the central core of the city. I expect that the effect of Near Eastern methods and the whole change in scale will be forgotten by the Americanists who finally complete the publication of Tikal research. That is only natural. Specialists do not take kindly to invasion by specialists from other fields.

With some fifteen excavations going on in Iran, Turkey, Pakistan, Jordan, Egypt, Italy, Ireland, the American Arctic, Greece, North Africa, and the South Pacific, I got around to most of the expeditions only when there was some trouble or when major decisions were to be made. But Tikal remained a particular problem, always requiring a visit and consultation each season for fourteen years. From the beginning Ed or Aubrey always saved a tomb or grave for me to excavate during the week or two of my stay. The one that sticks in my memory was deep in the central acropolis and contained among other things a group of clay pots with covers. When opened they were found filled with seeds. It was good to think of the man buried there, 1,500 years ago, equipped with the seeds to plant his fields in another world.

It is, of course, a myth that grain found in Egyptian tombs can be germinated. A thousand-year-old lotus seed was said to be germinated in China, but generally it is agreed that life in a seed does not remain vital for centuries. Discussing that fascinating question with Mouk Boyer, the president of the pharmaceutical company Smith, Kline and French, in Philadelphia, I learned that a chemist in one of their research laboratories was culturing the spores of germs and had been able to regenerate spores that had been latent for some time. We agreed to send him to Tikal with all his equipment when I knew that a tomb was to be opened deep inside one of the stone pyramids. When explaining this experiment to our Board of Managers, Dave Goddard, a noted biologist, spoke up to say that it was impossible; no spore of that age could possibly be regenerated. Aubrey Trik finally located the chamber tomb in Temple I after long tunneling through solid masonry. At once Mouk dispatched his chemist, with sterilized equipment (including his clothing), to Tikal so that he was ready to drop into the tomb the moment the capstone was removed. It was a rich tomb, with jade carvings, many painted pots, a skeleton, some magnificent engraved bones with figures of masked men in a boat, and Maya glyphs. The chemist scraped off deposits on the walls and on the skeleton, popped the material into sterile containers, and flew back to his laboratory in Philadelphia. Some weeks later he phoned to say that the germ spores, over 1,200 years old, had germinated, but unfortunately they were all familiar germs existing at present. He did prove that very ancient latent spores could be revived but did not find any strange ancient disease germs that might have given us a clue to the disappearance of Mayan civilization.

Later we were to learn that there are, however, some lethal germs or spores lurking in the Tikal ruins. Two young students excavating a chultun, a deep rock-cut storage pit, were suddenly taken critically ill with very high fever. Fortunately our doctor in Guatemala City was able to diagnose a very rare fungus disease and to save the eyes of both boys, which were badly infected, although full recovery took nearly a year.

Those annual visits to Tikal were not usually for special research projects like the germ experiment or the water search. Mostly they were simply to sort out management problems. Ed Shook, Aubrey Trik, and finally George Guillamin, the three different field directors during the years at Tikal, were not Ph.D. graduates in archaeology and hence were often at loggerheads with the professors and graduate students who worked there over the many years. Where and how to dig was always a problem, but added to this were the endless questions of what ruined buildings to remove to get at the earlier constructions and what structures to restore, and how. The field directors and I agreed that we must clear, consolidate, and maintain the important structures excavated, but not do an elaborate restoration job such as that done by the Mexicans at Teotihuacan and Palenque. The unique wilderness character of Tikal should be retained. But also we must remove some of the ruined buildings on the surface to get at, and restore, more ancient and intact buildings below them. In some cases we were publicly damned for the destruction of pyramids and temples overlying those below. However, the Guatemalan government and their archaeologists were always consulted and agreed with our decisions.

For me management problems came to a head one year when a group of graduate students from Harvard, employed by Ed, wrote to me to say that he, as a nonprofessional in their eyes, was not adequate as a field director and should be replaced by someone who would follow their "more professional" ideas about how to excavate the city. I had warned, without effect, the director of the anthropological division of the National Science Foundation that it would be unwise to pay graduate students in the field out of grants from the foundation, and this revolt was a natural result. With payment they became "professionals" in their own eyes and had the crust to criticize a man who had excavated in Guatemala for many years. That year it was a great satisfaction to ship them all home immediately. But then even some of our own graduate students from The University of Pennsylvania, left without supervision for a few weeks, were so rude and insulting to a group of tourists from Texas that they inspired a series of newspaper stories about "the impossible archaeologists" at Tikal. It is difficult to educate young and inexperienced students in the hard facts about who, in the end, pays for their opportunity to work at an exciting place like that. To them, I suppose, tourists are just a nuisance. And, of course, at times some of them are. Others, like those from the Rockefeller and Mellon families and foundations, contributed hundreds of thousands of dollars to make the Tikal project work. And some of the most inconspicuous visitors sent cheques for thousands.

When I was advised by the director of the Mellon Foundation that he was taking Richard, the young son of Sarah Mellon Scaife, to visit Tikal, I arranged to accompany them out to the site from Guatemala City. The director wanted a good safe aircraft to be chartered and did not want to trust the old battered DC3's flown by Aviateca. Hence I arranged for a twin-engined Fairchild for eight passengers. At the airport, boarding the plane, we all noticed a maker's label stating that the aircraft had been built in 1932. Many layers of paint on the fuselage were like those on an ancient bus or streetcar. As usual I reassured myself by remembering that the pilot's neck was at stake also, and he probably was confident that it could make it to Tikal and back over all those mountains and jungles with no place for emergency landings. But I had overlooked the fact that it was his first landing on that narrow, rough, and short airstrip, cut through trees over a hundred feet high. That was the most hairy landing I ever made at Tikal. We all emerged looking grim and white-faced.

John and Tina Dimick, and Tina's sister Alice Tully, contributed very handsome sums for the excavation and restoration of two of the temple pyramids on the central plaza, and John arranged for even larger sums from the Mellon and Rockefeller Foundations. The Rockefeller grants were, in fact, made as Dean Rusk's last action as director of that foundation before he became U.S. Secretary of State. Those major grants, together with the many grants from private individuals, carried the Tikal project through ten years. Then, as they all terminated about the same time, I and the Board of Managers decided we could not carry on unless the U.S. AID Program and the Guatemalan government took over a large part of the cost. Ed Shook and Adolfo Molina Orantes, our attorney in Guatemala City, tried to interest the Guatemala government (Tikal was by then the greatest tourist attraction in the country and hence a source of significant foreign exchange income), while I tried to interest our embassy in supplying AID funds. We were not successful. Our embassy decided that the Guatemalan government would not approve such expenditures from the AID funds.

But when we notified the government that we were closing down and terminated Ed Shook's second five-year contract as director, I had a letter from an unknown priest stationed in a small village outside Guatemala City, stating that he could arrange for substantial funds from the government through his friend the dictator, General Peralta. At the time it seemed a faint hope, but worth exploring. Young Ted Kidder, our associate director and most fluent Spanish-speaker, went down to talk with the priest and General Peralta. He returned with the astonishing news that the general would appropriate nearly $1 million over the next four years if we could get a plan through to him before the current congress was replaced by the new one. At that point Adolfo, using his great influence in the country (he was later to become the foreign minister), stepped in and made it all work. That meant four more years at Tikal (1966-1969) and the completion of the Museum's single largest enterprise in nearly a century of research. Aubrey Trik continued as director until assigned to be a roving architect for the Museum at other sites abroad, and he was then replaced by George Guillamin, a Belgian archaeologist with long experience in Guatemala.

Out of this grew a museum on the site at Tikal to house the treasures found in the site. It was conceived and financed largely by Americans living and working in Guatemala, led by a group of American women with determination. And they also involved responsible Guatemalans, like Adolfo Molina, in the support of the project and of archaeology in general, a move that would have an important bearing on the future of research there.

The archaeological reports of the work at Tikal, now being when published by Bill Coe and more than fifteen graduate students among the many who worked there, will give a new look to the history of the Maya people, but they will tell little of the drama of the work in progress with all of the hundreds of people involved in it. To me, in many respects, this is in fact one of the major aspects of digging into the past. Such involvement is the vitality, the meaning, and the purpose of archaeology. Without that intellectual excitement for thoughtful people, digging becomes a dull and academic business shot through with petty controversies about obscure theories and pedantic rivalries. Those theories change and disappear, but the astonishing ruins in the Peten jungle and the magnificent objects found in them remain to intrigue, astonish, and excite the thousands upon thousands of people who will come after us. I like to remember the people who drifted into the enterprise and left their mark upon it.

Aubrey and Helen Trik spent years creating the environment of the Tikal project that appealed to so many of the people who came there. With them I often took off with one of our jeeps over jungle tracks to the Subin River, where we would hire a dugout canoe and drift down to the Passion River, collecting exotic orchids from the trees overhanging the Subin. Both the Subin and the Passion were wilderness rivers then, with only an occasional Indian hut along their banks. The Passion overflowed into great jungle lakes and the fishing was marvelous. Tarpen was the most exciting game fish, but blancos and roballo were much more plentiful and very good to eat. Some of our happiest days were spent on the rivers in a large stable dugout manned by a Maya Indian, sometimes with the whole river purple with drifting blossoms from flowering trees. Aubrey designed a fishing camp on the Passion, built and owned by Ortiz of the Jungle Inn, in the Maya style but on stilts to keep it above flood waters. Helen furnished it in a comfortable and charming manner so that fishing parties from Tikal could spend a pleasant time there in the care of a houseboy-cook, also trained by her and kept up to her standards. At Tikal Aubrey's excavations of tombs and his meticulous drawings of buildings will survive in the Tikal reports, as will Helen's study of the drawings on the walls of standing buildings, but the atmosphere of the years of digging and the camps will surely dissolve away with the years and the smothering jungle.

The most perfect time to visit the central plaza at Tikal was at night with a full moon. Then the white limestone palaces and pyramids are luminous against a black background of forest, and one can most easily imagine the city peopled with its builders. Tikal was famous for its tall and steep pyramids (up to 235 feet) with temples and high roof combs appearing to drift in the moonlight above the forest. That is part of the special magic of the place.

One such night when Tina and John Diminick and Alice Tully were visiting the site with an opera singer friend of Alice's, we drove out to the plaza in two jeeps. Alice and her friend were some minutes ahead of John, Tina and I in the second vehicle, and when we drove up the steep ramp into the open plaza, there in bright moonlight were Alice and Edward tearing off their clothing, dancing about, and yelling as if in some pagan ritual. They had stepped out of their jeep directly upon a column of army ants marching across the plaza. The soldier ants guarding such columns attack at once and their sting is like a sharp electric shock. I remember Tina quite calmly asking her sister if the ants had penetrated beneath her girdle. Recovered, but still in his shorts, Edward climbed to the top of Temple II and we heard his opera singer's voice booming out snatches from Rigoletto and Carmen.

Some years later I was at Tikal with my elder daughter, Penny, and friends from Philadelphia on another such period of the full moon. It happened that both my daughter and Gates Lloyd shared a birthday while we were there. Lolly, Gates' wife, and I decided upon a memorable birthday party. We had brought a supply of wine from Guatemala City, and at Tikal we found a large supply of candles as well as a marimba orchestra made up of Tikal women. The orchestra with tables of food and wine was located on the north terrace, backed by towering pyramids and temples and facing out toward the open plaza with the cleared and partially restored white palace enclosing the opposite side. Candles were placed in rows on the several terraces rising to the temple on Pyramid II and before the door into the temple at treetop height. The night was so still there was hardly a flicker in the candle flames. Surely that is one birthday that Penny and Gates will never forget.

With the burst of jet-borne tourists and the heyday of popular interest in archaeology crystallizing in the early 1960s came a flood of correspondents, photographers, and television crews eager to record the story of the recovery of Tikal. The *Life** magazine photographers spent many days there preparing one of the most impressive picture stories of the operation. Similar stories appeared in magazines published in many countries. I was reminded of a similar excitement when

* See *Life*, volume 51, number 6, August 11, 1961, pages 45-48.

The University Museum and the British Museum were excavating at Ur in Iraq in the 1920s. Sir Leonard Woolley, our director of that dig, had told me how special trains from the north of England carried thousands of people to see the exhibition of treasures from Ur's royal tombs when they were first shown in London. But in our day we had television. One such filming was done for a TV series in Philadelphia called "Concept," managed by Marciarose Shestak, a TV personality in the city. She and I were to "talk-over" the film on site, and I can remember our difficulty over the script outline. She was soon exasperated with my "maybe," "possibly," "we think," "it could be," and demanded specific facts learned at Tikal about the ancient Maya. I could see why most archaeological TV programs sound like an elementary schoolbook and how it is that they miss what intrigues most thoughtful people, the mysterious, unanswerable questions that permeate every major excavation of the ruins of past civilizations.

To dramatize the whole operation, she asked about the hardships and dangers of work in the jungle, such as disease and poisonous snakes. I explained that we had had a yellow fever scare but that mosquito-borne disease had affected only the monkeys, because the mosquitoes carrying it were confined to the treetops. No human on the ground had contracted it. The only really serious poisonous snake was the coral snake and in all the years at Tikal no one had been bitten. I had never seen one. We were sitting on a log in the central plaza, and when we rose to move to another location, there, just under the log at our feet, was the only coral snake I had ever seen.

Those hard facts for the schoolbooks about the Maya are strangely elusive. For many years Americanists digging in the ruins of this unique civilization agreed upon certain basic "facts": the great stone pyramids were not tombs of kings like those in Egypt but rather the bases for temples built on the summit, hence not related in function; the many groups of pyramids, temples, and palaces found throughout the lowland jungles of Guatemala and Mexico were "ceremonial centers," not urban centers as in the Old World; one fundamental element in the early civilizations of the Near East, the wheel, was totally lacking in America; no traces of any direct contact between ancient civilizations in the Old World and those in the New have been proved, hence those in the New World were independently developed.

Then at Palenque, in Mexico, a large and rich tomb of some elite person was found at the heart of a great stone pyramid, and at Tikal we learned that they were all burial structures for the elite as well as temple bases. Excavation of some 100 house sites at Tikal and the elaborate palace structures in the central acropolis extending over four acres convinced everyone that Tikal was a true urban center with a permanent population of at least 10,000 people in the central six square miles of the city and many more thousands in the outlying suburban area. There is also evidence of extended family compounds and specialized industry. In an ancient grave in Mexico were found small terra-cotta toys in the form of carts and wheels. Clearly these New World people knew about the wheel even though, apparently, they did not use it functionally. And in Ecuador pottery of the Jomon type made in Japan in 2500 B.C. has been found, and some diggers now claim this is evidence of direct contact with the ancient cultures of the Far East.

Such discoveries, made during the period of my own career in archaeology, do not surprise me. With my first look at a Maya site in 1948 I was struck by the extraordinary similarity between stone sculptures (e.g., those at Quirigua) in the Maya world and those in Asia. Later, wandering about a wat in Thailand, it struck me that it was very much what a living Maya "ceremonial center" must have been. Of course, famous jungle ruins like Angkor Wat were built several centuries after

Tikal had died, but we are now learning that civilized living began in Southeast Asia before 3000 B.C., not with the arrival of Hindus and Buddhists about the time of Christ as once supposed. Time-space relations are shifting rapidly in the contemporary conception of our world; theories about human history are also changing. Many of us anticipate future theories that would now be totally inconceivable.

At Tikal, over the many years there, there was one "fact" that never ceased to puzzle me. Always, looking over recent finds in the workrooms, those crude stone working tools stuck in my mind like a lump in the throat. If they were found in a site without vast ruins of buildings, elaborate carvings in jade, and hieroglyphic inscriptions, they would be considered clear evidence of a primitive Stone Age culture. After coming from one of our excavations in the Near East where elaborate working tools were the norm, those crude Maya tools seemed completely out of place. It still stretches my imagination to think of an advanced civilization based on such primitive tools.

One other "fact," or coincidence, will always intrigue me. In our fairly recent application of scientific techniques in archaeology a method has developed for measuring the shifts in the earth's magnetic polarization. We are learning that at certain datable periods (C-14) magnetic north was many degrees east or west of what it is now. At Tikal it was noticed that one pyramid was oriented in relation to magnetic north of the century in which it was built. Without a steel needle and a magnetic compass, how could that be? A lodestone, presumably invented by the Chinese about 1000 A.D.? Or just a coincidence? There is no answer.

The great, and mysterious, questions about the Maya are still unanswered. Who were they and where did they come from? The earliest remains at Tikal, a few fragments of pottery and a grave, date from about 600 B.C. By the first century before Christ there are elaborate buildings and hieroglyphic inscriptions. Presumably they are related to the Olmec, a more ancient people on the Gulf coast of Mexico who produced very distinctive stone sculpture, elaborate buildings, and inscriptions comparable to the Maya, and to the earlier people of the Guatemalan highlands. But this only begs the question. What and who created the many interrelated early civilizations of Middle America? Is it really all a unique and isolated development in America or was there direct contact with Old World civilizations?

For me, one of the most puzzling questions is why and how the Maya created such a civilization and such a large population in a region like the Peten. The soil is shallow, poor, and apparently incapable of supporting a large population based upon the growth of maize. That there was a dense population all over the area is shown not only by the size of Tikal but by the great causeways, roads often as wide as a modern expressway, converging upon the city from the surrounding country. There are reasonable suggestions that the Maya grew a yamlike tuber with a greater yield per acre than maize, that the common people lived to a large extent on the fruit of the ramon tree, plentiful in the jungle, but now considered much inferior as a food to the familiar maize, or that they had developed intensive agriculture in the low marshy lands surrounding Tikal. Paleobotanical studies in the marshes show that the climate has not changed significantly, and one must think of the Maya living in the Peten much as it is today. And why did they build their greatest city only twenty-five miles from the great lake at Flores, while their only water in the dry season must come from laboriously constructed reservoirs?

There is evidence at Tikal that, in one sense, only adds to the mystery of why this unique civilization disappeared so quickly. About A.D. 900 the construction of new buildings, a never-ending process for more than 1,000 years, suddenly ceased. But people remained in the city to live and plunder the temples and tombs. They did not build, but they squatted in the growing ruins, even up to the eighteenth century. Mayan-speaking people still live in many regions of Central America. It is agreed that Tikal was not invaded (though to everyone's surprise an earth wall and ditch was discovered in 1966 running east and west for six miles about two and a half miles north of the central plaza, possibly for defense), there was no drastic weather change, no earthquakes, and no evidence of a plague. There is evidence of a rapid population increase preceding the collapse. The best possible guess is a social revolution in which the elite, religious ruling class was destroyed by a long-suffering peasant population who were fed up with the labor of the constant building of temples and palaces and the bureaucracy of political-religious hierarchy. Perhaps this explanation is only a reflection of our own particular moment in history and has no reality. In any case, Maya, like all the ancient civilizations, died, leaving its people to be butchered by the Spanish long after the great cities began to fall into ruins.

This is all a mystery common to much of the known world of the past. Ruined cities in the jungle, as in Central America and Southeast Asia, are just more dramatic than the lost cities buried under the mounds in the Near and Middle East. There is no explanation. But I suspect, some day, there will be a theory about the sudden rise and decline of energy in particular ethnic groups of people, for reasons now unknown, that will account for this universal phenomenon, at least to the satisfaction of that future generation.

The University Museum's research in America began in the late nineteenth century with Max Uhle's discovery of the remarkably well-preserved remains of an ancient civilization on the coast of Peru. It is still going strong. During my time the major work was in Guatemala, at Tikal and Quirigua, where

Robert Sharer continued working after the termination of the Tikal project in 1968. With other diggers he has also worked at several other sites in Central America, to me of most interest at El Mirador, north of Tikal, a preclassic city, recently discovered, of great size, with the largest temple building yet known in the Maya region.

Recently, I have learned from him that theories about the Maya and their development are undergoing dramatic change, primarily because there has been a breakthrough in deciphering Maya writing, but also because of intensive studies of the Maya in relation to other advanced civilizations in Central America and Mexico. It is now probable that the origins of these interrelated American advanced societies can be traced to some 2,000 years B.C.

Also during my time at the Museum, American research continued in the Arctic, the western United States, Mexico, and Peru, so that I kept in touch, in a general way, with the development of American prehistory. Several of my students in Arctic studies excavated sites in the north under the auspices of the Museum and wrote their Ph.D. theses on that region. But for the most part I was not personally involved, in the field, with other American digs.

There was one exception. Just before Loren Eiseley and I retired at age seventy, we decided to have one more crack at digging in Montana in search of men and mammoth. Loren had begun his research on the western plain and it was my original homeland, hence it was a kind of nostalgic journey into the past. We based our search at the ranch of Dan Downs (who had been the last foreman on my father's ranch), near where mammoth bones had been found. We made no significant discovery but roamed over the prairies and badlands, did some digging, and thoroughly enjoyed ourselves.

Excavations at Sybaris, Italy in the fall of 1961. Workmen struggling to keep ahead of the water rapidly filling their trench.
Photograph courtesy of The University Museum Archives.

CHAPTER NINE

Europe

T he Archbishop of Calabria, a neat little man in a purple cassock, purple shoes with silver buckles, and the grand manner of a dignitary in the Catholic Church, made the sign of the cross and then prayed for the success of our venture. When the prayer was finished, Enrico Mueller turned to me and exclaimed in a low voice, "My God! Imagine, an archbishop praying for the success of a pagan in his search for the remains of a pagan city!"

We were on the low, flat, marshy plain of Sybaris near the mouth of the River Crati on the southern coast of Italy, standing in the shade of a large excavating machine that moved a cubic meter of earth in each bucket. Ernesto Spina, the operator, beamed with satisfaction at the blessing of his new dragline. Before us were a deep hole partly filled with water and a vast pile of soft mud. The clatter of machinery was everywhere—the heavy engine of the extractor, the steady beat of the water pumps, and the roar of an electric generator. It was very hot, bright, and swarming with gnats. The crews that manned two different drilling rigs and the magnetometer instruments had come in from the outlying fields for the ceremony at the excavation. All of us, except the archbishop, were spattered with mud, stained with grease, and sweating in the humid summer heat of what was once Magna Graecia.

Not long after I had become the director of The University Museum I was confronted by a retired banker of Philadelphia, Mr. Orville Bullitt, who was then president of the Philadelphia Orchestra and also president of the University of Pennsylvania Hospital Board. He was known as a cantankerous, irascible fellow who found great pleasure in getting under people's skin with his sharp and irritating comments. From me he wanted an immediate, all-out search for the tomb of Alaric, which was supposed to be somewhere near the bridge over the Busento River at what is now Cosenza in Calabria. At the time it was the least likely possibility for utilizing the Museum's research facilities, and I tried to explain the impossibility of his idea without bringing down upon my head his most scathing comments. Ten years later everything had changed. At the Museum I had established an Applied Science Center for Archaeology (MASCA) with the purpose of adapting new technology, then developing so rapidly, to archaeological research. We had already put in operation radiocarbon equipment for dating ancient remains, the first to operate after Bill Libby's station in Chicago, and were then experimenting with other techniques including new electronic instruments for underground search.

By 1960 Carlo Lerici was using resistivity equipment at Tarquinia and Cerveteri to locate tombs, and because I had also used similar equipment for experiments in Mexico, I thought it wise to combine an American crew with the Italian crew at Tarquinia and Cerveteri with different kinds of electronic search equipment. At Oxford Martin Aitkin had adapted the proton magnetometer for archaeological search, and we added this to a German resistance instrument that we had found simpler and more efficient than the American equipment used in Mexico. Aubrey Trik, Jim Delmege, and I, with a student of Martin Aitkin's to operate the magnetometer, joined the Lerici crew at Tarquinia in the summer of 1961. After some difficulty with the magnetometer, probably caused by unusual magnetic storms at that time, we soon learned that we could pick up the entrance passage to Etruscan tombs in the same manner as the resistivity apparatus, and much more rapidly.

These tombs are rectangular chambers cut into bedrock, with a ramp cut down through bedrock to the entrance. The ramp, filled with surface soil, registers less electrical resistance than the bedrock through which it is cut and thus can be detected by the resistivity meter. Also, we learned, the fill is more magnetic than the bedrock and can be detected with a magnetometer. But, to our surprise, the proton magnetometer also registered the cavity of the tomb itself. Before long we were locating up to six tombs a day. There are thousands of such tombs at Tarquinia and Cerveteri that are, of course, unmarked on the surface, although on aerial photographs it is possible to detect the massed graves because they show up as light spots in the green fields. Rarely are they worth excavating. Practically all have been looted during the past two thousand years, and only one in perhaps a hundred or more has painted walls. With the periscope developed by Lerici we could drill into the center of the tomb, insert the periscope with a lighting attachment, and quickly discover whether it was worth excavating to expose wall paintings.

Once the system for location and examination was worked out, the mass production of tombs, for me, became a boring operation. Franco Brancaleone, the foreman of the Lerici crew, and I then began experimenting with the magnetometer at the site of the acropolis at Tarquinia. Measuring magnetic intensity every two meters in long parallel transverses across the site, we discovered that we could locate buried walls in the ruins. The stone walls were less magnetic than the soil in which they were buried. Franco was an energetic, restless, and eager sort of person always in search of excitement. He had found on the plain of Sybaris a deeply buried stone wall with his resistivity equipment, and with that lead we proposed to Carlo Lerici that we explore Calabria, both the plain on which ancient Sybaris was supposed to be and inland near Cosenza where Orville Bullitt had hoped to find the tomb of Alaric.

Lerici and I took the train from Rome to Paola, to be met by Franco with his car, and then drove across the mountains to Cosenza. Looking down over the present city of Cosenza we could see at once that any attempt to find the famous tomb was hopeless. After the last war the town had become the center for the administration of the economic development of Calabria. The whole valley around the bridge over the Busento River is now a city with twenty-story office buildings and apartments. If Alaric is still there, he is buried beneath many tiers of bureaucrats. Some clairvoyant in California had written to Lerici advising him that the tomb would be found at a certain point near the bridge. To our amusement we found that point at the center of a huge brewery complex.

But in the thinly settled plain of Sybaris we found the ideal location for a major test of electronic search equipment in archaeology. Senator Zanotti-Bianco's excavation of the Roman site on the plain was still exposed, and some distance to the north was the wall discovered by Franco. The earlier archaic Greek city of Sybaris could be anywhere within the 125 square kilometers of the plain and probably would be deeply buried because it was the only major Greek city ruin not yet discovered in Calabria, even though many had searched for it during the past century. That evening, back in Paola waiting for a late train to Rome, I wrote Orville an account of our day of exploration, explained the situation at Cosenza, and proposed that we tackle the century-old problem of Sybaris. A few days later in Tarquinia a cable arrived from Orville saying he would finance the attempt. Who could then guess that it would cost him over $150,000 and that I should spend eight years in the search?

We moved from Tarquinia to Sybaris in the fall of 1961 and with the magnetometer very quickly found that Franco's wall extended for at least one mile across the plain north of the Crati River. Excavations cut down to the wall disclosed that it was of Roman construction, but we hoped that an earlier Greek wall would lie below.

The most extensive farm on the plain was owned by Enrico Mueller and his wife, Anna, one of the Toscano family that had drained much of the plain in the 1930s. Both of them had long been fascinated with the problem of Sybaris, and they joined us in the search, becoming not only my hosts for many years, but our protectors in all the necessary arrangements with other farmers whose land was to be explored. On the farm, Enrico had a small mechanical excavator, which we used to expose the Roman wall. With that we soon discovered one of our major problems of excavation on the plain. At a depth of 3 or 4 meters the excavator broke through a dense clay deposit that capped a subterranean flow of water in sandy soils. Once that was exposed, groundwater surged upward like an artesian well, swamping the machine. We could go no deeper without pumps and heavier excavation equipment. The enigma of the "long wall" and the possibility of an earlier Greek wall below remained unsolved. However, the magnetometer was effective for a rapid survey of buried structures, and in spite of water problems in excavations the project was feasible. We fully expected the next season to solve the riddle of Sybaris.

In those early years of the search I was the president of the American Association of Museums and chairman of the National Research Council's Science Planning Board, attempting a look into the twenty-first century for a federal science exhibition at the Seattle World's Fair. Those responsibilities, together with my normal job of running the Museum and its many expeditions abroad, meant that I could spend only a few weeks in Italy twice a year. Hence our normal routine was a spring and fall campaign each year with a group from the Lerici Foundation in Rome and another group from MASCA of The University Museum. Over the years, scores of people were to join those campaigns, Dutch and Italian as well as American archaeologists, geologists, electronics engineers, hydraulic engineers, photographers, drillers, and many volunteers of all kinds. The Lerici Foundation financed the Italian, and Mr. Bullitt, through The University Museum, the American element. We were also joined by the Director of Antiquities in Calabria, Giuseppe Foti, and several members of his staff from Reggio-Calabria, who officially supervised all the research and also opened up continued excavations at the Roman site known as the Parco del Cavallo. In 1962 Elizabeth Ralph, Associate Director of MASCA, took charge of instrument surveys and thereafter was to spend more time at Sybaris than anyone else, assisting in excavations and all other aspects of the whole operation. Paola Zancani, who had excavated at the Parco del Cavallo with Zanotti-Bianco, was excavating a cemetery in the foothills above the plain at Francovilla, and as the most experienced digger in the region, became a mentor for all of us.

Like "the man who came to dinner," I continued to be a guest of the Mueller's in their rambling old house in Cassano-

Ionio, above the plain. Enrico often worked with me in drilling, digging, and surveying, supplying workmen for special jobs, machinery, repairs, and above all, advice and counsel in all the complexities the search was to develop. We became close friends. I watched their six children grow up, went to weddings in the family, learned some Italian but taught the children more English than they taught me Italian, and became a member of the family myself. In those years I think I learned more about Calabria and the Calabrese than I did about Magna Graecia and the Archaic Greeks. Enrico and I, from the terrace of his home in Cassano-Ionio, watched with amusement the marches of the Communist Party members through the streets. Both of us remembered how the American occupation forces cleared the plain of malaria with DDT and also financed the distribution of land to the poor, to head off the spread of communism in Calabria, and how communism became the strongest political force once the peasants had the land and little leisure to become interested in politics. He and Anna saved the Toscano landholdings by combining the individual tracts left to several different members of the family. It was the largest and most progressive agricultural operation in the province, aided by German manufacturers of farm equipment and German agricultural researchers. Enrico's commanding officer in the occupation of the Channel Islands was the father of our au pair girl in Philadelphia, and his barber in Cassano-Ionio had cut my hair in Frankfurt, as a released prisoner just after the war.

The threads running through one's life apparently interweave through time. Fred Rhinehardt, with whom I worked on Robert Murphy's staff at Allied headquarters, became the American Ambassador in Rome. He and his wife, Soli, were to join us for a picnic on the beach at Sybaris and to witness our discovery that we could so easily locate Etruscan tombs at Tarquinia with a magnetometer. He was also the one who arranged for a U.S. Air Force aerial survey of the Sybaris plain and helped to untangle constant difficulties with the Italian antiquities service in Rome. And through him I met the chairman of the board of the Ford Foundation, an archaeology enthusiast who was instrumental in arranging the large Ford grants that were to supply us with students in field research for many years. This interweaving of past and present impressed me particularly one evening at dinner with the Rhinehardts in Villa Taverna, where Senator Ernest Gruening of Alaska was one of the guests. I had not seen him for many years—not since, as governor of Alaska, he flew into Point Hope to watch our discovery of the strange Ipiutak culture found in burials on the tundra there. Later we met in the Piazza Navona in Rome to reminisce about our attempts at Soviet-American research in the Arctic twenty-five years before.

In the spring of 1962, Enrico had found Ernesto Spina, a Calabrese who was willing to ship in from Rome a heavy earth-mover, known in America as a dragline. With that and water pumps we felt sure we could excavate to the base of "the long wall" and reach the level of what our drills had shown to be the level of the Archaic Greek period, 700-500 B.C. Spina assembled his machine at the railroad station of Sibari. Then with Enrico, Jim Delmege, and me lighting his way with our car headlights, he moved it by night about two miles along the main road at a speed of one-quarter mile per hour. It was during that long night on the road that Enrico and Jim agreed to build a tourist hotel, to be known as "Bagamoio," on the beach at Sybaris. We were ready to begin digging by five in the morning and to enter into a competition with the Calabrian Antiquities Service, then attempting to reach the Archaic level below the Roman ruins at Parco del Cavallo, about one-half mile south of the long wall.

With the water pumps and the huge excavator we soon reached the base of the Roman wall to find it resting upon a

Greek wall made of well-dressed stone blocks of a type used by the Greeks of the Classical, rather than the earlier Archaic, period. Thus we knew at once that we had found a structure made after the destruction of Sybaris by the neighboring Greek colony of Croton in the sixth century B.C. If we were on the old site of Sybaris, it must lie still deeper and below the late-Greek construction. But as we dug deeper into the sand below the water-supressing band of clay, the water pressure increased until it swamped our pumps and filled our excavation almost to the surrounding surface. More efficient pumps were installed and the water was reduced so that the excavator could bail out the sludge at the bottom of the pit. Each bucket brought out many fragments of pottery and roof tiles that could be identified as Greek, and when we reached a depth of about 6 meters many of those fragments were of the Archaic (Sybaris) period. At about the same time, the Antiquities Service excavation at Parco del Cavallo also reached the Archaic level below the Roman and late-Greek levels and with their first Archaic pottery fragments they decided we should announce the discovery of Sybaris.

I was skeptical. A few potsherds do not make a city, and it seemed to me premature to rush into an announcement on Rome's evening news broadcast with nothing to show for our "discovery" but a few tiny fragments of pots. On our hair-raising drive to Cosenza to record the news statement in time for the seven o'clock news in Rome we argued the point to no avail. In flowing and excited Italian Giuseppi Foti and Tine announced the dramatic discovery of Sybaris after nearly 100 years of search, and I lamely concluded in halting and awkward Italian (rehearsed on the road) that we had found some Archaic Greek sherds and hoped we might eventually locate the famed city ruins. As I feared, the next day on the site television, radio, and newspaper crews arrived in a swarm to photograph the fabled city of Sybaris. Mud holes and a few potsherds, which meant nothing to reporters, were a shocking anticlimax.

Not long after that the Director of Antiquities in Rome accosted me at an archaeological congress in Venice to accuse me of a false announcement about the discovery. The argument grew furious and ended when I called him a son-of-a-bitch. That started a running battle with the Antiquities Service that was to plague me for years. An article that I wrote for the Illustrated London News about the search, the premature announcement that hit the world press, and the credit given to an American expedition all added fuel to the conflict. Only the intervention of Freddie Rhinehardt and the Morgan Guaranty Trust (then headed by Tom Gates, an old friend from Philadelphia) made it possible for us to continue. Also my involvement in America's securing of funding for the preservation of Abu Simbel convinced the Italian construction company, Ital Consult, that they should give me a hand with the diplomatic problems in Italy. At that time they hoped to get the contract to lift Abu Simbel on hydraulic jacks, rather than to move it as it was finally done by a German company.

On the site our problem was that we found no structures of the Archaic Period beneath the late-Greek and Roman structures in our excavations—only fragments of Archaic pottery in the liquid sand beneath those later structures. With the excavator and pumps we made three major cuts to the 7-meter level (in 1962 and 1963) with no signs of Archaic structures, not even the foundation stones of a building. Perhaps the Archaic ruins lay somewhere else on the plain or on the foothills surrounding the plain.

By that time we had learned that our proton magnetometer could not record ruins that lay deeper than 3 to 3.5 meters, and our drills raised Archaic sherds only from below the 6-meter level. Hence it was obvious that to locate structures of Sybaris in the plain we must develop a new and more effective apparatus for search at that depth.

With the financial support of Howard Pew and the Sun Oil Co. I had hoped to develop a sonic device that would penetrate to that depth, and through them worked with Varian Associates and with Petty Geophysical Co. in Texas, to build and test such equipment. At that stage, electronic technology was not sufficiently advanced to produce a successful instrument. We turned to the production of a more efficient magnetometer to be made by Varian Associates. Shelly Breiner, one of their engineers, arrived at Sybaris with a whole minibus-load of electronic gear for experimentation, primarily equipment used to measure magnetic intensity in the Heaveyside layer in outer space.

He and Beth Ralph were to spend weeks on the plain experimenting over deeply buried structures that we had located with the drills. The day they succeeded remains with me as the most exciting moment in the whole eight years of work on the plain. Shelly sat before a battery of jury-rigged recording equipment in the minibus, Beth hovered over a generator to keep it running at a steady output, one of our workmen at the end of a 200-foot cable carried a sensing device across the plain, and I waited for the sonic scream that should come from the amplifiers if the thing worked when he passed over a certain point where the deeply buried structure lay. Suddenly the scream, which could be heard for at least half a mile, was all about us. It came at just the right point, and we knew they had succeeded in their scheme for a more efficient magnetometer. That was known as a rubidium magnetometer, but by the time the instrument and the results of their tests were returned to the design engineers at Varian, cesium was substituted for rubidium in the sensing device and within the year a new cesium magnetometer was operating at Sybaris.

The Lerici Foundation also developed a more efficient

hydraulic drill, mounted on a truck. With that, and our power-driven auger drills, Franco Brancaleone and his crew were to drill over 1,500 holes to a depth far below any cultural debris, over most of the plain of Sybaris. Many thousands of sherds raised by the drills followed a systematic arrangement everywhere,—Roman potsherds down to 3 or 4 meters, late-Greek from 4 to 5 or 6 meters, and Archaic sherds below that. There was one notable exception, however, in a region about one mile north of the Roman site at the Parco del Cavallo. There Archaic sherds were found at 4 to 5 meters in depth. While Beth continued to survey hundreds of acres of the plain with her new cesium magnetometer and Franco continued to drill, we decided to try another test cut into the peculiar zone where Archaic sherds were found at a surprisingly shallow depth.

To that depth we thought we could manage a conventional dig without the excavator, utilizing only shovels and pumps. All went normally until we again passed through the clay layer into the sands below—then, as usual, the groundwater surged up under pressure to swamp all work with shovels. Enrico knew a retired engineer who had worked draining the Sybaris plain, and we decided to bring him out of retirement in Rome to solve the water problem of our dig. He tried a kind of caisson made of planks to hold back the liquid sand and water so that we could continue hand digging with shovels. That too was swamped and collapsed. He gave up and went back to retirement. But we were almost down to the known level of the Archaic sherds and I could not quit. With our best workmen, and those who would risk it, we rebuilt and braced the caisson and continued down. This was even worse than digging through the thawed muck of the trenches at Kukulik on St. Lawrence Island in the Bering Sea. At least the walls would stand there and one was not in imminent danger of being drowned in a hole.

At last we were down to the Archaic sherds and masses of roof tiles that Paola Zancani identified as of the Archaic period. Among them was one block of cut stone—the first sign of any Archaic building. Antonio was the last workman to leave the hole after we had passed through the level of sherds. In his joy with having got out alive and having finished the job, he danced about the edge until it caved in and he fell the 5 meters into the mess at the bottom. When we fished him out he was weeping and convinced his chest was crushed. I got him into the car and rushed him to the doctor in the hospital where a thorough examination was possible. But when that was over, I watched the doctor paint his whole chest with iodine and grin at me behind Antonio's back. We drove back in high spirits— Antonio completely cured of his crushed chest.

At that point it was necessary for me to return to the States again. David Ridgway, a young British archaeologist from the British School in Rome, was willing to take over and expand our excavation to see if an actual Archaic structure could be found. But both he and Paola were so horrified at the idea of digging in such a manner that I soon had a cable saying they had decided to close it down. We had struck a shallow level (40-50 cm) of Archaic sherds and roof tiles with no superimposed levels of late-Greek and Roman deposits as was normal in the area, and still were not able to conclude that we were on the site of the fabled city.

The next season was the most heartbreaking. Beth had found, with the new cesium magnetometer, a large structure lying 6 meters deep to the north and west of Parco del Cavallo at what must be the Archaic level. Apparently assured at last of finding a major structure of Archaic Sybaris, I employed a contractor to install a well-point system that could pump water from below the excavation, thus allowing us to excavate "dry" down to and below the 6-meter level. Spina and his dragline were again employed to remove the mass of earth above the

buried structure. At first all went well, but at the 4-5-meter
level the sodden walls of our huge pit began to collapse and
flow into the excavation. Pumping of course continued twenty-
four hours a day, and in spite of the flow the excavations
managed to continue down to the 6-meter level, barely staying
ahead of the inflow from collapsing walls. At last we were
ready to uncover by hand the structure so accurately located
by the magnetometer. Workmen with shovels quickly removed
the last few centimeters of earth, and then to my horror I saw
that it was a brick-and-cement structure of the Roman period.

After all those years and the expense of drills, pumps,
excavator, magnetometers, and skilled workmen, our sure
thing had turned into just another damned Roman building. I
had had enough. A long letter to Orville explained why I was
throwing in the sponge. Then a few days later a phone call
from America reached me in a bar in Rome. Lively as a cricket,
Orville, at seventy-five years of age, was not ready to quit. I
would return to the U.S. and we would plot a new course.

In Philadelphia Orville had run down a new kind of mobile
drill, which could be purchased in Italy. With that we could
rapidly drill areas where deep structures had been located and
by lifting potsherds from the surrounding debris determine the
period of their construction and outline their form. By this time
the Lerici Foundation and the Antiquities Service had
withdrawn from the joint effort, and we would go on alone.
Aerial photos made by the U.S. Air Force and also
experimental infrared sensing devices carried in the plane were
of no use to us. All structures in the plain lay too deep to be
spotted by patterns of vegetation growing over them, and
nothing came of the infrared device.

Orville, his wife, Susie, and Ann Ingersoll joined me again at
Sybaris the next year for our experiments with the new drill.
Certainly the drill was one of the most efficient machines we
had used on the site. This auger drill, lifted by hydraulic

pressure, brought up potsherds from any level, and when it struck stone or roof tiles we could detect it at once. Soon we were outlining the foundations of structures in a field about 1 kilometer north of the Parco del Cavallo at levels where only Archaic sherds appeared.

One evening, with Beth's magnetometer survey charts spread out on the floor all about me, I suddenly realized that there really was only one specific area on the whole plain of Sybaris that was magnetically "noisy." That is, in the terminology of magnetometer surveys, one specific area showed great variability in magnetic intensity while the rest of the plain was "quiet"—magnetically invariable. The magnetic "noise" was clearly due to buried archaeological structures and hence there was only one area of major settlement on the plain covering about 2 square kilometers—a reasonable area for the original city of the Sybarites. Late-Greek and Roman settlement, judging from the buried sherds, covered the southern part of this area, while ancient Sybaris covered the whole area.

With the location and delineation of major stone foundations in the older section, outside the area of later Greek and Roman settlement, and the magnetic pattern on the plain, I could then be sure that we had found the remains of the famous city that had become a symbol of luxury and decadence in our time. But the six test cuts we had made over the years and the 1,500 drill holes also indicated, beyond any reasonable doubt, that there was nothing left of the city but scattered foundations of buildings and masses of pottery fragments. Nowhere had we found debris of the city more than 1 meter thick, and it was apparent that no extensive and very expensive excavation would reveal another Pompeii. I advised Orville and the Italian government that large-scale excavations were not worth the effort and the cost.

Publicity, however, can move mountains. There had been so much in the press and on television about Sybaris after eight years of search that my negative advice was of no avail. Giuseppe Foti, Director of Antiquities in Calabria, came to Philadelphia to celebrate the discovery of Sybaris with us at The University Museum. I wrote the final paper on the search for the *American Journal of Archaeology*, and all our work there was discontinued. Then Foti wrote to say that the Italian government, using contractors and a huge well-point system of pumping, would begin the thorough excavation of the site. That continued for years at very great expense, with no significant results except to convince the more conservative diggers that this was in reality the site of the city. The dream of a new Pompeii of the Greek Archaic period in south Italy that would attract tourists from around the world did not materialize.

Orville Bullitt wrote his first book, *The Search for Sybaris*, in his late seventies and then wrote two more before his death at eighty-five. When I apologized to his children for all of his money I had spent, their reply was cheerful and unanimous, "We are delighted. You kept Pa off our necks!"

In the introduction to Orville's *Search for Sybaris* I wrote: "As a political negotiator during and after the last war, there was a time when I concluded that myth and history are indistinguishable. If consensus of opinion writes history, then myths, which have the authority of faith, must be a part of what we accept as the facts of history. Still, much of the excitement in archaeology surely lies in the discovery of hard, solid evidence that an episode in recorded history is real, in the sense that one can see and feel some remains in the earth with relate to that episode." It was that kind of excitement that spurred Orville and me to continue our search for solid evidence of myth-history after the Italians began the systematic excavation of the remains of Sybaris.

Paola Zancani-Montuoro had excavated so many bronze objects from the tombs near Francovilla, above the plain of Sybaris, and had traced so many other bronze discoveries in the general area that she was convinced there had been a major bronze industry somewhere in the region in ancient times. In the Odyssey, Ulysses refers to the bronze work of Temessa somewhere in southern Italy. Orville was pleased to finance the new quest, and I was happy to do the digging if Paola could spot a likely site. She went to work in the library of the Vatican tracing the location of the earliest bishoprics in Calabria recorded by the Church to see if she could find any reference to a place called Temessa. Some months later she wrote to say that Malvito still exists as a small hill-town in northern Calabria. Ancient Temessa should be somewhere near present Malvito. Near that town, on a mountain peak above San Sosti, there is the ruin of a chapel or sanctuary recorded on medieval maps at a site called Artemesium. In the spring I joined Paola for a look at Artemesium.

That site is one of the most picturesque locations for an archaeological dig I have seen anywhere in the world. High in the mountains, it looks down over a deep gorge that is the most obvious pass between Sybaris on the Gulf of Taranto and Paestum, its colony, on the Tyrrhenian Sea. Through that pass must have moved many pack trains of Greek goods for trade with the Etruscans, avoiding the Phoenician-controlled Straits of Messina, to create the fabled wealth of the Sybarites. It all looked good on several counts—even to rumors of an ancient copper mine nearby. Paola felt certain that some of the pottery fragments we found on the surface there were from the Iron

Age, but they were of the crude kitchenware variety, very hard to identify, and I was puzzled that we found no fragments of easily identifiable painted Greek pottery. However, I could not resist such a dramatic site, whatever it was.

For the excavation I was joined by my daughter Penelope, a classicist, Charles Hare, who joined us as surveyor, and Marianne Maskant, a Dutch archaeologist. We rented a house in San Sosti from which we could see the peak of Artemesium high above, moved in all the digging equipment from the site of Torre Mordillo, and began our daily treks up and down the mountain. The only identifiable ruins were the chapel and a stone water reservoir, but test cuts soon exposed stone walls, and at places a considerable deposit of refuse filled with potsherds. But as we went deeper and deeper there was no significant change in types of pottery, and all of it was crude kitchenware that looked to me like the nondescript medieval ware found at so many sites in Italy. My method of large-scale digging with a crew of workmen deployed in several test cuts was something of a trial to the Dutch archaeologist trained in the more meticulous digging of her generation, but with a target like Temessa, we could not settle down to years of digging a medieval site. With mules, Charles Hare and I roamed over the neighboring mountains in search of the rumored copper mine and could only find where two German engineers had dug in an earlier search for the hypothetical mine.

After some weeks I was convinced we were not going to find an ancient level at Artemesium (confirmed by later radiocarbon dates for the deepest levels as medieval) and that digging should be discontinued. But before abandoning the site I urged Orville and Susie to fly over from Philadelphia to see what we were up to. Because they were then in their late seventies, I was a bit worried about the long steep climb for them from the end of the road far up to the peak. Susie was an experienced horseback rider, but Orville was definitely not of the fox-hunting set. We mounted Susie on a reasonably good horse, which I had been using, and Orville on a burro. They made it up the precipitous foot track without too much trouble, but neither of them would ride down again. The descent on foot was difficult even for youngsters, and upon their arrival back at base camp almost too tired to eat lunch, all of us were filled with admiration.

That descent from the mountain very nearly ended in tragedy just before we abandoned the site and after the Bullitts had returned to Philadelphia. Paola had Dennis Haynes, an English professor of classical archaeology, and his wife visiting with her in Calabria and brought them up to San Sosti to see our excavation. They drove up to the end of the road and to our base camp on a shoulder of the peak in a Volkswagen, where they parked at the edge of a cliff that dropped several hundred feet straight down. After their climb up to the peak and our farewells, the three of them climbed into the Volkswagen for their return to San Sosti. But in turning Professor Haynes must have put the car in forward gear when he thought it was in reverse, and shot straight over the edge of the cliff. We all thought they were finished. But when we rushed to look over the edge, there was the car, upright on its wheels, standing undamaged on a ledge of rock. They were not even badly shaken up. I remembered that a road-grading machine was at work on the road some distance below and arranged with the operator to bring it up to cut a ramp on the face of the cliff down to the stranded car. Paola and the Hayneses sat quietly in the car until the ramp was finished and then drove back up on to the road as right as rain.

Undaunted by our failures to find Temessa, Orville persisted
in financing my search for the hard, material evidence of the
myth-history of ancient Europe. His long-standing ties with
France and his fluent command of French led us into
magnetometer searches at Vix, in Burgundy, where the famous
huge bronze krater had been found in a fifth century B.C.
tomb (we did find a second rich tomb), to the south of France
at sites thought to be Greek, along the Channel coast, and to
Aleria in Corsica where a rich Etruscan cemetery was known.
We had some success at several sites, but I found that
archaeological collaboration with the French was impossible.
As in most of Europe there are now many more archaeologists
than there are promising archaeological sites to be explored,
and competition is bitter.

Some years ago, after I had retired from The University
Museum and was working with the Nature Conservancy in
Washington, Orville, then in his eighties, phoned to say that he
was not too old to finance more digs, and proposed that I take
over the search for a Phoenician settlement believed to lie near
or beneath the Roman ruins at Lixus on the Atlantic coast of
Morocco. He was then on his third book, and was compiling all
ancient accounts of the Phoenicians and Etruscans. The new
ground-radar sensing device (developed by Bruce Bevan of
MASCA) proved to be a great success in locating deep,
superimposed levels of occupation at Lixus. However, I could
not work out a long-range plan for excavation with the
Moroccan Antiquities Service.

In the conclusion to his book *Search for Sybaris*, Orville
wrote: "One lovely day I was standing watching the work. The
sea and sun were at my back with the rugged mountains rising
in the distance through a faint haze across the plain. This was
the same beautiful scene that had brought the Greeks to this
spot so many hundreds of years ago, and thoughts of the past
kept recurring. These silent fields had been the setting where

there had been life and activity, slavery, riches and decadence, and the site of the largest Greek city of its time. The life and culture of these people were to influence the western world for countless ages, although here they had disappeared and, until now, had left no trace of themselves or their very existence."

Nearly 100 years ago a banker and a professor of divinity, excited by recent archaeological discoveries near Mosul in Iraq, inspired the foundation of The University Museum. With atomic-nuclear sensing devices undreamed of at that time, a banker and a professor of anthropology-archaeology found the same excitement probing the earth in Italy, France, and Morocco searching for the reality of myth-history. Now I wonder just how much of the world view of those nineteenth-century thinkers had been carried on by the two of us speculating on the nature of history in the late twentieth century? Would they anticipate the decline of Western political and economic domination throughout the world in the next century, and did they have any inkling of what science and technology would do to our theories about the universe?

Surely they too must have pondered the meaning of the lost worlds of ancient civilization rediscovered in the earth and the implications for the future of our own. But theirs must have been a much more solid, substantial universe, based on a hard core of indivisible atoms, with God in His heaven and all well with the earth. Science would achieve wonders—but not pull the rug out from under them. For Orville and me, who had watched our world pass from horse-power to atomic energy, a human population increase from two to four or five billion, and the universe dissolve into a mysterious balance of energies, there was something nostalgic about the discovery of hard evidence for the mythical city of the Sybarites—rational, logical Greeks who, probably, thought about the nature of their world much as did the two nineteenth-century founders of The University Museum.

Perhaps the search for that solid, substantial earth and heaven we have lost so recently is a half-conscious drive for the many thoughtful people who take to digging in the earth for reassurance.

The author holding pet gibbon surrounded by children in the
village of Ban Chiang, Thailand, 1974.
Photograph courtesy of the Ban Chiang Project of The University Museum.

CHAPTER TEN

The Far East

In northeastern Thailand near the Laos border there is a town called Ban Chiang, established by immigrant Laotians about 200 years ago. In 1973, accompanied by my wife, Marina, and Nikom Sutiragsa of the Thai Fine Arts Department, I watched scores of the Ban Chiang villagers digging under their pile-supported houses in a kind of do-it-yourself archaeology that reminded me of the organized Eskimo women diggers at Point Hope, Alaska. It is against the law in Thailand to loot archaeological sites, but I noticed uniformed policemen watching the operations, almost as interested as I. The prize was pottery, painted with red and white or buff curvilinear designs that were reminiscent of ancient Yangshao pottery from China.

Nikom had done some systematic digging at the site for the Fine Arts Department and was very popular with the local people. At house after house we climbed up a ladder to the verandah, took off our shoes, and while waiting for tea, examined our hosts' recent, unsold collections of pottery, bronze, iron, stone, and bone objects. Many of the less decorated pots were left under the houses to hold water and grain for the chickens—pots now worth several thousand dollars apiece. When we declined to buy anything, our hosts usually presented us with all kinds of objects (now in the Thai Museum) including some handsome painted pots that Marina hated to part with.

Thanks to the behavior of atomic particles in mysterious instruments, developed since the first atomic explosion, I knew, sitting there in a Thai village surrounded by rice paddies and water buffalo, that some of those pots were at least 6,000 years old and that they would soon become not only rare collectors' items but the symbol of a revolutionary discovery in the record of human history. Looking down into the pits excavated by Nikom and other Thai archaeologists near the central village wat (temple), I could see uncovered burials with pottery and bronze and iron objects lying in place as found with the skeletons. They lay at different levels in the earth and with closer examination it was clear that iron objects were found with the upper burials and bronze objects with the lower. Here were represented both the Iron and the Bronze Age in man's history, but at that stage almost no one was willing to accept the idea that a complex technique of metallurgy had existed in the Far East as early as, and probably much earlier than, metal manufacture in the Near East—generally agreed to be the cradle of civilization.

The crux of the matter lay in a technique for dating pottery by thermoluminescence that, at that time, was being developed by MASCA in Philadelphia and the Archaeological Laboratory at Oxford. At Oxford they were more interested in the theory of the technique, probably because a number of graduate students there were working out doctoral theses in the lab, while in Philadelphia we were more interested in empirical experiments developing a practical application for dating in archaeology. Mark Han, a chemist, Beth Ralph, and Bill Stevens, head of the Physics Department at the University of Pennsylvania, finally succeeded and published the first account of the method for archaeology in *Nature* about 1965. In 1968 Bill Kohler, a volunteer worker in the Museum, brought to us from Thailand fragments of pottery from Ban Chiang in a collection made by Princess Chumpot. Lisa Lyons, of the Ford Foundation in Thailand, wrote to tell me about the site, with the information that pottery there was found with bronze tools. From the first, she recognized the importance of the site and urged us to do something about it. But it was not until Mark Han gave me his thermoluminescence dates for the Ban Chiang sherds that I became very much interested. Some of those dates were as early as the fifth millennium B.C., others in the fourth.

In late 1971 and 1972 new constructions in Ban Chiang produced a large number of painted pots, and collectors began to move in with devastating results. None of my colleagues in professional archaeology were willing to accept the possibility that bronze was made in the Far East as early as the fifth or fourth millennium B.C., but my own experience by that time had convinced me that anything was possible, and after years of experiment with the new thermoluminescence dating technique I had much more confidence than most. Once on the site I had no serious doubts at all about a very ancient Bronze Age in Thailand—the question was how to prove it.

George Dales and Ben Bronson of The University Museum had excavated a mound in Thailand a few years before my visit there, and I was pleased to learn from Captain Sompop, Director General of the Thai Department of Fine Arts, that they had made a very good impression. Unlike many Europeans with a colonial tradition, they had accepted Thai archaeologists as equally professional in the field and as colleagues equivalent to those in the West. There had been proposals for an international dig at Ban Chiang organized through the United Nations, but Sompop much preferred to work with The University Museum alone and with Lisa Lyons, an old hand in Thailand, popular with everyone in the Fine Arts Department. It was therefore easy to arrange for a long-term Thai-University Museum excavation in northeastern Thailand. She also told me of Chet Gorman, an American who had excavated Spirit Cave, discovered Non Nok Tha, and discovered and excavated other sites in Thailand over a period of years. George and Ben were then engaged at other sites in Pakistan and Java, and we needed an experienced person, known to the Thai, to direct the work at Ban Chiang. Chet was then somewhere up near the Burma border, three days' walk from the nearest road. With great misgivings I was prepared to walk in to find him when by good luck he happened to walk out, so that I could meet him in Bangkok. In spite of the huge red beard (Lisa had written, "Can't you ever find an archaeologist without a beard, which the Thai don't like!"), Chet was obviously the man.

Chet's opposite number for the direction of the Ban Chiang dig was Pisit Charoenwongsa, of the Thai Department of Fine Arts, a young man with great ability, good sense, and quiet dignity for whom I soon developed a profound respect. Chet's appointment in the Museum and the University of Pennsylvania was achieved, and arrangements were made for a full season at Ban Chiang in 1974.

During the dry season we were back in Bangkok with Chet, Pisit, and Lisa to prepare and initiate the first season of digging. It is a long drive of several hours from Bangkok to Udorn, where there was then a very large U.S. Air Force base supporting B-52's, which flew out each day to bomb the Viet Cong in Viet Nam, Cambodia, and Laos, and another hour's drive to Ban Chiang. There was also considerable guerilla fighting along Thailand's northern border, mixed up with the normal banditry associated with smuggling. It was said that

Nationalist Chinese troops, relicts of Chiang Kai-shek's army, who controlled the smugglers' trade, were fighting Thai army patrols along the border. It was not clear who was actually engaged, but, of course, in the American press all irregulars fighting the Thai were communists. In any case travel at night in northern Thailand was discouraged at that time, and because we were long delayed in a beer-fueled discussion with a group of Australian archaeologists along the road, we entered the unsettled zone long after dark. Pisit, carrying all the Thai funds for the dig in cash, was worried. Chet explained that there was nothing to worry about, he was armed, and pulled out of the glove compartment a tiny automatic pistol. Marina and I had our quiet laugh in the back seat of the Land Rover, thinking of armored cars, tanks, and automatic rifles used by modern bandits in Southeast Asia. In Ban Chiang the next day I watched a jeep unload a group of young men, not in uniform, but with automatic rifles, and wondered just who they were.

By 1974 there was so much native digging going on under each pile-supported house, with steeply rising prices for the painted pots, that it was difficult to find an undisturbed area for a controlled, systematic excavation. But Pisit, having the authority of the Thai government, the first season to appropriate a village side and back yard and the second season (1975) he to close off a street and lay out a small area where there was no previous digging. Arrangements with the village authorities took time, and while we waited, a Japanese archaeologist arrived in Ban Chiang with a proposal that the Japanese join the Thai and the Americans for the excavation. All of us were polite, and I stalled off the persistent man by saying that such a plan of course must be approved by the Department of Fine Arts. Later in Bangkok, before returning to the U.S., Captain Sompop gave us a farewell dinner, and after liberal doses of the infamous Mekong whiskey, I commented that remembering the Second World War I did not believe that

Thai, Japanese, and Americans could work very happily together at Ban Chiang. Sompop thought for a moment, then grinned mischievously and said, "That's all right, I'll give the Japanese a site on the River Kwai." And he did.

Working with the Thai, after my attempts to work with the French, was a tremendous relief. They seemed to me relaxed, confident, sophisticated people—no chip on their shoulders—with whom I could joke, laugh, and kid just as I had with the Danes for so many years. Thailand was never a colony, and that must make all the difference. It was good to be back in Thailand after almost twenty years and to remember the conversations with Western-educated young Thai at Jimmy Thompson's house in Bangkok. Then they had us all in stitches describing the antics of thousands of Americans in "The Golden Ghetto" who were supposed to look after the massive economic and military aid then being poured into their country. And it was a joy to read the English edition of Thai newspapers. They contained a wider coverage of international news then The New York Times and editorial comment that nearly always put a finger on life's human comedy.

The young Thai and American archaeologists worked well together in a highly meticulous excavation of that first broad cut into the Ban Chiang mound, seeking to determine the various layers of occupation, the nature of the burial deposits, and material for radiocarbon dating that could prove the great age of metalworking in Southeast Asia. As a survivor of earlier generations of diggers, I could appreciate the need for very careful excavation, but worried about the scale of digging. After all, what could one sizable pit tell you about a low mound in the rice paddies that was a kilometer in diameter and 3 or 4 meters deep? There must have been thousands of burials in that mound alone, judging from the native digging all over the place, and I had seen four other similar villages on similar mounds also producing masses of pots and metal objects. The Thai assured us that there were scores of such deposits in northeastern Thailand. We could find the evidence to convince all the skeptical diggers in the West about the age of bronze, but I think it will take many years of digging by many expeditions to understand just what went on in Thailand, and all of Southeast Asia, so long ago—and only if all those remains are not destroyed to supply the collectors' market.

From earlier Thai excavations and the pit being excavated in 1974, I could conclude that some unknown people with remarkably advanced technology had lived on that site in pile dwellings, burying their dead beneath the houses, probably for several thousand years. The place was then abandoned for centuries to be reoccupied by immigrant Laotians in recent times. Moreover, it was obvious that at least some of the people buried there were not of the same race as the people of Southeast Asia today. Among the hundreds of burials I have excavated myself in different parts of the world, I had never seen one skeleton as large as some of those exposed by the Thai dig. In a region of relatively small, light-boned people of today, those skeletons were startling. Could these be some relatives to the tall, big-boned people of northern China?

Like Malaysia, Thailand has been famous for tin production since at least the tenth century A.D. Both tin and copper, the constituents of bronze, are found there in quantity and at depths accessible to ancient men. In southern Thailand, at a tin and lead-smelting plant where I went to arrange for analysis of the bronze tools and ornaments from the Ban Chiang excavations, I found that they were trucking many tons of ancient slag from deposits in northern Thailand, primarily to recover lead remaining in the slag after the ancient extraction of tin. This again, like the number of bronze-producing sites in the north, and the astonishing number of metal objects found in them, convinced me that we had stumbled onto an ancient bronze industry of unknown age and magnitude, which might well turn out to be the region of origin for metalworking. Eventually it may solve the riddle as to where the tin came from that supplied that alloy for copper-tin bronze in the Near East.

With a wholly new look at the ancient history of the Far East (Prince Dhani, in Bangkok in 1957, had expressed to me the familiar and universal view that civilization began there with the introduction of Buddhism and Hinduism not long before the birth of Christ), I got in touch with the men at the Texaco Oil Co. headquarters in New York to see if they might wish to finance a long-term archaeological research plan in Southeast Asia for The University Museum. That company had discovered the oil field in Sumatra just before the Second World War and were drilling the first well when the Japanese took over. By a curious twist of fate the field was just beginning to produce when the Japanese were chased out, and Texaco went back to reap the profits on the Japanese investment. And by 1973 the Americans were selling most of the Sumatra oil to the Japanese. The Texaco men were amused to learn that I had worked for their company selling kerosene to Chinese traders in the Philippines forty-three years before and introduced me about the office as an old hand for Texaco in the Far East. They were interested, very much, at what was turning up out there. Caltex, the international company then operating the Sumatran field and refineries, had an Indonesian manager in Jakarta who would make the final decision. It was decided that I should see him there after investigating the Ban Chiang site in the winter of 1973.

Ben Bronson was then working with Indonesian archaeologists in the exploration of sites in Java, and so The University Museum was already known to the Indonesian diggers. The Caltex manager turned out to be an archaeological enthusiast himself and was pleased to back up the wishes of the New York office. But for Caltex to make a contribution of perhaps one million dollars to such a research project they would need the approval of the Indonesian National Oil Consortium. A meeting with the general in charge of the National Company was necessary but could not be set up at once. In the meantime, Caltex arranged for us to fly in a company plane from Jakarta to their headquarters in Sumatra, where the local manager would organize an expedition into the jungle to explore the ruins of a temple that had been reported.

I had been in Sumatra briefly more than forty years earlier, but I was not prepared for the astonishing contrast between Java and Sumatra that struck me as we flew over the island: Java, one of the most densely settled lands anywhere in the world, and Sumatra (at least the northern part) a very sparsely settled jungle where tigers were still supposed to be a threat to oil company explorers and where strange little hunters of the Stone Age still occupied the forests. At first, in the ultramodern headquarters of the oil men, resembling a suburban town in America, it was difficult to realize our surroundings. But at night on the screened verandah of the guest house facing a dense jungle we could actually hear the call of tigers in the bush.

The manager, perhaps pulling my leg with a tall Texas story, told me that one of the American wives, known to be something of a tippler, particularly on Saturday nights, had raised the whole town with cries that a tiger was in her bedroom. After two Saturday night alarms, most of the town was convinced it was probably just the whiskey. But the next week one was finally found there chasing one of her pet poodles.

Tiger stories were my favorite. A handsome skin was brought out to prove one of the stories that later appeared in a book of poetry written by Loren Eiseley after I had recounted the tale to him in Philadelphia. An oil-prospecting team in camp in the jungle were playing poker around a table in one of the tents when a tiger strolled in, selected one of the men, and killed him. True or not, the tale is now immortalized:

> While the oil drillers in their tent played deuces wild
> There at a table by the Coleman lamp, a tiger softly padding
> Came to the door, stepped in and circled gently
> The entire party in a stricken hush, chose one man at the door
> And took him out, away, bones, flesh and all...
>   the one who died we found
> His cards spilled on the table there, he held the worst,
>   the poorest hand.
>
>   From the "Innocent Assassins"
>   by Loren Eiseley, 1973.

Our expedition into the jungle was led by a Sumatran whose favorite expression was "pas de problem." But there were some problems. He himself got lost in the jungle only a few yards from our calvalcade of jeeps. In every village we passed there were police or soldiers who said it was forbidden to pass there into the jungle. Our leader solved those problems by inviting the police to come along. We were soon escorted by several jeeploads of them. They made short work of our ample supply of sandwiches and drinks. We did eventually find the ruins of a temple by a broad river deep in a jungle as wild as the southern part of Borneo. It was no Angkor Wat, but any temple in such a wilderness excites a sense of the mysterious. I was reminded of those unknown temples in the Peten of Guatemala discovered by oil prospectors while we worked at Tikal, and as before in Southeast Asia, pondered the curious resemblance between lost jungle civilizations in Asia and America. Those in America are, of course, generally much older, and so far as we know now there is no historical connection. But how does it happen that men separated by thousands of miles of ocean and centuries in time created such similar records of their passing? The site was, in any case, worth investigation by Ben and his Indonesian colleagues in their search of northern Sumatra for remains of the Srivijaya kingdom based in Palembang about the eleventh century A.D.

The general in charge of Indonesian oil production was away when we returned to Jakarta so that no decision could be reached about Caltex support for our research in Southeast Asia. Correspondence with the office in New York continued, and we returned for further meetings in Jakarta in 1974 after the beginning of excavations at Ban Chiang. But when we landed at the airport in Jakarta we found to our utter surprise that there seemed to be no way of reaching the city from the airport. It was jammed with people who told us that a riot or revolution was taking place in the city; no taxi or bus would risk the drive. Cars were burning in the streets, mobs were everywhere, and the army was trying to take control with tanks. Later we learned that all this was sparked off by the visit of Tanaka, the Japanese Prime Minister, in protest to Japanese economic and financial domination of Indonesian industry. I found that Marina seemed to enjoy the revolutions, after her experience in Paris during the riots of the 1960s, but I, having had many experiences with mobs and revolutions in Guatemala, Ecuador, and Iran, dreaded another involvement in the madness of uncontrolled mobs (for example, being trapped in the office of the Minister of Finance in Quito by a mob of Indians armed with machetes).

We managed to find a man with an Australian-made taxi who was willing to risk the journey, at a bandit's fee, because he thought the mob was burning only Japanese-built vehicles.

The lonely journey along streets lined by troops, tanks, and armored cars, as well as blazing vehicles, went well enough until we nearly reached our hotel. Then we were surrounded by a screaming crowd of people who tried to overturn our taxi. Gunfire dispersed them, and we swung into the hotel drive parallel to a crowd racing away from a burning Chinese nightclub just across the street. Inside the hotel we found the lobby filled with soldiers and wounded civilians brought in for shelter. The young Dutch manager of the hotel, who remembered us from the previous visit, was helpful but wild-eyed and urged us to wait in the bar until a room could be found for us. In such an affair I felt easier being besieged in the bar with American oil men and Indonesian troops than somewhere out there in the streets at the mercy of madness, but it was difficult to suppress Marina, who wanted to go out to see what was happening.

Nothing could be done in the city during the next several days until the troubles were sorted out, but after two days, with the army in control, it was possible to fly out to Bali for the cooling-off period. It is an island I had wanted to visit for many years, ever since reading of the surviving Hindu culture there in graduate anthropology studies at Yale, and listening to Kennedy and my classmates talking of his research in Bali as well as several other islands in Indonesia. It was no disappointment. In spite of the swarms of tourists and hippies, the strength of Balinese society survives in its wonderfully colorful and forested hills. It is encouraging that some few traditional societies can survive the leveling and depressing shock of Western technological society. One wonders if these are the ones that will outlive the present world-dominating system we call Western civilization.

Back in Jakarta the grant from Caltex still could not be resolved. I did not know at the time that the general was in serious trouble with a number of banks around the world and that a crisis was brewing in the Indonesian oil-supported economy. That was to become clear only in 1975 when we returned to Java for a third time to find my old friend from Libya, David Newsome, the U.S. Ambassador in Jakarta. It was like old times to stay with David and Jean at the residence and to have David again involved in negotiations with oil companies, fund raising for University Museum research projects. Meetings with the general were repeatedly postponed, and after ten days I was ready to admit defeat. Sometime later we learned that the general had decided that $1 million for archaeological research in Indonesia should not go to the Americans but to Indonesian diggers. With what is now happening in the world it was no surprise, but still there was a feeling of chagrin after three trips to Indonesia and more than two years of negotiations.

In the meantime the first season had been completed at Ban Chiang and the site was becoming internationally famous among antique dealers and collectors. Through them, Bill Honan, editor of *The New York Times Magazine*, heard of our excavations there, then called me at The University Museum to say that he was writing an article about the trade in Ban Chiang pots. We had some radiocarbon dates from charcoal found during the first season, but the samples were small, limited in number, and not sufficient for reliable dating. Still they did tend to confirm the thermoluminescence dating, and I decided to give Honan the whole story as we saw it then rather than have a lot of misinformation published in the *Times*. When his article, called the "Case of the Hot Pots," was published in June 1975, even archaeologists on our own staff at The University Museum, like Jim Muhly, wrote letters to the Times disclaiming my conclusions about the age of bronze in the Far East, and Bob Madden at the University of Pennsylvania advised the president that I was endangering the reputation of the University. Both have now been won around. But traditions die hard. Most archaeologists now accept the revolutionary idea that metalwork is very ancient in Thailand and may be older than in the Near East, but still reserve judgment on the place of origin. There are now claims for the most ancient metallurgy in Southeast Europe as well, and a tendency to increase the age of metal in the traditional "cradle of civilization."

The *New York Times* story precipitated a spate of articles in the mass media such as the Washington Post, Newsweek, and Time magazine. Joe Alsop, who had done a book on the Bronze Age in the Mediterranean, and was for a time one of the Board of Managers at The University Museum, did a lengthy story for the Washington Post and told me that he had more response from that story than any of his controversial political stories written over many years.

The worldwide interest in what was turning up in Thailand meant to me that Southeast Asia would soon become the most significant theater in the world for archaeological research. Moreover, it was still an area in which Western archaeologists were welcome if they took a sensible view of the shifting emphasis on leadership and influence from West to East. With the future in mind, Marina and I visited Malaysia and Borneo in 1974 after seeing the first season of work at Ban Chiang well underway. In both countries we found leading diggers well aware of what was turning up in Thailand and the refreshing way in which The University Museum was going about collaboration with the Department of Fine Arts there. Also, they knew that the Ford Foundation in Bangkok, thanks to Liza Lyons, was backing the research and was interested in supporting such research in other countries in that part of the world. Liza's job as the head of cultural affairs for the foundation's activities in all Southeast Asia gave her the opportunity to create a whole new epoch of archaeological collaboration there, a system by which young people from Thailand, Malaysia, Borneo, Burma, Cambodia, Vietnam, Indonesia, and the Philippines could be trained at The University Museum and the University of Pennsylvania, as well as at excavations in Thailand and other countries in the region.

Many years before I had reported upon some very remarkable discoveries at Niah Cave in northern Borneo and had sent one of our curators there to work with British archaeologists. He was one of those rare curators at the Museum who did not like field research, and nothing came of it. The cave still produces the gelatinous birds' nests for gourmet Chinese soup as well as guano, much prized for fertilizer. It has been occupied by men for many thousands of years. Burials in the cave indicate that the ancient Chinese were there presumably to collect the famous birds' nests as they do today.

In Kuching in Sarawak (now east Malaysia) we met Chinese and Malaysian archaeologists at the famed museum where Wallace had independently hit upon the theory of biological evolution made famous by Charles Darwin. As one would expect, the museum was much like late-nineteenth century natural history museums in England and, like Kuching itself, had an indelible stamp of the British Brooks family, rajahs of Sarawak for so many years. Nancy Grace, from Philadelphia, who had gone up the Nile with Kelly Simpson and me during the Nubian salvage campaign, joined us in Singapore for the trip to Borneo and went with us to Niah Cave.

On the long drive to the river where we could get a boat to travel inland, I understood for the first time just what worries so many environmentalists. For many miles we passed through vast areas of tropical forest being cut down for oil palm plantations as well as newly planted areas. This, with the insatiable demand for lumber, is clearly destroying one of the world's great tropical forests, as in Southeast Asia, Africa, and Central America. Just what happens to that land, and to the world's weather, is anyone's guess, but there is no doubt that we are losing many species of plants and animals each year because of the destruction of specialized environments. For me these excursions in East Asia, more than forty-five years after my travels there, were another revelation for my comprehension of what had happened so rapidly around the world in just one lifetime, a period so brief, as an archaeologist thinks of time, that it seems almost instantaneous. The colonial system is gone, East Asia is rapidly coming to dominate the trade in manufactured goods, population has increased enormously producing a pressure on the environment that even outstrips that in the West, and the focus of dominant human activity appears to be shifting in that direction. It is said that if you plot the lines of the earth's magnetic declination they will curve toward the centers of dense human population. Is there some unknown electromagnetic field that also shifts human energy concentrations from one region to another as the centuries pass?

At least for an afternoon going up the river to Niah Cave, and a day exploring that fantastic cavern in limestone hills, in a dense forest, time played no tricks on me. It seemed unchanged since Stone Age men had lived in the vast entrance chamber, or since the ancient Chinese had discovered those birds' nests. Probably none of them had constructed a raised plank walkway for the two miles between the cave and the river that the guano packers now use to bring out their bags of the fertilizer, but they must have had some sort of construction of logs to cross all those swamps and ponds. Nancy was so excited she walked all the way in during the evening and again with us the next day. The archaeological service in Kuching had an old, delapidated hut on the river where we spent the night sleeping on floor mats. A native woman fed us on the famous birds' nest soup and a jungle chicken, and all went well except for the "facilities," built on piles over the river with the usual large hole in the floor. But the river had recently flooded, the floor was covered with the most slippery mud I had ever encountered, and after my hair-raising experiment the women decided to use the kitchen.

In Brunei, where the Sultan with a great admiration for Winston Churchill had built an extraordinary museum of Churchill memorabilia, we looked over archaeological sites with the national archaeologists. But I was most impressed with the collection of ancient bronze cannons. Perhaps that is what gave this tiny, independent, oil-rich state its medieval flavor, at least for me. Like Kuching, Brunei is the cutting edge of the modern population explosion with its new technology moving rapidly into the primeval jungles of the island. Probably Nancy does not think of it in quite the same way. She remained in Borneo to travel inland, upriver, with a group of primitives to their settlement still in unmolested jungle. Her account of the aboriginal life in the river villages, and the swamping of her boat on the return trip, did not sound as if the ancient way will soon disappear. Marina and I wondered just what happened to her box with her two wigs, carried everywhere, when she spent the night up to her ears in the river clinging to the swampy bank until rescued by another river boat.

In Thailand the second season of digging at Ban Chiang was completed in 1975, with a second large pit excavated to the base of the deposit. Chet and Pisit then shipped to The University Museum in Philadelphia eighteen tons of pottery, metal, stone, and other materials from the two cuts. With students and many volunteers, work on the collections would continue for at least three years until the whole collection was returned to the Fine Arts Department in Thailand. More adequate radiocarbon analysis confirmed a date of at least 3600 B.C. for the manufacture of bronze at the site. Their meticulous excavation and the painstaking study of the materials, together with C-14 dating, has convinced most of the doubting professionals of the reality of an astonishingly early metal technology in East Asia. However, I remain somewhat skeptical about conclusions based on so small a section of the vast deposit at Ban Chiang that has been riddled with native diggers. Even the two pits, close together near the center of the site, showed a different stratigraphy and somewhat different materials. There is no reason to suppose that they hit the oldest deposits there or that an area 1 kilometer in diameter would be homogeneous throughout. Judging by the amount of bronze and the advanced casting techniques represented in the oldest deposits found in two seasons, I would expect that the age of bronze there, or somewhere in northeast Thailand, will turn out to be older than now agreed. Additional digging at Ban Chiang is expected to continue and, we hope, at some of the many other related sites in the region.

These recent tours in the Far East create for me a provocative idea that archaeology will follow a shift in the center of human vitality. Archaeology as we know it began in Western Europe in the nineteenth century at the height of European influence throughout the world. Theories of human history originating there or from excavations by Westerners in other parts of the world still dominate our ideas about world history. What happens as vitality shifts to the East? Perhaps the discoveries at Ban Chiang are only a signal of what will happen to man's future theories about his past.

"What in the World" broadcast in the 1950s; Schulyer Caaman, Sir
Mortimer Wheeler (who hosted the BBC version of the show)
and Wiltman Krogman.
Photograph courtesy of The University Museum Archives.

PART IV

Speculations on the Nature of Archaeology

Experimenting with balloon aerial photography at Jim Pritchard's
excavations at Sarepta in Lebanon in 1972.
Photograph courtesy of the author.

CHAPTER ELEVEN
Science and Archaeology

One morning in what was then called the Brazilian Coffee Shop in The University Museum, Loren Eiseley and I, in one of our frequent discussions about anthropology, history, and the present state of affairs, cooked up the idea of a science center for archaeology.

I was at that time chairman of a science planning board, appointed by the National Science Foundation, to mastermind a Science Exhibition at the Seattle World's Fair. Loren was increasingly interested in the history of science and technology.

Frequent meeting with the planning board over a period of two years had left me more than ever impressed with the impact of technology on the present generation and the probable effect on the next. Loren, who had become an international literary figure after the publication of his *Immense Journey* and subsequent books concerned not only with the past but with the present and the future, was also speculating about that unpredictable impact. We agreed that the new technology probably would have a profound effect on

[251]

archaeological digs just as it had on so many fields of research. In terms of technological spinoff from pure scientific research everyone thinks of jet aircraft, atomic energy, space travel, electronic communications, and a host of chemical and mechanical applications that have totally reorganized everyday life in one generation, but many of us are still more impressed with the new tools for research. These tools, derived from atomic-nuclear studies, surely have altered our whole concept of the nature of the universe we live in.

For years Loren and I taught a class in the University, together, in a kind of pedagogical experiment. It was basically speculation on the study of history and became a rambling dialogue, with the participation of the students, that was never the same in any two years. We never did manage the course outline required by the department nor did we write the book that Loren continually proposed. I did not see how I could possibly collaborate with a skilled and famous writer like Loren. In any case we were both deeply involved as anthropologists and archaeologists in thinking about the force of technology in the course of history and that led naturally to the Museum Applied Science Center in Archaeology (MASCA).

Unfortunately, Loren accepted the job as Provost of the University, about that time, and was so occupied as the fall-guy for University administration that he was unable to join me in the active organization and operation of MASCA. His administrative worries, however, did not entirely interrupt our continuing discussions, and during his term he was able to transfer the Department of Anthropology to The University Museum with offices in the old Widener amphitheater, so that he and all the other anthropologists became physically as well as officially a part of the institution. Moreover, he became the Professor of the History of Science as well as Curator of Early Man. With our offices in the same building, our teaching experiment, and a strong friendship that began at the

American Museum in New York shortly after we had left school, it was natural that so much of my direction of the Museum should be influenced by Loren's ideas.

The National Science Foundation financed the major costs of MASCA, under my direction, for the next fifteen years. Gaylord Harnwell, the physicist who became president of the University in the early 1950s, had managed to set up a radiocarbon laboratory in the Museum very soon after Willard (Bill) Libby had convinced us that the new system of archaeological dating would work (about 1951), so that we already had the nucleus of a center in the Museum. It was operated by Elizabeth Ralph, a physicist selected for the job by Gaylord from his physics department. That had also been financed, in part, by the National Science Foundation, and after two years of discouraging troubles in getting it to function (the first station to be set up after Libby's original station in Chicago) it finally functioned. Beth Ralph was then not only dating archaeological sites being excavated by the Museum but, with Gaylord and Bill Stevens, working on the development of the technique to obtain more accuracy and to discover the cause of many uncertainties in the system. I then learned how the physical scientists, like archaeologists, seek the greatest probability rather than absolute facts—something that continually eludes all of us.

In England, sometime in the early 1950s, I had run across Professor Case, at Oxford, who was utilizing a conductivity meter to locate buried earthworks at archaeological sites near Oxford. He had borrowed the technique from engineers, who used it to find sand and gravel deposits for road building. His success with this electronic instrument for measuring the conductivity, or resistance, in subsoils reminded me of Paul Fejos, at the Wenner-Gren foundation in New York, who had tried to interest American archaeologists in the technique, without success, a few years before. Also I remembered Professor Joesting, at the University of Alaska, using such equipment in search of gold-bearing deposits, just before the war.

Back in the United States, while we were recording a "What in the World" TV program with Mat Stirling as a guest, I found that Mat was spoiling for something to do (he had just then retired from the Smithsonian Institution), and we hit upon the idea of trying resistance apparatus at an Olmec site in Mexico. I found such an instrument, made by a company in Minnesota, bought the thing sight unseen, and arranged to meet Mat and his son Matthew in Mexico City after my return from Tikal that year.

Mat decided that Cerro de las Mesas was a good place to experiment. He had excavated part of the site fourteen or fifteen years earlier; it was on an old flood plain with deep deposits, and there were many earth-built mounds that could be tested for archaeological remains. Mat had driven his car down from the U.S., and with it we were able to visit a number of sites in eastern Mexico bordering on the Gulf Coast. This was my first exploration of the Olmec country with a specialist in the field who could bring alive that strange Maya-like civilization that had preceded the Maya by several centuries, produced the first glyphs in the Americas, so far as we know, and left to us their mysterious stone carvings, some of which are huge heads that look like Africans in football helmets. Radiocarbon was then giving us dates of some 1200 years B.C. for the early Olmec sites.

Luckily, young Matthew was a hi-fi buff and understood something about electronic instruments. Under his management we soon had the instrument operating at Cerro de las Mesas. Four metal pins, connected by wires, were driven into the ground in line 2 meters apart and then connected by cable to a small box containing the recording apparatus and the battery. With the punch of a button, a current was passed through the metal pins, and this gave us a digital reading of the electrical resistance in the ground, presumably to a depth measured by the distance between the pins. The pins were then moved forward along a measured line so that we could record the variability in resistance on a graph. Then a series of parallel lines were run until we had a sizable grid recording greater and less resistance over an area of a few hundred square meters.

Our first "hit" was a spot of very high resistance, relative to the surrounding area, that was in a likely looking section of the site. Excavation, carried out by our Mexican workmen, who were all graverobbers selling antiques to the trade, very quickly exposed a stone monument. It was a long rectangular object standing about 2 meters high, known as a stela, with elaborate carved figures in relief and also hieroglyphics. Our mutual congratulations, however, were soon dashed. Mat recognized the steal as one he had excavated fourteen years before. We could see a photo of it in one of his publications on the Olmec.

In any case we convinced ourselves that we could detect such features in the ground with electrical resistance equipment because large stone objects apparently produced more electrical resistance than the surrounding earth. Many other features were discovered in this way over the next few weeks, including a buried stone stairway running up a pyramidal earth mound, and a burial rich in jade carvings, so much sought after by the antique dealers. The jades were just too much temptation for out workmen. One of the finest disappeared while our backs were turned. With Mat's long experience digging in Mexico, he took over negotiations with the workmen, fired two or three of those apparently implicated, and stopped any future looting. But we did not recover the carving.

Actually, one of our problems at Cerro de las Mesas, a site including centuries of post-Olmec cultures, was the trade in such objects. Each day men, women, and children would arrive at the site with baskets of pottery, clay figurines, jade objects, and stone tools, all dug up somewhere in the vicinity by the peasant farmers who were accustomed to itinerant buyers. It was the number of such things that surprised me. None of this was supposed to be exported from Mexico, Mat and I could take nothing back to the U.S., but we disliked seeing some quite rare objects lost to dealers. We decided to buy the best things for the Museum in Mexico City. The cost was not great, and in a few weeks we had scores of museum pieces for the Mexicans.

The Mexican experiment was to result in many years of experiment with electronic search equipment (the current technical term would be remote sensing equipment). In Italy, working with a proton magnetometer at Tarquinia and Cervetri, and at Sybaris developing the thorium and cesium magnetometers, I was to learn that a highly skilled electronics expert is necessary to maintain and operate the new atomic-nuclear equipment in the field. Beth Ralph took over that job as well as the C-14 laboratory and went on to work in Italy, France, Yugoslavia, Greece, Iran, Iraq, Turkey, and the U.S. Once a member of the National Women's Hockey Team, she was tough enough to walk the hundreds of miles of magnetometer survey lines required to make the large magnetic grids at many sites during the next ten or twelve years.

At times we drew a blank, as at Helike and on the island of Santorini (Thera). Professor Spiridon Marinatos, who had heard of our work at Sybaris, came to see me in Rome with a proposition that we join him for surveys at Helike on the Bay of Corinth, and on Santorini. At Helike the wires supporting the grapevines made our magnetometers useless. We tried searching the sea bed just off the site (where the ancient Greek city was said to have sunk beneath the sea) in an aluminum boat, with no luck. On Santorini the land was clean with no surface obstructions. But we soon learned that the soil of that exploded island was so magnetic that our magnetometer would not function there either. However, while Beth was making her grids, Marinatos discovered the now famous Minoan site that was to make the island even more famous. He and I arranged a joint University Museum-Greek Antiquities Service excavation of the new site, but after our first season, with too many Americans there and too much publicity about an American excavation, Marinatos continued the work as a wholly Greek enterprise. We remained friends, and our C-14 lab in Philadelphia undertook the dating of the site during the next several years.

There were difficulties and uncertainties about the C-14 samples and the dates they gave for the last occupations of the site, presumably destroyed with the volcanic explosion of the island. The dates obtained focused on a period about 1500 B.C. and corresponded with other C-14 dates on material from the sea bottom around the island that was associated with the ash fall from the explosion. Marinatos and other Greek archaeologists were happy with these dates for the end of the Minoan period; they seemed to confirm the rather complex archaeological dating based on connections with Egypt. Then, at the first international conference on Santorini, concerned with the volcanic destruction of most of the island, and the possibility of that destruction causing the end of the Minoan civilization, I received a cable from Beth in Sweden informing me that the new correction factor for C-14 dates had been accepted by the international C-14 conference there. That meant the revision of all C-14 dates during certain periods when C-14 in the atmosphere had not remained constant. Our 1500 B.C. dates for the Minoan site should read 1650 B.C. For prehistoric archaeologists a correction of 150 years was of no significance, but for classical archaeologists, so long conditioned to archaeological dates worked out with many logical conclusions about the interrelations of ancient cultures connected in some way with Egyptian and Sumerian inscriptions, such a shift was almost heretical.

Marinatos had planned to reveal the C-14 dating of his site at the conference and then call upon me to verify it with all the analysis made by our lab at The University Museum. After the cable I tried to warn him, but he was too busy with the conference to listen. My announcement, coming on the heels of his satisfactory statement that C-14 had confirmed his archaeological dates, was a shock. It was the most unpopular statement I have ever made at a conference. Claude Shaeffer summed up the reaction by observing that we apparently used Egyptian archaeological dating to correct C-14 analysis and then used C-14 to correct Egyptian dating! Actually the correction factor was based on long studies of growth records as recorded in tree-rings, and those studies were begun when several C-14 labs began to note that Egyptian dates did not correlate with C-14.

MASCA and my own involvement with scientific techniques in archaeology for so many years, surely stems from that first encounter with Aristide de Grosse in 1949. His idea that radioactive isotopes could be used in a technique to date ancient organic materials was, at the time, about as preposterous as landing a man on the moon. However, my experience during the war years had begun to crack loose many of the firm beliefs and convictions one normally acquires as a student and young professor, so that I was seriously intrigued by something that sounded like science fiction. When he took the idea to Bill Libby in Chicago and we then received the funds for experiment from the Wenner-Gren Foundation, thanks to Paul Fejos, an explorer at heart, it was a tremendous satisfaction for me to work with the C-14 committee and Libby to supply ancient organic materials and to see the technique gradually achieve reality. Cracks in my student armor also expanded in our regular meetings at Libby's laboratory at the University of Chicago, listening to the arguments of men like Harold Urey (who, at that time before the hydrogen bomb, observed that fears about the effect of bomb explosions on the earth's atmosphere were groundless), and many others working in a far-out world of nuclear phenomena.

The heartbreaking delays in getting our our C-14 lab to function at the Museum and the puzzling results of some of those early analyses using solid carbon in the counters did nothing to dampen my interest. Why did burned bone and burned antler give different dates? Why did several analyses of the same material sometimes give different results? Were the Egyptian dates, based upon hieroglyphs associated with the king lists, wrong, or was C-14 in error? How could the system be improved? Many archaeologists took the attitude that the exact scientists had produced a magic box that was either right or all wrong, and if it did not confirm archaeological dates of which they were convinced, it was wrong. Few really seemed to grasp the idea that it was a matter of the greatest probability. One single analysis on their particular material meant almost nothing. Archaeological literature was filled with meaningless dates, based on C-14 analysis of one small sample of organic material presumably associated with a particular culture.

Soon after the Museum lab began to function, other C-14 stations were established, notably in the Netherlands, Australia, England, and the U.S. It was then possible to correlate results on the same material and to pass our problems with the system back and forth among several people equally concerned. The first major improvement was the substitution of carbon dioxide for solid carbon in the counter. Other improvements soon followed, and with them more questions. After one of the early atomic bomb tests in the U.S. Beth called me to say she had just been in touch with the Australian lab and they had reported evidence of bomb fallout in their lab just two weeks after the blast. No one then knew how fast mixing in the atmosphere could take place. Soon we were all worried about the effect of fallout on all C-14 stations. The bombs were increasing the amount of C-14 in the atmosphere. Moreover, we were detecting an increase in carbon dioxide in the world's atmosphere, presumably the result of burning fossil fuels during the past century. It became necessary to correct each analysis for both the increase of C-14 from bomb tests and the increase of carbon dioxide from a century of fossil fuel burning. Those were beginning days in nonmilitary uses of the spinoff from atomic weapons and the breakout from security control of nuclear phenomena, which in a few years were to change our whole concept of the nature of matter.

Several years ago the problem of Egyptian archaeological dating came to a head. The reign of certain pharaohs can be correlated with the Christian calendar because the ancient Egyptians recorded the dawn appearance of the star Sirius in a certain year of that Pharaoh's reign, and that particular rising can be calculated astronomically. Hence the reigns of certain pharaohs in the famous Egyptian king lists, for example, those carved on the walls of a temple at Abydos, can be fixed in terms of our calendar. But those "fixes" are rare and the lists are very long. How accurate are those lists as a whole? There is much room for debate.

In Arizona Andrew Douglas had worked out a tree growth record by measuring the thickness of annual growth rings in the cross-section of long-lived trees such as the sequoia and the bristlecone pines. Working back from living trees to ancient logs in Pueblo Indian house ruins by overlapping pronounced tree-growth "signatures" (such as two thick rings succeeded by three thin ones), he established a tree-ring calendar going back many centuries. It was used for many years for accurate dating of Pueblo ruins.

That calendar, more recently expanded to about 6700 B.C. with ancient bristlecone pine wood (the oldest tree in the world), was the means of solving the Egyptian problem. Our lab in Philadelphia, and several others in America and abroad, carried out a very long series of C-14 analyses on the wood from the separate dated rings (only the outer rings of a tree are living in the sense that they are accumulating C-14 from the atmosphere) in cross-sections of more than 4000-year-old living bristlecone pines and from ancient, buried logs from such trees. In this way it was discovered that the C-14 content in the atmosphere had not remained constant, as Libby assumed, but had shifted so that radiocarbon dates of about 5000 B.C. are about 800 years too young. With some variations, the divergence of C-14 dates with the true dates increases with age. No one is sure of the reason, as yet, but there is a theory that the dates will converge again about 10,000 years B.C. if or when they can be checked. Beth Ralph and Henry Michael, of The University Museum lab, have worked out a correlation factor chart for C-14 now generally used by archaeologists. Henry has long been in pursuit of more and more ancient buried bristlecone pine logs and was one of the first to use the lab's new ground-radar equipment to search for them in California.

With news of this discrepancy in C-14 dating some archaeologists immediately assumed that the whole method was a failure, and some even began to throw out all C-14 dates. It took time to explain, and it is no wonder I had a bad time upsetting the comfortable 1500 B.C. date for the explosion of the island of Santorini and the hypothetical end of the Minoan civilization. Even at the last international conference there, dating of the site was unresolved and I noticed the characteristic classical archaeological distrust of C-14 dating. In the past few years, however, radiocarbon dates placing the thera explosion 75 to 125 years earlier were confirmed by ice-core dates and frost tree-ring dates. The latter places the explosion in 1627 B.C. and was published by Henry Michael and Phil Betancourt in 1987 and 1988. There are, certainly, errors in C-14 dating of archaeological sites, and any attempt to date something to a specific century is pretty dicey, but for prehistoric sites thousands of years old it is now the accepted method.

The nuclear dating of pottery, now called thermoluminescence (TL for short), intrigued me from the beginning when I heard of the first experiments at the University of California. Pottery is the most common object in most archaeological sites, and if you could date that you would avoid the inherent error of dating charcoal or other organic material at a site that might not be contemporary with the specific culture you were attempting to date. Beth Ralph, Mark Han, and Bill Stevens (then head of the University's physics department) set up the equipment in the lab when the method was only an idea and began experiments, specifically for archaeological dating. Series of potsherds from superimposed levels of deposit in many sites excavated by the Museum, particularly in the Near and Middle East, were used to compare with the C-14 dates for those levels. Mark became the operator of the equipment and with advice and suggestions from Beth and Bill continued to improve methods of grinding up potsherds, heating the fine powder quickly and at high temperatures to release photons for improved recording equipment, and calculating glow curves. By 1966 Beth and Mark were able to write in the British magazine *Nature* that the method was finally worked out for archaeological dating and with future refinement would become a standard method. In the U.S. I announced this achievement at a meeting of the American Philosophical Society for publication in the proceedings of an archaeological symposium.

There are still "bugs" in the method, and many archaeologists are still skeptical about it. Probably they expect too much of the "exact" sciences. In all these methods there are uncertainties, and there are bound to be unexplained errors, or what appear to be errors. At the lab, watching whole series of stratified potsherds come out of the TL dating in the right order with dates corresponding to those made by C-14, I have been impressed with the system and am still not surprised when other dates turn out to be inexplicable.

Probably the most amusing example was the dating of the Julsrude collection of pottery figurines. Arthur Young, a friend in Philadelphia, had seen some 30,000 clay figurines in Mr. Julsrude's collection in Mexico that were very queer indeed. They looked very little like the usual ancient Indian figurines, and some seemed to be figures of dinosaurs. Julsrude was sure they were very ancient and had been excavated in Mexico by Indian farmers. Most archaeologists were sure they were fakes unloaded on a gullible collector. Rather to the embarrassment of our American curator, Linton Satterthwaite, I put a number of them on exhibition at the Museum with the question, "What are these things?" We also did some TL dating. To our utter surprise they dated some to 5000-6000 B.C. We made more tests. All very ancient. Arthur was delighted at the upset to the archaeologists and was provoked that I would not announce the dramatic results proving Mr. Julsrude right. However, an archaeologist friend of mine had made a study of the collection and had actually found the Mexican who was making them. Something was obviously wrong. Years later Mark did some more TL analysis on the same figurines and found they had aged several thousand years! There is still no explanation as to how they could acquire large doses of radioactivity in the Museum in a few years.

Unfortunately, Mark Han, the young man in the lab who became so proficient over the years working out a precise method of measuring thermoluminescence, left to work with the Dupont Company. But there are now many TL stations, and I have no doubt the method will eventually come to general acceptance with the understanding that it can only be a matter of probability.

For a laboratory attempting to adopt many new scientific techniques for use in archaeological interpretation it makes no sense to do extensive basic research in physics, chemistry, electronics, and so on. There are hundreds of labs working in private industry, the universities, and government on many new techniques that might be applied for our special purposes. Hence, our object was to find what and where. Our information center culled a large number of scientific journals for ideas and also made the information available to other archaeological centers. I took to lecturing on archaeological techniques through the RESA groups of scientists at the big research centers like those of Dupont, Alcoa, and Hercule Powder. In return we received many possible ideas. Also we brought into the lab volunteers, often specialists retired from industry or government labs. One of these was a gentlewoman who had been working with electron microscopes and had an idea that she could distinguish ancient from modern gold objects by a study of surface crystallization. Ancient gold objects are very easy to fake and impossible to detect. Faked gold objects of course may contain gold mined thousands of years ago. After some time her research progressed and was promising, but by that time our lab was swamped with requests from museums and collectors to prove or disprove the authenticity of art treasures with C-14, TL, and other methods involving the analysis of materials. Quite suddenly I came to the conclusion that all this work, for our lab, was pointless. We were set up to improve interpretation of remains in the earth, not to adjudicate arguments about fakes. And in any case, if collectors and museums believed their objects were authentic and the fine arts experts could not agree on whether they were or were not, then why spoil their pleasure in such things? From then on I tried to discourage all such work in the lab.

For many years the Museum's excavations in the Near East exposed mud-brick buildings that soon disintegrated through wind and weather, once exposed. Even before MASCA was established I was in touch with chemists at the Rohm and Haas Company in Philadelphia seeking some chemical method for preserving such structures. Experiments were made in Iraq and Iran, without success. Chemicals tried would not penetrate the dried mud, and the surface continued to crack away. We also tried Rohm and Haas chemicals on the stone winged bulls of the Assyrians standing before the Baghdad Museum. Otto and John Haas became interested in the research of the Museum, and Otto joined the Board of Managers. Sometime after the establishment of MASCA Otto suggested that one of the Rohm and Haas chemical engineers, Darryl Butterbaugh, recently retired, might like to work on the old and so far insoluble problem as a volunteer. Otto himself became an associate director of MASCA.

Within the next three years Darryl, with the help of his colleagues in the Rohm and Haas laboratories, had discovered compounds of acrylic chemicals, newly developed by that lab, that would penetrate mud-brick and also stone. Moreover, these new chemicals would seal off water penetration and yet allow water vapor to pass out through the mud-brick or stone, a process that has something to do with the coating of individual molecules in the treated material. Finally, the treatment strengthened the structures by a factor of four or five times. Later he also discovered a chemical that would stop the disintegration of all limestones, including marble, caused by "acid rain" in the atmosphere. Tests of all these things were made in the pueblo country of the Southwest, in Iran, in Guatemala, and at other sites including colonial brick houses in Philadelphia. Early on, Otto and I thought that this new and highly successful technique could be commercialized to finance the operation of MASCA. But I learned that you can invent the best mousetrap and still not be able to sell it in our modern world without quite a lot of effort going into marketing. That process is continuing, outside the academic world, with a fledgling company in Ireland called Scarab Ltd. Tests are being made on many structures including St. Paul's Cathedral, the Parthenon, and probably soon the Taj Mahal.

My old friend Nancy Grace, hearing of this new technique, insisted that we try it on her house in Philadelphia, where colonial fired-brick walls were cracking away and allowing water to seep into the house. Darrel and his wife, Jan, themselves applied the treatment. The next morning I had an urgent call from Nancy to say that a pungent odor of chemicals was all over a bathroom. I called Darrel who exclaimed, "My God! Tell her not to smoke in there, it might blow up." It did prove that the chemicals would penetrate fired brick, clear through the wall. Nancy tells me the treatment is a great success and has saved her many thousands of dollars.

Fenimore Johnstone, heir to the Victor Talking Machine Co., now RCA, came into the Museum one morning, sometime in the late 50s, to suggest that we try underwater archaeology. He had been making underwater cameras since the war years and was personally interested in undersea exploration. Fenimore had long been a supporter of the Museum, financing ethnographic research in South America as well as one of the first of the ethnographic films, in Brazil in the early 30s. Naturally I was much interested. He then brought in a naval officer, in charge of diving teams, for discussions on how to go about it. It was soon very clear that Museum research funds were far too limited to pay the salaries of professional divers. The naval officer finally concluded that the only way was for us to train Ph.D. candidates to dive. Obviously the place to begin such exploration was the Mediterranean. To my surprise, Rodney Young, the head of our Mediterranean section and a rather conservative archaeologist, was all for the attempt. Neither of us could think of a way to start until, some time later, Rodney heard of Peter Throckmorton's archaeological dives off the coast of Turkey and his discoveries there. Rodney also dug up one of his graduate students, a young man recently transferred from Johns Hopkins University named George Bass, who was willing to take instructions in scuba diving in

Philadelphia's Y.M.C.A. After that, George joined Peter to dive on a Bronze Age wreck off Bodrum in Turkey. That set George off on a career that was to make him world-famous in ten years and to put underwater archaeology on a firm professional base.

What George did was to change adventurous looting of ancient sunken ships into systematic archaeological excavation on the sea bottom through the development, not only of standard archaeological method, but of new technology for underwater archaeological research. Those techniques included airlifts for removing sediments, undersea television, adaptation of our magnetometers and mine detectors for archaeological search, side-scanning sonar (George tested the Navy's first equipment of that kind because his costs were less than the Navy's own), and, finally one of the first midget submarines.

The Electric Boat Co.'s first commercial job (all Navy before that) was the tiny *Asherah*, built for The University Museum. Surrounded by nuclear submarines that made the Asherah look like a flea, Ann Bass christened it with a bottle of champagne. It was so small it could be flown around the world in cargo planes. Yet it could take two men down several hundred feet, with two wing motors, and through viewing ports allow them to scan the sea bottom. I think the high point of George's contribution was reached when his crew in the Mediterranean spotted a wreck with the new side-scanning sonar, and through three shore-based radio stations, located the ship precisely on the sea floor—so precisely that the *Asherah* could submerge directly upon it—no small trick in the open sea. For a time we had *Asherah* bobbing about in the fish pond at the Museum entrance, just to show our members what archaeology was doing in those days.

When George had his first full-scale underwater excavation of a wreck off Bodrum fully under way, I stopped by to see how he was making out. Some twenty young men and women were living in a ramshackle rented house in Bodrum, presided over by a very efficient Ann Bass, and stocked with equipment of all kinds. Eating and sleeping arrangements were primitive (no funds wasted on comforts) and morale was high—one of the most cheerful, exciting, and efficient operations of the fifteen or twenty we had going around the world at that time. Out on the barge, anchored over the wreck, there was the ear-splitting roar of generators refilling the compressed air tanks, diving equipment in piles, divers resting in the sun, and one irrepressible fellow keeping them happy with his guitar and his songs. They decided the "old man" should try his first dive on the wreck. I was buckled into a wet suit, breathing tube, flippers, air tank, weights, and a bayonet for sharks, then heaved overboard. It was a disaster. It seemed to me that all that gear went adrift and that I was entangled in everything. I didn't know if I were head down or head up, and instead of air I breathed sea water. After an age when I felt I should have arrived long since at the wreck, several divers deposited me again on the barge with shouts of laughter. I was told, and I don't believe it, that my bottom never went under. Surely that is a job for young people with a lot of training, not for me.

Those years experimenting with electronic equipment, combined with my own excavations and the constant inspection and negotiations having to do with many university excavations directed by museum curators, kept me traveling constantly in several countries. Jim Pritchard was then the associate director of the Museum, and it was no worry to be away from my office there for a month or two at a time. We saw eye to eye on all fundamental questions about museum policies, and at home things were going well, including the construction of a new $6 million academic wing financed to a large extent by private contributions. It was a period of great popular interest in archaeology in which the many University Museum expeditions, their newsworthy discoveries, and their worldwide scope played a leading role.

The astonishingly rapid development of science and technology in the postwar years, based on atomic-nuclear research, certainly has had its effect on archaeology, particularly with the new dating techniques, but the effect seems to me curiously out of step with the general trend in current scientific thinking. We now utilize many scientific techniques in dating, identifying materials, reconstructing climatic and environmental changes, and searching for ancient remains in the earth, but this does not mean archaeology is a "science." Moreover, the theoreticians have borrowed terms like "model," "working hypothesis," and evolutionary schemes to guide their interpretations of what happened in the past, assuming that they can be tested in digging in the same way that scientists test their theories in repeatable experiments in the laboratory—an assumption I think is misleading.

In the 1960s and 1970s we heard much about "the new archaeology," a blend of anthropology and archaeology, in which diggers, utilizing a knowledge of the customs and behavior of living primitive people, and artifacts found in ancient sites, tried to reconstruct the social, political, and economic life-style of the people represented by those remains. I was reminded that on my first trip to the Soviet Union in 1938 I found the Soviet diggers attempting the same thing. All their archaeological reports ended with a theoretical section fitting their discoveries into a prescribed level of cultural development somewhere between the original primitives and the ultimate Communist state. They were a bit embarrassed and apologetic about this, explaining that it was necessary in order to obtain funds from the state to carry out future excavations.

Such theories, I believe, stem from the period before the revolutionary discoveries in the physical and biological sciences brought about by atomic-nuclear tools for research. Now, with a new vision of the natural world we live in, I would guess that the next generation will see fundamental changes in the way we interpret archaeological remains of the distant past.

"What in the World" broadcast in the 1950s; from left: Carleton Coon, Margaret Plass, Mat Stirling try to identify an artifact as the author (far right) looks on. *Photograph courtesy of The University Museum Archives.*

CHAPTER TWELVE

Why Do We Dig?

"What is a grown-up man like you doing down there playing in a sand pit?" Or so Alfred Kidder used to quote an old gentleman in the Pueblo country of the southwestern United States who was watching him excavate an ancient Pueblo site.

That is one of the simplest, and most difficult, questions for any digger to answer. But if your job is to manage a museum of archaeology and anthropology, organize expeditions around the world, and raise the money to pay for them, certainly you must find some answer.

The Museum records were full of statements by my predecessors pleading their case—usually in connection with fund drives. Somehow they all sounded like old familiar tunes that may have served their purpose then but did not exactly "send" a postwar generation of the 1950s. I have been trying to answer that simple question for many years. The beginning of an answer, at least, came to me in a television studio in Philadelphia in 1948 or '49 when that new medium was just beginning to find its stride.

Eleanor Moore, director of the Museum's Department of Education, was a wise and creative woman who was then leading the way in the use of museums by schoolchildren. She had grasped what television could do and, with a scriptwriter, was producing occasional programs for one of the local stations. I was scheduled to appear on one of those just when Helge Larsen was to stop off in Philadelphia on his way from Alaska to Denmark, so, quite naturally, we planned to do something on the Eskimo while Helge was there to perform.

But Helge and I got so involved in discussions about future work in the Arctic that we forgot about the program and the script written for us until late in the evening before we were to go on the air. When we looked at the script we both began to laugh at the idea of saying such things to each other, and since it was too late to change it, decided to ditch the script and extemporize our own show.

In that early period all broadcasts were "live." Once you went on the air at the appointed hour you and the studio were stuck with whatever happened until the hour passed.

In the studio, as "visuals," were a number of objects made by Eskimos. As we went along ad-libbing our conversation it occurred to me to pick up one of the objects and as a "straight" man ask Helge what it was. Soon I began to notice that the young men in the crew on the studio floor were missing their cues. Afterward I learned from them that it was not only the odd things that Helge said about such strange objects, but the original, extemporaneous, and unexpected conversation. The director, with no script, was furious, but the crew loved it.

Strange things made by strange people in strange places obviously have some kind of appeal to those who live in the mechanical, mass-produced, regimented world of the twentieth century, and the unexpected must be a boon to those who live in a planned society. Anyway, I saw the possibility of taking archaeology and anthropology to the millions via television. Perhaps out of that would grow a satisfactory answer to that simple question: why archaeology?

The studio management was not interested in an archaeological quiz show—too high hat, too stuffy. The father of our assistant registrar, Caroline Dosker, however, did take an interest. Irwin Leslie Gordon had been the first publicity director of the Museum and was at this time the public relations chief of the Reading Railroad. For some weeks he and I and various television people argued about the possibilities of such a program until Charley Vanda, manager of the WCAU studio, agreed to give it a try, probably because he hoped to get an advertising contract with Reading Railroad.

At first it was a very bad amateur performance. I sat on a box made to look like a pirate's treasure chest and periodically got up to fish out some odd object, which was then identified by a panel of three "experts." They tried to agree on the age, the origin, and the purpose of each object.

The chest was too awkward so we tried out a pretty model who minced in with an African wood sculpture, a Persian pot, or a Melanesian woman-catcher. The experts, who had never seen any of the objects before they appeared on stage, were often wrong, but you could practically see them think and often what they said was surprising, very funny, and invariably interesting. It was a regular weekly event. After a few weeks it was clear that the public was watching and liking it. It occurred to me that the experts, like any other performers, should be paid by the studio. But when I proposed this to the manager of WCAU, he was so shocked at the idea of paying professors on an educational program that he immediately terminated the show.

To the surprise of everyone, the studio was besieged with letters from the Philadelphian audience demanding that the program be restored. The manger called me, agreeing to a modest fee for the panel, and proposed that we get down to a serious production with a director, three cameras, a set man, a producer, and a professionally designed TV program. Someone in the studio came up with the idea of calling it "What in the World." A bright young producer from Hollywood conceived the idea of having each mysterious object materialize out of a cloud of smoke produced by dry ice, and of introducing mood music that set an entirely different tone to the whole affair. Also he was ingenious enough to recognize that if the audience was told, offstage beforehand, what each object was, they would have the titillating satisfaction of seeing the professors sweat it out when they themselves already knew the answer.

Within six weeks "What in the World" was taken up by the Columbia Broadcasting System and was appearing weekly all over the United States. Soon it received the Peabody Award, and a story about it appeared in *Life* magazine. Strange objects from strange places made by unknown people suddenly became interesting to millions who had never heard of archaeology and anthropology, or who thought of such subjects as dry as dust and boring. This first American network television series on archaeology appeared about the same time as the first best-seller on the subject, Ceram's *Gods, Graves and Scholars*. Thanks to television, archaeology moved into the mass media.

The program continued over a period of fifteen years in the U.S. and soon after its beginning was adopted by the BBC in England under the title "Animal, Vegetable and Mineral." It happened that Rik Wheeler, later to become Sir Mortimer, was a houseguest of ours at Valley Forge on a day of one of the weekly broadcasts. I thought he would be a "natural" as a guest on the program. He certainly was. And he was so enthusiastic that he and Glyn Daniel soon convinced the BBC to try it out in England, where it was equally successful for several years. It was also adopted in Denmark, Canada, and Mexico—but not in Austria. Heinie-Geldern in Vienna thought that the Austrian National Television system should produce it for Eastern Europe and arranged for me to bring over some tapes for our discussions with the station manager. After seeing them he said, "It's a marvelous idea but it is impossible in Austria. No professor in this country would make a fool of himself like that."

While we were broadcasting concurrently on CBS in America and BBC in England, David Attenborough thought it would be amusing to air-express the objects used in one program in the U.S. for use in England, and vice versa, and then exchange tapes to be shown with the next program in each country. That became a game in which each panel of experts tried to outdo the other in correct answers. At one time I had a cable from the BBC saying that they were doing a very special program and would we send over the usual six or eight objects for it. Normally, Geraldine Bruchner, the Museum's registrar, and I selected objects for each program, but in this case Carl Coon and Ted Kidder, the regular members of our panel, joined us to select objects that were almost impossible to identify. That BBC program was something of a fiasco because the English panel failed to identify any of the six objects shown, and most embarrassing for them because that special program was done for the Queen and Prince Philip, who were in the studio.

In the early days, when all programs were live, I had a "panic button" to switch the voice off the air in a crisis. It was primarily necessary because of Carl Coon. Half the tension in the studio was the result of our fears as to what he might say. Often his language was unprintable. But at times he had us all laughing so hard that no one remembered the panic button. There was the occasion when I asked Professor Allbright what his personal friends called him. (We always used first names or nicknames on the air.) He blushed and said that no one ever called him by his first name. Irrepressible Carl popped up with "What does your wife say, 'Roll over, Professor Allbright'?" And then there was the time he began to swear at Margo Plass because she insisted that a small ape skull was that of a monkey—and his announcement that a carved figure of the Madonna and Child was a mother with a child with adenoids.

The first surprise was to learn that all kinds of people were listening. Conductors on the commuting trains, taxi drivers, people in bars, business men on transatlantic ships, and the schoolchildren wandering about the Museum often would recognize my voice or face and stop to comment on the program. Tom Kendrick, the director of the British Museum, told me, with tongue in cheek, how he had been holidaying at some resort in England, and happened to comment that he knew Rik Wheeler—and became a celebrity. Many years later, students in classes at the University would tell me how they became interested in archaeology as children listening to "What in the World."

The "gentlemen of Philadelphia" who founded The University Museum and established its tradition of active field research around the world interpreted for the intelligent public could not have imagined television and an audience of many millions, but I think they would have agreed that intelligent entertainment is far better than pedantic educational programs if you intend to reach a broad public. As the director of Educational Television in America once said, "Anything labeled 'education' on television is the kiss of death." Many of us learned during those early days of television that there are millions of intelligent people in all walks of life who are avidly interested in most fields of learning. But they do not wish to be lectured to like schoolchildren. I think the BBC has long since learned that lesson while the networks in the United States have not.

The rapid growth of public interest in archaeology during the 1950s and the early '60s meant that The University Museum was plagued by people who wished to go on expeditions. With ten to twenty expeditions operating in the field each year in a dozen different countries around the world, the Museum was often in the news as well as on the air each week. Each field director, of course, chose his own crew, usually from graduate students in archaeology at the University of Pennsylvania or at other universities in the United States and abroad. But my office caught the brunt of callers and letter writers seeking a position on one of those expeditions. One young lady, I remember, gave one of her special qualifications as her ability to drive a car with a gear shift. But the ones who bothered me most were the youngsters who wanted to choose archaeology as a profession. I talked with scores of them over the years, not wanting to discourage them nor to mislead them by too much encouragement. Conversations with them, and with my own students in the University, invariably raised those questions as to what archaeology was all about, why one digs, what it was for. Because of television and the news stories of the Museum's many expeditions, I also took to the lecture circuits around the United States and was invariably faced with the same questions in Dallas, Cincinnati, Buffalo, or San Francisco.

Three men in the Museum, Sam Kramer, Carl Coon, and Loren Eiseley, were highly successful writers of books intelligible to laymen, and they too were concerned about the answers to these simple, but most difficult questions. It was obvious to all of us that the Museum's collections, all having to

do with archaeology and anthropology, should be used to speak
to the interested public because the Museum was founded for
that purpose. But when you get right down to the construction
of exhibitions, how do you do it? After the neglect of the war
years, all exhibitions in the Museum needed redoing. There
was no exhibition staff, and in any case if we wished to explain
and answer questions with exhibits, the digger-curators should
do them. Face-lifting and refurbishing of exhibitions was going
on all over the Museum under the direction of a series of
designers employed for specific jobs, but the first real "think-
piece" was the "Hall of Man," primarily conceived by Carl
Coon but also advised by at least a dozen of us with our own
ideas.

The actual installation of that exhibition was done and
redone three times. The best and most original section was an
introductory panel painted by Al Bendiner as a caricature of
the whole history of man, but in the last desperate rush to
finish the exhibition, after two years, for an opening night,
with most of the curators themselves painting and hammering,
someone painted out the most lively part of it. The gallery was
designed for the viewer to move from left to right through the
story of man, but on the opening night we suddenly realized
that traffic in the United States moves on the right. Everyone
saw the story backward. Writers, particularly a group of them,
are clearly not at their best in exhibition design and
installation. The Hall of Man, conceived by writers and
curators as an educational exhibition explaining archaeology
and anthropology to laymen, was not a success.

Jacques Lipschitz, one of our regular guests on "What in the
World," was an authority on ancient and primitive art as well
as a world-famous sculptor. He practically bristled with ideas
about museum exhibitions. Employed as an exhibition
consultant, he spent one whole day experimenting with the size
of a base for a small Sumerian sculpture, with no conclusion,

and then retired as a consultant. I found a young Indian man in Mexico City whose exhibitions in the Museum were outstanding. He did a gallery on the Royal Tombs of Ur, which was still in place in the Museum after nearly thirty years, but it was a conventional job, just done very well for that period.

Four museum innovations in that period were a success. The conventional idea of No Smoking in museums had always seemed to me ridiculous. A stone or brick building with stone floors and largely nonflammable exhibitions, is hardly a fire risk. Storerooms of flammable objects is a totally different matter. We introduced lounge areas in each gallery with ashtrays and reading material and thus urged our visitors to relax and enjoy themselves. (Very strict rules against smoking in storerooms were posted everywhere, but with faculty and students working in them it was never possible to enforce the rules completely.)

Watching the uniformed guards, either asleep in corners or trying to educate visitors with a lot of mis-information, it occurred to me that they were a pest to the public and of little use for security. I dismissed the whole lot (and had a major robbery the day before they left), while at the same time employing an equal number of cleaners and general handymen of all work in the galleries dressed in work clothes rather than uniforms. Men who are busy do not molest the visitors and are not a challenge to youngsters, who always want to do guards in the eye. Once we had settled the ensuing dispute with the Union and allayed the fears of the staff, it worked well, particularly in terms of a much happier maintenance crew.

At that time several museums had snack bars or lunchrooms for their visitors, but they were invariably down in the basement next to the restrooms. We decided to install a "Brazilian coffee shop" at the center of the Museum, on the main floor, near the entrance and next to the sales desk. It was to be an exhibition area as well, with comfortable and attractive chairs and tables, really good coffee, properly made in attractive surroundings and the location remained a success. The business of the sales desk boomed, and the coffee shop became famous in the University as well as the city. Moreover, it became a coffee-hour meeting place for the whole staff and the place where everyone could air ideas or grievances. Most of my really important meetings with the staff members were held there and were completely informal.

Finally, after several years, and a comprehensive, personal study of museums in fifteen different countries, I borrowed one of Charlie Cunningham's ideas for the rejuvenation of his museum in Hartford, Connecticut. He convinced me that the usual preview of new exhibitions for the conventional "members' night" was worn out and that the postwar public wanted something new and different. We began the members' parties, cracking our heads to think of original ideas to entertain people in the Museum. "What in the World" games, where the members competed to identify a number of strange objects, or joined in a mock program just as it appeared on the air, attracted overflow crowds on members' nights. But there were also belly-dancers, Roman dinners, American Indian games, folk dances, exotic entertainers from abroad, and "reports from the field." The reports—short, ten-minute accounts by field directors of what was new in each expedition—became a regular event each fall, and still continue.

An occasional dinner party for the members was an old custom at The University Museum, but the popularity of the rapidly expanding members' nights soon made dining in the Egyptian or Chinese gallery a standard affair for University functions as well as for many groups outside the Museum and the University. When Rudolf Anthes arrived from Germany to take charge of the Egyptian section, there were often several dinner parties in his gallery each week. For his generation and his country that was indeed an innovation. With a twinkle in his eye he asked if he was to manage the nightclub also.

With a grant from a foundation in New York, I began a systematic investigation of the use of museums in the United States, Mexico, Canada, and Western Europe, in an attempt to discover what museums would become in the postwar period and, particularly, what we might do with The University Museum to interpret archaeology and anthropology for the public. That meant months of traveling to scores of museums, discussions with directors and curators, and debates about purpose, function, use, and theory. An emphasis on "education" was apparent everywhere, but many museum people were skeptical about education in the limited academic sense.

In the U.S. in the 1930s the great majority of privately founded museums were forced to turn to city and state for funds, since private gifts and grants could no longer bear the costs. "Education" was then a magic word with city and state authorities, and effective in obtaining public funds. But by the early 1950s that justification for museums was already wearing thin. It was significant that grants for museums in Philadelphia were then made through the Department of Recreation, not Education. Europeans, pressed for funds to restore museums after the war, and almost entirely dependent on public funds, were borrowing much of the educational theory pioneered by American museums twenty years earlier, and many of the directors were not happy with it. Several of us remembered the educational exhibits in Moscow, just after the Revolution, when thousands of illiterate peasants were crowding into the city and were taught sanitation, public health, the use of toothbrushes and flush toilets, and other basic elements of civilized living, by means of explicit educational exhibits. That was very effective at the time. Moscow in the 1950s was a very different city. Then those great private collections of painting made before the Revolution were being established in public museums for the pleasure of an educated public.

In Europe, as well as in America, chain-gangs of schoolchildren were being led through the galleries by dedicated teachers drumming into them the facts about painters, sculptors, and historical objects. I sympathized with all those little boys who pulled a pigtail or tripped up a companion just to create a diversion. Is it really sensible to move the schoolroom into the museum? I remember one very wise young director who removed every sign in his museum with the word "education" and refused to allow any teacher to accompany a group of children through the galleries. With him I watched the happiest school kids I had ever seen in a museum. I think there is no doubt that the great majority of schoolchildren, at least up to the age of adolescence, really enjoy museums on their own. And, except for a limited number of academically oriented adults, I believe most people think of museums as recreation, as places where they go for pleasure, contemplation, intellectual interest, and relaxation. Of course, museum directors are always being dressed down by irate visitors who complain that there is not enough information on the labels. Experience has taught me, like a lot of other directors, that these are the people who loved the schoolroom, and who never got over it. They forget that most of us *do* get over it.

In Rome I saw a new sculpture gallery that was so well done that it took your breath away. And I have never forgotten it. In Holland, at the Mauritzhuis, I saw classical Dutch paintings and furniture in the setting for which they were originally produced, and have never forgotten it. I also saw far too many museums filled with rows upon rows of glass cases incarcerating things that might have been lovely or fascinating if one were not distracted by numbers and a forest of glass.

Probably the worst were archaeological museums, with thousands of stone tools and pots arranged in scores of glass cases according to age and location, sometimes "enlivened" by maps and charts. Usually there was no one in such museums except for an occasional scholar or collector struggling to see what was written on a label at the back of the case.

Excavations in the Near and Middle East and Central America had taught me that there is tremendous excitement in the discovery of things in the earth that alter our conventional conception of man's history. Television had taught me that people in all walks of life are also fascinated with such things. Wandering through the museums of the Western world and talking with men and women whose job it was to give meaning to the worlds' treasures from the past had left me in a quandary. I was then well aware that Calvinist-Puritan morality in the Western world dictated a "serious" view of life in which everything must have a "purpose," moral, social, or economic "improvement"; that the practical success of science in changing our environment lent stature and prestige to the whole idea of science, and that the arts of history, social philosophy, economics, anthropology, and archaeology were being called science in order to participate in such prestige. Many of my contemporaries were writing about the dynamics and processes of cultural history, implying that some day someone would put all the "facts" of archaeology and anthropology together in a scheme of things that would make a better world. But I was increasingly skeptical of this whole theory of the social sciences, unconvinced that they really were science as I understand the physical and biological sciences, and particularly dubious about any "scientific" scheme of the past that would improve human existence in the future.

Certainly dull and pedantic educational exhibits were not the answer. Brad Washburn, at the Boston Museum of Science, learned that very quickly. During the most exciting period of beginning space travel, he had some of the leading people in space research design an exhibition to educate the public in what was happening. It was organized as a systematic, step-by-step series of exhibits that the viewer was to go through like the chapters of a book. But most of them did not. They wandered about being momentarily interested in a group of things but rarely followed through the prescribed course. The exhibit was short lived. Later he told me that, traveling in Scandinavia, he hit upon the idea of a "smorgasbord" exhibit—independent units of exhibit that alone might spark an intelligent interest sufficient to take the viewer into the library for a thorough look into a particular subject.

For me there is still no resolution of that quandary of how to give meaning to our theories of the past to a vitally interested public, nor, particularly, how to use museums for that purpose. Sometime in the 1950s I came to the conclusion that the best we could do at the Museum was to create a congenial environment in which people could find pleasure and relaxation in the contemplation of beautiful and fascinating things from the past that might inspire them to dig into books and work out their own ideas about what happened and what is happening. My greatest satisfaction from years of thinking about museums was to have the occasional visitor drop in to tell me of the unique atmosphere of The University Museum. Often it was to wax enthusiastic about a museum with few glass cases and all the exposed objects that really meant something to them; or the friendly, relaxed atmosphere with dramatic lighting and installations of beautiful things made by ancient and strange people; or the comfortable places to sit and relax with no uniformed guards to plague them. But for the most part it was something intangible, uninstitutional—a more natural human environment.

With at least a temporary resolution of the question of how to give meaning to archaeological research in a museum and for the public at large, I could then give a direct answer to all those who continually asked, "But what is archaeology for?" When I said, "It is just for fun," they were often shocked, or incensed by what they thought was flippancy. Then it was necessary to let them down easily by explaining that archaeology was not a science in which you could prove what happened in the past or what might happen in the future, but an art that advanced a sequence of theories about what might have happened. It was essentially fascinating speculation.

There are so many theories about cultural and historical process, even attempts to engineer human society, based on a knowledge of the past, many different cultures, and of human behavior. The dialectic materialism of the Communists is one such theory, which, I think, has influenced many contemporary archaeologists in their attempts to discover some predictability in the archaeological record of past societies. It is not convincing. For me archaeology remains intellectual entertainment of the highest order. It needs no justification in the sense of applied science. As thoughtful people probe deeper and deeper into the functions of DNA, the behavior of atomic particles, or the structure of distant planets, for the intellectual pleasure of learning, so we search for traces of our ancestors in the surface of the earth, just to know.

In biology, chemistry, and physics there is a spinoff that fundamentally affects our lives. In archaeology there is none except for an expanding knowledge of what we think may have happened in the past and what we think this means in relation to man's place in the universe.

Popularization of archaeology had, and probably still has, a bad name among scholars in the discipline. That is sad because it restricts the impact of one in many fields of learning in the twentieth century that are expanding the conception of our world. Literacy and contemporary communications release ideas to great numbers of people who, in turn, generate original thought. Teaching, in an academic sense, is by nature a limited thing. Communications are worldwide. Often the untutored come up with the most original ideas.

In the late twentieth century I was still directing the Museum toward its original purpose of the late nineteenth century— research interpreted for the intelligent public. But our world was greatly changed. Literacy and mass communication were responsible for carrying ideas to the millions, and I had learned from television about the universal interest in man's past. Unlike the hard sciences we had no effect on day-by-day living, but like them, I think, we were having an effect upon the way people in general are beginning to think in this generation.

The author and friend off to pick apples at the author's home, Oldhay, in Cornwall, England. *Photograph courtesy of author.*

CHAPTER THIRTEEN

Retrospect

My first clear memory is the purchase of a horse. Billy and Bird were a team of fast trotters used by my parents when their two-cylinder Reo automobile was laid up for repair. Billy, frisking about the ranch buildings, struck his knee against a disk cultivator, receiving a gash that was to give him a stiff knee for life. I must have been about four years old when I heard my father and a cowboy deciding that Billy would never improve and should be shot. It must have taken a certain amount of courage to interrupt with an offer to buy the horse for the five pennies I then had in my piggy bank.

However, Billy was famous for his uncanny intelligence, a favorite of everyone about the ranch, and no one wanted to put him down. Father considered the offer very seriously and then agreed with the stipulation that I would only ride him bareback so that I would not be hung up in the saddle when he tripped and fell. He was a tall and long-legged horse by western standards, and I was very small. When he fell, which was often with his stiff leg, I sailed over his head. Then, looking embarrassed with his head hanging, he waited for me to recover and walked off with me to find a fence, often a long way off on the prairie, where I could climb a post and jump aboard. We became inseparable. He took me to school on my first day, when I was six, and thereafter grazed about the one-room schoolhouse while I learned to read "the robin had two blue eggs." Twenty years later his pure white, long-haired winter skin lay on the floor of my study at Yale.

After Billy's natural death from old age, in mid winter, there were many horses in my life—some I remember by name, like Nig, Babe, and the Buckskin, a pony acquired from the Indians on a reservation near the ranch, who was a perfect devil. But Billy is the one I remember best, probably because he was the first and also because of his almost human intelligence. Naturally, on a cattle ranch in eastern Montana in the early years of the twentieth century, horses were an essential part of life, taken for granted as working animals with none of the fuss made over riding horses today. In winter most of the saddle horses were turned out to fend for themselves on the open range in temperatures ranging as low as fifty degrees below zero. A wild horse could be bought for three dollars, and a well-trained cow pony for fifty. As with all working animals, intelligence, speed, and endurance were most important, but still cowboys were always pleased to find a handsome and spirited animal to keep as their own personal mount in traveling from ranch to ranch.

For most of my life I have managed to keep one or two saddle horses, and I think for me they have been a symbol of the preindustrial, mechanized, urban society—that 5,000 years of civilized living based on manpower and horsepower when most of mankind lived upon the land producing food with hard physical labor—the kind of life I knew as a youth.

I was only one year old in 1908 when my parents joined the westward migrations of that period into the high plains east of the Rocky Mountains. These were the lands between Texas and Montana where a rush of homesteaders were taking over the grasslands of the open range held by sheep and cattle ranchers since the time of the Indian wars. Old Indians from the reservations, with whom I traded horses as a small boy, could remember Custer's last stand, the old buffalo trails could still be seen on the prairie, and old-timers in the bars still talked of the good old days of wagon trains, gun fights, and Indian skirmishes.

At first my parents filed on a homestead in the valley of Seven Mile Creek, about twenty-five miles west of Glendive, Montana. With them were mother's parents, Herman and Anna Holzhausen, and their two sons, Hugo and Red. They too filed on homesteads in the same area, and all were required to live on their land tracts for two or three years in order to "prove the claim" for individual ownership.

Of course, I do not remember those first years of homesteading. By the time I bought my first horse father and his elder brother, Rob Rainey, from Black River Falls, Wisconsin, had become land dealers, selling railroad lands to settlers from Wisconsin. Those two must have been anathema to the big ranchers whose open-range land was being eaten away by "squatters" from the east. However, before I was ten the Rainey brothers joined the ranchers. They formed a "land and cattle company" to import, at first, long-horned cattle from Texas and later the first Aberdeen Angus cattle to be seen in Montana. Then they, too, became concerned with the preservation of an open range. Thereafter their conflict was with the sheep ranchers, one of whom ran sheep only a few miles to the north. It was a conviction among cattle ranchers that sheep ruined a grazing forever.

Mother's brothers, Red and Hugo, remained in Montana for some years working for the Rainey Land and Cattle Company. Red preferred the life of a cowboy and stayed with the cattle, while Hugo, who preferred machines, became the mechanic for a series of antique cars (my father never took to riding horses) and eventually for the huge tractor that was used to plough virgin grasslands for wheatfields during the First World War. Both, as long-standing residents of the bunkhouse, must have had much to do with raising and disciplining my brother Rex and me. I remember, also, that Red delighted in watching over our small sister, Viva, born six years after me, taking her up into his saddle for a ride when she could barely walk and keeping an eye on her as she toddled about the ranch. Red also looked after me during the bitter winter of the influenza epidemic of the First World War when I was ten. To avoid contagion in Glendive, where the family then lived, I was sent into isolation on the ranch with Red and Dan Downs. Most of our time was spent breaking ice so that range cattle and horses could get drinking water, but also inventing new dishes to vary our diet of dried and preserved foods.

The years of successful ranching and wheat growing in one of those periods when it rained consistently on the high plains meant that my brother and I became cowboys at a very tender age. At six or seven I was put up on Babe, one of our best-trained cow ponies, who, on her own, would cut out a steer from the herd during the spring roundup. All I had to do was hang on in her fast dashes and quick turns in the milling herd of animals. But by the time I was ten or eleven I could throw a lariat over the head of a calf, double-hitch the rope to the saddle horn, and dismount to throw the animal down while the horse kept the rope taut.

The animal roundup was the most exciting part of the year. Additional cowboys were employed to ride over thirty or forty miles of open range collecting cattle with our brand—the R-lazy-B—to be brought in to holding pastures around the ranch. Young animals were then roped, thrown, branded, and injected against disease, and the males were castrated. It was hard but often hilarious work, particularly when some clumsy cowboy, like fat, red-faced Elmer, got tangled in the ropes. He seemed to be thrown more often than the calves and always came up sweating, more red-faced than ever and grinning.

At the end of the roundup, sometime in June, full-grown steers were selected for the beef market and driven to the railroad in Glendive, bound for the stockyards in Chicago. One year, I remember, there were 3,000 head in the drive, some of which I think, came from neighboring ranches. They were moved slowly over a twenty-four hour period the twenty-five or thirty miles to the bridge of the Yellowstone River just outside Glendive, and then broken up into small groups to cross. If too many animals got onto the bridge at once, it would begin to sway, giving us a sickening feeling, and felt as if it were about to collapse. Sometimes there was a shortage of cattle cars so that the herds had to be held on very poor grazing land about the town. Many thousands of pounds of beef could be lost in a few days.

Two or three men from the ranch accompanied each trainload to see that the cattle got water and to see that none were trampled in the cars. Once, when I was thirteen or fourteen my father gave me the job so that I could meet him in Chicago. The one thing I can remember most about it was facing my first dish of raw oysters in the bar at the Blackstone Hotel. To me, then, it seemed incredible that people could eat anything so horrible. At first I suspected my father's familiar practical jokes, but I saw others at the bar eating the things and downed the dozen without being sick.

It must have been about this time, traveling with Father that he began to indoctrinate me with his particular prejudices—a process which I suppose is normal in the education of boys. He was a Democrat whose political philosophy is indicated by his choice of my second given name, Gladstone (the first, Froelich, was in memory of a jolly little waitress who fed the students while he was in medical school and was learning German). He was also an agnostic with a preference for reading Icelandic sagas and the Indian Vedas, a trial to my mother who was a devout and Protestant Christian. In addition to his ideas as to who was, and who was not, a gentleman, he had very distinct principles, rigid in maintenance without any religious sanction. These principles were forced upon me with the razor strap, but also by his evident disgust at any backsliding.

Probably his most dominant characteristic was a sense of responsibility. Whatever happened for many miles about the ranch, it was always Father who took the responsibility and looked after it: a scandal when a neighbor boy shacked up with the schoolteacher, a cowboy crushed by the belt of the threshing machine, an insane woman who had to be taken to the asylum tied up in the back of his car, women in difficult childbirth, sick cattle, bankrupt and homeless families, or the construction of a local telephone line. He was not a busybody, just one of those men whom people naturally depend on.

It is curious what one remembers of paternal instructions. One day, in a discussion about what every young man should know, while driving from Miles City to Glendive, he stated that I should never eat sweet cakes with my wine or have anything to do with a red-headed woman. I have often wondered just what episode that represented.

Consistent rain in the high plains came to an end as it always has periodically on the grasslands, sometime in the mid 1920s. Wheatfields became dry fields of Russian thistles (tumbleweeds), the range land shriveled into sparse burned prairies where even the buffalo grass was stunted, small trees and brush along the stream beds died away, and dust hung in a red sky. Range cattle died by the hundreds, and some nameless disease decimated the expensive Aberdeen Angus bulls and cows. With persistent drought a dreary exodus of Montana families began. Some moved westward to the Pacific coast, like the later migration from Oklahoma made famous by *The Grapes of Wrath*, and some returned to the east. Among the latter was my family.

My father had become interested in a new type of gasoline engine and became the managing director of the Lever Motors Corporation. That took us to Wheaton, Illinois, a suburb of Chicago, and into years of wishful thinking. It was always just about to succeed and never did. The engine was designed and built for passenger cars, trucks, and aircraft, tested on the roads and in the air with notable success, yet was never produced commercially. Once, just before the Great Depression when my brother and I were at the University of Illinois, father phoned to say that General Motors had offered to buy the engine for a large sum of money, and we celebrated a wealthy future. The company barely survived the depression and dragged on in one way or another until my father's death at eighty-seven.

For that whole period the thing that impresses me most was my mother's resilience. She was always a remarkably cheerful person, but the trials of those years were enough to break the spirit of a saint. She managed somehow and cheerfully kept our spirits up through all those disappointments. It must have been a very hard life for her, but you would never know it. She retained that quality until her death at ninety-three.

The physical environment of one's childhood and youth must have a powerful bearing upon one's world view. I was sixteen when we left Montana for Illinois and a suburban kind of life in the environs of a huge city. But each summer during the last two years of high school and four years of college I returned to work for Dan Downs on his ranch only a few miles south of where I was brought up. He was one of those ranchers who managed to survive the long period of drought until the rains came again, and when I last saw him in 1975, he was producing bumper crops of wheat on 2,000 acres with the most modern industrial farming machinery, even though he was in his late seventies and had steel pins in both hips.

In my time with him, during the late 1920s, he ran a few cattle and cultivated about 150 acres of grain, all with horses. He could pay me only forty or fifty dollars a month (and I think that was really more than he could afford) for the hay and grain harvest. I rose at five in the morning to round up the work horses, feed and harness them, and eat breakfast, and was then off to the fields at seven. Normally we worked until twilight before returning to supper. But after that we had to milk a few cows by hand. Sometimes we took a Sunday off.

I disliked urban and suburban life and was happy to be back on the open plains, even though it meant very hard work for long hours pitching hay and grain. With the occasional free day, however, I could saddle a horse and be off on the open range of rolling hills around Timber Fork, reliving my childhood in the country that was homeland. The space, emptiness, paucity of people, and timeless quality of ancient prairie land altered and reinterpreted all that I was learning in the schools and universities about the history and behavior of human beings as well as their place in the cosmos. There were, in some way, two worlds, one academic and one natural, one artificially man-made and one in which men like me were simply incidental players in a drama of vast interrelated forced interacting in some incomprehensible system that could crush and obliterate the busy man-made world as easily as an ant colony. In such an environment, empty space under the canopy of bright stars, it is easy to understand why ancient nomads should conceive of earth as shielded by a heaven filled with gods and spirits to look after the lonely existence of wandering mankind.

In retrospect I now think the experiences of my childhood and youth, as well as later years of travel and work in the hinterlands of many different countries, is unusual today and, in part, responsible for my skepticism about current reconstructions of human history. Exploding population during the past century, the massive increase in urbanization in the developed as well as in many developing countries, and the spread of Western technology throughout the world are rapidly turning the rural food-producing population into a minority. An urban-industrial-technological society, dominated by Western theories, tends to lose something of the wonder and mystery characteristic of the natural world of the more ancient and once dominant rural society.

Originally, in the mythology of Western civilization (that complex of religion, philosophy, tradition, and belief), mankind was created by God in his own image as a creature apart from all other living things, and destined to utilize the natural world for his own purposes. Now with the general acceptance of the idea that humans evolved from lower forms of life we still believe that man with his superior brain power is destined to manage natural forces for the survival and increase of the human species—a process developed in the twentieth century with its massive growth of human population, increase in life expectancy, and the reduction of hard physical labor through the invention of machines. Quite suddenly, near the end of the century, we have become aware of crucial environmental problems created by science and technology, and the growth of human numbers. How valid are our Western theories now and can they solve the problems they have produced? I think that question hinges on the knowledge of man's place in nature.

As an archaeologist I have become uneasy about theories of the past primarily based on one particular world view, that of Western mythology, dominant until the mid-twentieth century.

In recent years Oriental archaeologists have begun to dig in Asia on a scale equal to the West during the past century. The results in that vast and less-known region, with a different world view, surely should change the direction of reconstruction, particularly for the prehistoric period. In like manner, Oriental scientists working in the research laboratories in the West and at home have already shifted our conception of time to something more in tune with Oriental mythology. It is reasonable to expect that their theories of man's place in nature, such as that implied in the Buddhist doctrine of reincarnation, should also shift Western thought at a time when we are all faced with crucial environmental problems.

It is significant that the science and technology we hope will solve those problems are also discovering just how critical they really are. We are learning that humans, far from being set apart, are intimately related to all living things and must sink or swim with them. We are also learning that what men have contrived may foul up the whole biosphere.

That curious conflict stemming form our growing knowledge of man's complete dependence upon a still unfathomable natural world, and the prevailing hope that we can manipulate it with science and technology for our survival, apparently leads us into one crisis after another. Contamination of air, sea, land, and even the stratosphere, becomes critical. Saving thousands of living species now threatened with extinction is urgent. (An old blacksmith, finished shoeing my horse and drinking an Irish coffee, finally exclaimed in a discussion of the state of the world, "I think it is time for the bomb.") Could this be the age of ultimate crisis?

After I retired from the museum and archaeology I became the director of The Land Preservation Fund of The Nature Conservancy in Washington (probably because of my comment that we should now arm the animals and put a bounty on people), and I was impressed with the dedicated young people who ran the organization. The more I learn about the worldwide drive to preserve the environment, usually inspired and manned by the young, the more encouraged I become about the changing attitudes of the late twentieth century. And I have noted with great interest that many of these young conservationists are quoting educated and articulate American Indians, who attempt to describe their ancient and aboriginal ideas about man's relation to the world about him. My work in the Arctic and in the Far East has convinced me that there is an ancient connection between American Indian and Far Eastern theories—theories that may have a profound effect on the way we go about future attempts to preserve our environment.

Because the use of atomic weapons in war is now clearly suicidal it is possible that they can be outlawed, just as firearms were outlawed in the internal wars of the Japanese in the sixteenth century, and thus eliminate one of the greatest threats to human survival, but is it possible to do the same with the longer-range threat to the environment that involves worldwide industrial economy, world population, and a great many group conflicts?

Anyone involved in the long-range study of human history must conclude, I think, that grouping and group conflict are as deeply engrained in human genes as the herding instinct and conflict in many species of animals. Such conflicts, ranging all the way from family feuds to national states and religious beliefs (for example, the conflict between Christianity and Islam that has afflicted the Western world for more than a thousand years), seem to be as old as Man. So far as one can imagine, an effective drive to end an increasing destruction of the biosphere will require an international political system and a powerful central control that is unacceptable at the present time. It will also require a compromise between differing world views and religious beliefs. At the moment this does not seem likely.

However, the human species has proved to be remarkably adaptable, and as the crises deepen into a certainty recognized by all people, the force of circumstance may well shift current beliefs and submerge instinctive conflicts in a common will to ensure a future.

I now work in tiny, walled medieval fields clearing brambles and nettles to restore the sheep fields of my distant Celtic ancestors—these small, dark Britons who were pushed back toward Lands End by invading Anglo-Saxons. There is a Stone Age site just above the spring that supplies the house today, and on the moor beyond are many stone circles left from the Bronze Age men who supplied copper and tin for the Western world. When I dig a post hole below the barns, I find the record of changing styles of pottery and porcelain discarded by men who lived here by the spring for many centuries.

Sometimes I dig in my garden with Roy Marshall, a stocky, black-bearded man of the moor. We discuss the night's frost, the state of the apple blossoms, and the prospects of the crops. I look across the tight little valley of the Penpont Water and think that these same thoughts and concerns have echoed and re-echoed about this valley for endless generations.

In my study I read of quasars, whose light that we now see left them when the earth was born, theoretically some four billion years ago. I read of the possibility that certain actions of particles in the nucleus of an atom appear to reverse time; in the quantum theory it is possible that several worlds exist at the same time. But in the meadows on the hillside watching a buzzard glide in the wind, I am sharply aware of living in different worlds—one of senses and one of theory. I *know* only what is sensory experience and imagination; the rest is belief and theory distilled by generations of men and crystallized in written records like the Bible, the surviving classics of the Greeks and Romans, the ancient Chinese Book of Changes, or the empirical scientific documents of my generation.

Reality is the energy of thought in any moment in any space. There is no beginning and no end. There are only moments of experience strung together with belief and theory to create one man's life. He in turn re-creates the world about him, and the past, as a reflection of his particular society and his generation.

Publications

1935   An Indian Burial Site at Crystal River, Florida. *The Quarterly Periodical of the Florida Historical Society* 13 (4):183-192.

1935   A New Prehistoric Culture in Puerto Rico. *National Academy of Sciences* 21: 12-16.

1936   Eskimo Chronology. *National Academy of Sciences* 2 (6): 357-362.

1936   A New Prehistoric Culture in Haiti. *National Academy of Sciences* 22: 4-8.

1936   A Compilation of Historical Data Contributing to the Ethnography of Connecticut and Southern New England Indians. *The Archaeological Society of Connecticut Bulletin* 3: 1-89.

1937[1976]   *Archaeological Excavations at Kukulik, St. Lawrence Island, Alaska.* Preliminary report by Otto William Geist and Froelich G. Rainey, prepared under the direction of the Commissioner of Indian Affairs in cooperation with the University of Alaska. Washington, DC: U.S. Government Printing Office. (With Otto W. Geist); reprinted 1976 by New York: AMS Press.

1937   Old Eskimo Art. *Natural History* 40: 603-607.

1939   Archaeology in Central Alaska. *Anthropological Papers of the American Museum of Natural History* 36 (4): 351-405.

1940a   *Puerto Rican Archaeology.* The New York Academy of Sciences, Scientific Survey of Puerto Rico and the Virgin Islands 18 (Pt. I).

1940b   Archaeological Investigation in Central Alaska. *American Antiquity* 5: 299-308.

1940c   An Ancient Town Site in Alaska. *El Palacio* 47: 227-228.

1941a   Eskimo Prehistory: The Okvik Site on the Punuk Islands.
                *Anthropological Papers of the American Museum of
                Natural History* 37 (Pt . IV): 453-569.

1941b   The Ipiutak Culture at Point Hope, Alaska. *American
                Anthropologist* 43 (3, Pt. 1): 364-375.

1941c   Native Economy and Survival in Arctic Alaska. *Applied
                Anthropology* 1 (1): 9-14.

1941d   *Excavations in the Ft. Liberte Region, Haiti.* Yale
                University Publications in Anthropology 23. New Haven.

1941e   A New Form of Culture on the Arctic Coast. *Proceedings
                of the National Academy of Sciences* 27 (3): 141-144.

1941f   Culture Changes on the Arctic Coast. *New York Academy
                of Sciences, Transactions* 2 (3): 172-176.

1941g   Mystery People of the Arctic. *Natural History* 47: 148-
                155, 170-171.

1941h   Alaskan Work Reported. *El Palacio* 48: 259-260.

1942   Discovering Alaska's Oldest Arctic Town. *National
                Geographic* 82 (3):318-336.

1943   Alaskan Highway—an Engineering Epic: Mosquitoes,
                Mud, and Muskeg Minor Obstacles of 1,671-Mile Race to
                Throw the Alcan Life Line Through Thick Forest and
                Uninhabited Wilderness. *National Geographic* 83: 143-
                168.

1946   Quinine Hunters in Ecuador. *National Geographic* 89
                (3):341-363.

1947   The Whale Hunters of Tigara. *Anthropological Papers of
                the American Museum of Natural History* 41 (Pt. 2): 231-
                283.

1948   Ipiutak and the Arctic Whale Hunting Culture.
                *Anthropological Papers of the American Museum of
                Natural History* 42: 260-266. (With Helge Larsen)

1950a   The Museum Takes Inventory. *University Museum
                Bulletin* 15 (4): 3-18.

1950b   The University Museum, Its Collections and Expeditions. *Fairmount Park Art Association 78th Annual Report.* Philadelphia.

1951a   The Arctic as a Strategic Area. *The General Magazine and Historical Chronicle* 54 (1). Philadelphia.

1951b   Eskimo Archaeology in 1950. *Bulletin of the National Research Council Proceedings of the Alaskan Science Conference of the National Academy of Sciences, National Research Council*, no. 122: 48-49.

1951c   Radiocarbon Dating, a Summary. *Memoirs of the Society for American Archaeology* 8: 58-65. (With Frederick Johnson, Donald Collier, and Richard F. Flint)

1953a   The Significance of Recent Archaeological Discoveries in Inland Alaska. *Memoirs of the Society of American Archaeology* 9: 43-46.

1953b   Afghanistan. *University Museum Bulletin* 17 (4): 41-56.

1954a   University Museum 1954: Tradition and Change. *University Museum Bulletin* 18 (4): 5-51. The University Museum, Philadelphia.

1954b   "What in the World"—a Museum Television Show in Anthropology. *The Museologist* 51: 2-4. Rochester Museum of Arts and Sciences.

1955a   The New Museum. *University Museum Bulletin* 19 (3): 2-53.

1955b   Spearheads to Spacemen. *Bulletin of the Rochester Museum of Arts and Sciences* 28 (6): 93-94.

1955c   Restoration of Mayan Tikal. *Science* 122: 1010.

1955d   Eskimo Whale Hunt. In *Indians of North America: A Historical Panorama*, ed. by Matthew W. Stirling. National Geographic Indians of the Americas (Pt. 1). Washington, DC: National Geographic Society. Pp. 389-393.

1956   A Compilation of Historical Data Contributing to the Ethnography of Connecticut and Southern New England Indians. *Archaeological Society of Connecticut Bulletin*, reprint no. 3: 3-49.

1957	*Problems of American Archaeology.* Published in the U.S.S.R.
1958	*Archaeology in the American Arctic.* Published in the U.S.S.R.
1959a	The Vanishing Art of the Arctic. *Expedition* 1 (2): 3-13.
1959b	Radiocarbon Dating in the Arctic. *American Antiquity* 24 (4): 365-374. (With Elizabeth K. Ralph)
1960a	Archaeological Salvage in Egypt, An Example of International Cooperation. *Expedition* 2 (4): 2-3.
1960b	Electronics and Archaeology. *Expedition* 2 (4): 19-29. (With M. W. Stirling and M. W. Stirling, Jr.)
1960c	The Changing Face of Archaeology. *Expedition* 2 (3): 14-20.
1961a	Techniques Program of the University Museum. *Bulletin of the Philadelphia Anthropological Society* 14 (1): 1-4.
1961b	Physics and Archaeological Salvage. *Archaeology* 14 (4): 287-292. (With R. E. Linington)
1962a	Archaeological Techniques and International Cooperation. Paper presented at *International Congress on Techniques and Direction in the Archaeological Problems of Today.* Venice, May 1962. (With Carlo M. Lerici)
1962b	New Instrument Techniques in Archaeology. *Proceedings of the Symposium on Detection of Underground Objects, Materials, and Properties,* 19-20, March 1962. U.S. Army Engineer Research and Development Laboratories, Fort Belvoir, Va., pp. 151-155. (With Elizabeth K. Ralph)
1962c	The Museum Expands. *Expedition* 5 (1): 2-3.
1962d	Electronics to the Rescue in the Search for the Lost City of Sybaris: Discoveries by a Joint U.S.-Italian Expedition, Part 1. *Illustrated London News* 241 (no. 6436, Dec. 8): 928-931.
1962e	Engineering Devices Used in the Excavation of the Lost City of Sybaris: Discoveries by a Joint U.S.-Italian Expedition, Part 2. *Illustrated London News* 241 (no. 6437, Dec. 15): 972-974.

1962f   Reflections on the 75th Anniversary of the University Museum. *Expedition* 4 (3): 12-13.

1963a   Archaeological Techniques and International Cooperation. *Consiglio Nazionale Delle Richerche*: 141-147.

1963b   The Applied Science Center for Archaeology. *American Journal of Archaeology* 67: 294-295.

1963c   The Applied Science Center for Archaeology. *American Antiquity* 29: 237-239.

1963d   The Applied Science Center for Archaeology Fellows. *American Anthropological Association* 4 (6): 3-4.

1964   Abu Simbel. *Carnegie Magazine* 38 (10): 329-332.

1966a   Archaeology and Its New Technology. *Science* 153 (no. 3743): 1481-1491. (With Elizabeth K. Ralph)

1966b   New Techniques in Archaeology. *Proceedings American Philosophical Society* 110 (2): 146-152.

1966c   Return to the Arctic. *Expedition* 8 (3): 2-8.

1966d   New Tools for Archaeology. *Science Year, The World Book Year Book* (submitted Spring 1966).

1966e   Technological Revolution and Archaeology. *Bild der Wissenschaft Redaktion* (submitted Fall 1966).

1967a   *The Search for Sybaris,* 1960-1965. Rome: Lerici Editori. (With Carlo M. Lerici)

1967b   The Archaeology Explosion. *Expedition* 9 (3): 2-7.

1969a   The Location of Archaic Greek Sybaris. *American Journal of Archaeology* 73 (3): 260-273.

1969b   The Search for Sybaris. *Expedition* 11 (2): 10-13.

1969c   In Search of Egi Zuma. *Expedition* 11 (4): 2-11.

1970a   Archaeology. *Encyclopedia Britannica Yearbook of Science and the Future.*

1970b   Tikal, A Fourteen Year Program Now Completed. *Expedition* 12 (2): 2-9.

1971a   Dating the Past. *Encyclopedia Britannica Yearbook of Science and the Future.*

1971b   *The Ipiutak Culture. Excavations at Point Hope, Alaska.* Addison-Wesley Publishing Company Modular Program.

1972   Archaeology. *Encyclopedia Britannica Yearbook of Science and the Future.*

1973   Archaeology. *Encyclopedia Britannica Yearbook of Science and the Future.*

1974a   Archaeology. *Encyclopedia Britannica Yearbook of Science and the Future.*

1974b   Science and Archaeology. *Archaeology* 27 (1): 10-21.

1974-1975   Speculations on the Future of Archaeology. *Folk* 16-17: 25-32. Copenhagen.

1982   The Road to Ban Chiang: A Dialogue of Events Leading to The University Museum's Participation in the Expedition. *Expedition* 24 (4): 5-12. (With Elizabeth Lyons)

1986   An American in Cornwall. *Cornish Scene* 1 (5).

1992   *Reflections of a Digger.* Philadelphia: The University Museum of Archaeology and Anthropology.